Law and Empire in Late Antiquity

This is the first systematic treatment in English by an historian of the nature, aims and efficacy of public law in late imperial Roman society from the third to the fifth century AD. Adopting an interdisciplinary approach, and using the writings of lawyers and legal anthropologists, as well as those of historians, the book offers new interpretations of central questions: what was the law of Late Antiquity? How efficacious was late Roman law? What were contemporary attitudes to pain, and the function of punishment? Was the judicial system corrupt? How were disputes settled? Law is analysed as an evolving discipline, within a framework of principles, by which even the emperor was bound. While law, through its language, was an expression of imperial power, it was also a means of communication between emperor and subject, and was used by citizens, poor as well as rich, to serve their own ends.

JILL HARRIES is Professor of Ancient History in the University of St Andrews. She is the author of *Sidonius Apollinaris and the Fall of Rome* (1994) and, with Brian Croke, of *Religious Conflict in Fourth-Century Rome* (1982). She is co-editor, with Ian Wood, of *The Theodosian Code: Studies in the Imperial law of Late Antiquity* (1993).

Law and Empire
in Late Antiquity

Jill Harries

PUBLISHED BY THE PRESS SYNDICATE OF THE UNIVERSITY OF CAMBRIDGE
The Pitt Building, Trumpington Street, Cambridge, United Kingdom

CAMBRIDGE UNIVERSITY PRESS
The Edinburgh Building, Cambridge CB2 2RU, UK   http://www.cup.cam.ac.uk
40 West 20th Street, New York, NY 10011–4211, USA   http://www.cup.org
10 Stamford Road, Oakleigh, Melbourne 3166, Australia
Ruiz de Alarcón 13, 28014 Madrid, Spain

First published 1999
Reprinted 2000

Printed in the United Kingdom at the University Press, Cambridge

Typeset in Plantin 10/12pt [VN]

A catalogue record for this book is available from the British Library

Library of Congress Cataloguing in Publication Data
Harries, Jill.
    Law and empire in late antiquity / Jill Harries.
        p.   cm.
    Includes bibliographical references and index.
    ISBN 0 521 41087 8 (hardback)
        1. Justice, Administration of – Rome.   2. Public law (Roman law)
    I. Title.
    KJA2700.H37   1998
    347.45′632 – dc21   97-47492   CIP

ISBN 0 521 41087 8 hardback

Contents

Preface

This book should be sub-titled 'travelling hopefully'. Its route has been planned in the light of long-standing preoccupations of my own, with some help from friends. The Theodosian Code has long been used as evidence for late Roman history, without much attention being granted, at least by historians writing in English, to the status of that evidence. The conference on the Theodosian Code held at the University of St Andrews in 1990 and the resulting publication, edited by myself and Ian Wood, were a start in that direction. This book takes some points further, in particular in relation to how imperial law was made, and how and whether it worked as intended. This enquiry will entail a re-examination of what we are to make of the rhetoric of the laws: if a certain scepticism over government pronouncements is in order now, there can surely be a case made for subjecting imperial legal propaganda and its motives to similar scrutiny. But we should not focus only on the centre, where imperial law originated; its reception and use by the citizens of the wider Empire is of equal importance. Two perspectives must, therefore, be used, that of the legislator, and that of those who used the law for their own purposes.

In order to arrive at the end of this journey at all, many attractive by-ways have been, regretfully, ignored. I have nothing to say about 'vulgar law' – except that the concept requires a re-examination I shall not attempt. Nor can I take account of the distinctive culture of Jewish Law. I also omit discussion of the formation of canon law, and the influence of imperial law-making procedures on the quasi-legislative activities of Church Councils. There is also, I suspect, something to be done on Christian attitudes to the Mosaic Law as part of the evolution of late antique legal culture in general. All these are projects for the future. I have restricted the main focus of the study to the period between Diocletian and the death of Theodosius II in 450 – thus giving a central role to the Code of Theodosius, rather than that of Justinian – although I stray outside it as far as Hadrian (117–38) in one direction and Justinian (525–65) in the other.

I first became interested in law in its social and cultural context in the 1980s, inspired in part by my then colleague, John Richardson's, researches on the law of the Roman Republic. By the end of the decade it was clear that the Theodosian Code, long neglected by Roman lawyers, was a potential growth-industry among late antique historians. The conference at St Andrews was a recognition of this and I owe much to all who participated in it and to those who contributed to the subsequent publication. I am especially grateful to Boudewijn Sirks, Simon Corcoran, Judy Evans Grubbs, Peter Heather, David Hunt, Geoffrey Rickman and Michael Whitby for their help at the time and academic inspiration since, and to Ian Wood, who brought his formidable mediaeval talents to the joint-editorship of the published version. John Matthews, a star contributor to the conference, will, I am sure, in due course produce a significant study of the Theodosian Code; his support and help over the years have been invaluable and, without him, this book would not have been possible.

Progress was much accelerated in the last two years by the kindness of various benefactors. In 1995, the Principal of the University of St Andrews allowed me to plan for 'thinking time'; I hope the product may be some return for his astringent encouragement. The Leverhulme Trust made generous provision for my teaching replacement at St Andrews for a year of Research Leave in 1996–7. For the first part of that year I had the privilege of holding a Visiting Fellowship at All Souls College, Oxford and place on record here my profound gratitude to the Warden and Fellows of the College, who provided the ideal combination of academic stimulus, material opulence and contemplative *quies* for the pursuit and completion of inter-disciplinary research. Individual acknowledgements for conceptual and bibliographical assistance with matters legal are due to Peter Birks and Stephen Cretney and to my fellow-visitors, Greg and Joy Parr, and, on the anthropological side, to the Warden of All Souls, and to David Parkin. Thinking was also assisted in entirely non-academic ways by four grey squirrels and the unrivalled beauty of the trees of Beechwood and Iffley Turn.

I am also grateful to many colleagues for their help with, and criticism of, various chapters of this book, as variants of them saw the light of day in the shape of papers delivered in Oxford, Cambridge, Cardiff, Milton Keynes and the University of South Carolina at Columbia. Among them, I would especially thank Chris Kelly, whose forthcoming work on (the absence of) corruption in Late Antiquity will be very relevant to some suggestions offered here; also Peter Garnsey, Keith Hopkins, Geoffrey Greatrex, Kate Cooper and Conrad Leyser, Richard Miles, Janet Huskisson and Andrew Lintott. Special thanks are due to Gillian Clark, for

reading most of this manuscript and various offshoots, and for her sensitive criticism and useful suggestions throughout. Ralph Mathisen and
Hagith Sivan gave their all to achieve the great social and academic
success of the conference on the Shifting Frontiers of Law in Late
Antiquity at Columbia, SC, in March 1997 and I owe much to them both.

Books cannot, of course, exist without publishers. Pauline Hire agreed
a version of this project several years ago, and has waited patiently for it
since. I am grateful to her and the publishing staff of Cambridge University Press for their hard work.

There are two scholars the influence of whose work is paramount in
this book. Fergus Millar shaped our concept of the 'responsive' early
Roman emperor and the implications of his thesis for analysis of late
imperial rule are far-reaching. Tony Honoré, through his publications on
the Theodosian Code and the late Roman quaestors, has shown how
imperial legal texts were created; no less significant is his wisdom on legal
culture, as reflected also in his studies of Gaius, Ulpian, imperial lawyers
and Tribonian. If this book has any merits, they are due to the stimulus of
the insights of both and their unstinting generosity in sharing them with
me.

Introduction

What is a tree? For lawyers, and litigants with trees on their land, this question could be important. 'Most of the ancients', according to the Severan legal commentator, Ulpian, thought that vines were trees, likewise ivies, reeds and willows. A plant could not be a tree unless it had developed roots and 'that also is deemed to be a tree, the roots of which have ceased to live' or which, if uprooted, could be put back again or transplanted. The stock of an olive was also a tree, whether or not it yet had roots. The roots were not included in the term 'tree'.[1]

Ulpian was a learned and prolific jurist, an expert commentator on law whose interpretations carried authority. His discussion of what a tree was is extracted from a work, not on arboriculture, but on detailed matters of law. The object of the discussion was to ascertain when, or in what circumstances, an action[2] for the secret felling of trees could be brought. In order to define the office, legal experts had to deliberate about what a tree was, how 'felling' should be defined (that was, not bark-stripping, cutting with a saw or pulling up by the roots), who was liable, what was due to the owner(s), what was meant by 'secret' and whether or not an alternative action, for theft, could also be brought. Authorities for one opinion or another, the 'ancients', unspecified, or named earlier experts in the law – Pomponius, Trebatius, Labeo – were cited and agreed with or refuted.

Jurists approached their learned discourses from a number of angles. One method was to define a problem and its solution in terms of question and answer. For example: 'It was asked whether an heir should be given a hearing, who, before a complaint of unduteous will is brought, wants payments made returned to him. He replied that a man who discharged a *fideicommissum* (trust), in the knowledge that he was not obliged to,

---

[1] *Dig.* 47. 7. 3 (Ulpian, *Ad Sabinum* 42).
[2] See Buckland (1966) 605, 'the Law of actions is the law of litigation, the law governing the submission of claims to a tribunal for settlement'. Cf. *Dig.* 44. 7. 51. Nihil aliud est actio quam ius quod sibi debeatur iudicio persequendi.

cannot reclaim on this ground...'[3] A second was to ask 'what if...' and answer in hypothetical terms; still on 'unduteous wills', Ulpian asked 'What, for example, if a brother was plaintiff and the heirs in the will were of different standing? In such a case, the deceased will be considered to be partly intestate, partly not.'[4] A third, in which one can detect the hand of a past or future imperial lawyer, was the prescriptive mode; 'One who administers justice should not do so in cases involving either himself, or his wife or his children or his freedmen or others, whom he has with him.'[5]

The last form, the statement of a rule, without discussion, was the one preferred by emperors. No author of an imperial law would have indulged himself with seeking to define a tree. While juristic commentators were, in general, deliberative and discursive, seeking to define principles and rules, emperors were concerned to tell people what to do, and what not to do. Prescription could, however, be combined with education: Theodosius II wrote of his planned Code of imperial law that its function would be to act as a 'teacher of life', telling the user 'what should be observed and what avoided'.[6] The demands of government therefore set imperial legislators on a potential collision course with the more deliberative aspects of the juristic legal tradition. Nor was the conflict resolved, and the extreme language of much of what survives in late antique imperial law-codes has caused scholars to despair of the law of late antiquity, or to ignore it altogether.

Late imperial law must be understood as a form of hybrid creation. Emperors themselves did not have a legal training or, indeed, in some cases, much education of any kind. They had the right to decide what the law was. On the other hand, many drafters of imperial laws, known from the mid-fourth century on as quaestors, were in fact men with a good understanding of law, who had read some juristic writings and had some understanding of legal principle. When, therefore, emperors deferred to the advice available, it became possible for the legal tradition reflected in the 'opinions of the ancients' to be merged discreetly with the apparent dirigisme of late imperial legislation. Not that this was always the case. Although many individuals pursued study of the law on a private basis, no independent judiciary existed to check the potential whims of the imperial legislator, or make rulings on whether a proposed constitution (imperial enactment) was 'lawful' or not. Emperors were therefore entitled to respond, or not, not only to legal pressures but to social and

---

[3] *Dig.* 5. 2. 21. 1.   [4] *Dig.* 5. 2. 24.

[5] *Dig.* 2. 1. 10 (Ulpian, again, formerly *a libellis*, in charge of petitions, later to be Praetorian Prefect to Severus Alexander). For his career and writings, see Honoré (1982); Syme (1972).

[6] *CT* 1. 1. 5 (429). Compare, on Chinese law, MacCormack (1996) describing the Confucian vision of law as the educator of the people.

political pressures as well. This right was in fact essential to the emperor's own legitimacy as a law-giver; he could expect his constitutions to be backed by the consent of society as a whole, the 'consensus universorum'.[7]

For those purist lawyers who regarded their discipline as being, for the most part, hermetically sealed from the outside world, this was (and is) an unsatisfactory situation. The contamination of the purity of the legal discipline and the undermining of long-held legal principles by perhaps temporary or irrational social pressures is an understandable cause for concern. It is true that in Late Antiquity protests could be made, for example by persecuted Christians, that the emperor was acting unlawfully,[8] meaning that both proper legal process and legal safeguards had been abolished, but in the law-making process itself, 'political (i.e. imperial) interference' was built into the system and it occurred to no one to question that this should be so. The result may have been to undermine classical principles in some areas, but in other respects the emperors' openness to social change may have made their legislation more responsive to public needs and changing social mores than it would otherwise have been.

Nor were the demands of law necessarily in conflict with social change. Historically Roman law had always contained a moral dimension, meaning that it was responsive to the social mores of the time, and it was an accepted part of juristic theory that the application of some laws was heavily dependent on social attitudes.[9] For example, one of the defining texts for citizen law was the Praetorian Edict, codified in *c.* 130 CE. This declared that an action could be brought if someone were shouted at 'contrary to good morals'.[10] Having asserted that not all shouting was actionable, Ulpian answered the crucial question, 'whose morals' were to count. The answer, derived from the first-century jurist, Labeo, was that those of the city were to count, not those of the offender.[11] In other words,

---

[7] A debateable concept even now. For the 'lawfulness' of taking into account 'public clamour'/'genuine public concern', defined as 'a petition signed by some 287,300 members of the public, with some 4,400 letters in support . . . a petition signed by nearly 6,000 members of the public . . . and over 20,000 coupons cut out of a popular newspaper (*The Sun*), with over 1,000 letters . . .', see *The Times*, Law Reports, 13 June 1997. For ancient concepts, from Aristotle on, see Oehler (1961).

[8] Lactantius, *De Mortibus Persecutorum* 22. 4 (under Galerius), eloquentia extincta, causidici sublati, iure consulti aut relegati aut necati . . . Licentia rerum omnium solutis legibus adsumpta..

[9] Cf. Cicero, *Topica* 73, observing that 'vulgi opinio', popular opinion, influenced the decisions of *iudices*.

[10] *Dig.* 47. 10. 15. 2, qui adversus bonos mores convicium cui fecisse cuiusve opera factum esse dicitur, quo adversus bonos mores convicium fieret, in eum iudicium dabo.

[11] *Dig.* 47. 10. 15. 6. Idem (Labeo) ait 'adversus bonos mores' sic accipiendum non eius qui fecit sed generaliter accipiendum adversus bonos mores huius civitatis.

in this case, whether or not an offence had been committed depended, not on strictly defined legal rules but on what was acceptable social behaviour in the *civitas* or *polis* as a whole.

Jurists thought, and modern lawyers think, in terms of their own intellectual discipline, exhibiting, in varying degrees, concern for legal principle, justice and fairness, definitions, rules, precedents and all the intricacies of real or imagined courtroom situations. Much of what was written by legal specialists was (and is) hard to cope with for the non-specialist[12] (the tree example set out above was chosen for its, perhaps unrepresentative, accessibility), and the importance of Roman law as law in the wider administrative, social and literary culture of the Roman Empire has received, until recently, little attention. For further progress to be made, historians who use law as a source must be aware of, and respect, the separateness of law as a discipline, with its own assumptions and intellectual tradition. To treat laws as just another literary or documentary source, without considering how law as text came into being, is to risk misunderstanding the texts themselves and drawing from them highly questionable historical conclusions.

Much of this book is an attempt to provide an alternative reading of late Roman Law as a source for Late Antique history. The writings of Fergus Millar and Tony Honoré have drawn attention to the responsive character of imperial legislation and the importance of the mechanisms and the people who brought it into being. This has important implications for attitudes to law on the part of those who went to some lengths to get a (favourable) imperial ruling, and the multiple influences – legal, bureaucratic, social, rhetorical – which contributed to the generation of the text of an imperial constitution. It will be argued (chapter 4) that to discuss Roman Law in terms of 'obedience' or the reverse is a misconception of what law is for and contributes to a mistaken assessment of its real effectiveness, even in those limited areas of life where it might apply. For it must be remembered that law had its own tacit frontiers; many people went about their business, and even settled disputes with each other or before adjudicators under rules of their choosing without resorting to Roman law at all (chapters 9 and 10). It should not therefore surprise that systems not quite like those envisaged by the Theodosian Code crop up in the sources; customary or local usages worked and, provided all agreed to the outcome, it was in no one's interest to interfere.[13]

---

[12] Which makes the bridge-building between Law and Ancient History by Olivia Robinson (1997) especially welcome.

[13] 'Vulgar' and 'local' or 'provincial' law are outside the scope of this book. Traditional Roman tolerance of local practices, provided they were compatible with the aims of Roman government, would naturally extend to local methods of dispute-settlement and internal regulation.

It will also be argued that one should not believe everything emperors, or their elite imitators, said or wrote was true, even when there appeared to be consensus, on, for example, the corrupt behaviour of judges (see chapter 8). While perceptions are important for cultural history, their truth is not always self-evident. Emperors in their laws resorted to a language of power designed to hold their officials to account; this has been, wrongly in my view, interpreted as evidence of extensive wrong-doing on the part of officials, and especially of judges. A similarly assertive and critical attitude is also evidenced in the widespread condemnations of abuses of power in historians, speech-writers, bishops and other authors. What this reveals is a culture of criticism, not that there was, necessarily, more to criticise in the fourth or fifth centuries than there had been earlier. Of course, there was much to fear in the operation of the Late Roman autocracy, and every reason to conciliate its agents and palliate its worst excesses. But the powerful and the weak alike also actively exploited the content and the language of imperial law to further their own ends. Petitioners of moderate means insisted on justice, using the emperor's words against him, while, on a more socially elevated level, the eloquent advocate or patron, echoing the rhetoric of the emperor's laws, represen-ted themselves, their friends or their clients as 'victims' of their 'powerful' opponents, and used their influence to highlight abuses perpetrated by others and, in the process, to make accountability a reality.

1   The law of Late Antiquity

Law was, in theory, the 'art of the good and the fair'.[1] Many citizens of the Roman Empire thought otherwise. As so much of what was written about the operation of law derived from a discourse about law, which confused perceptions, tendentious rhetoric and fact, some sense of the framework of the contemporary debate is required. The terms were cogently set out by Priscus of Panium, the Greek classicising historian, who, in 448, was sent with others on a delicate mission to Attila the Hun. In his *History*,[2] Priscus recalled an encounter with a Greek-speaking former citizen of the Roman Empire, who had been taken prisoner and settled with the barbarian. One reason for the latter's dislike of Roman rule was the iniquities of the legal system. His criticism focussed especially on the system in operation. The laws did not apply equally and if a wrongdoer came from the wealthy classes, then he might escape punishment, whereas a poor man, because of his ignorance of how to conduct such matters, would undergo the penalty prescribed by the law – if he did not die before the case was concluded, after protracted delays and much expense. The worst thing of all, he said, was that what should have been obtainable from the law could be acquired only by paying money.

In his defence of the Roman system, Priscus emphasised the ideal of law, rather than its malfunctions in practice. Justice, he argued, was administered according to rule and enforced, thus preventing one lawsuit leading to another, and, as law existed to help litigants, it was right that it should be paid for, just as farmers should pay to be defended by soldiers, and when litigants had wasted money on cases they had lost, this was their fault. The real grievance, which was the level of expense required to go to law, was not addressed. Nor was Priscus prepared to concede that the judiciary might be at fault. He attributed the law's delays to conscientious scruples on the part of judges, rather than the complexities of the judicial procedures of trial and appeal; it was right, he said, that a judge should take care not to make a mistake by being in too much of a

---

[1] *Dig.* I. I. I (Ulpian, *Institutes*), see n. 4.   [2] Priscus, fr. 8, *FHG* 4, pp. 86–8.

hurry. The laws applied to everybody and even the emperor had to obey them.[3] If rich men oppressed the poor in lawsuits, they could only get away with it if no one noticed – and that was true of poor men also.

As the second speaker, Priscus had the advantage of being able to offer a refutation of his opponent point by point. His method was to act as an advocate for the ideals of fairness and justice on which the law was based, while glossing over its malfunctions in practice. Law was given its place in the balanced functioning of the state as a whole, as a system of enforceable justice, to which even the emperor was subject. The aim of the whole literary construct was that the empire, which Priscus served and was, at the time, representing as ambassador, should be vindicated and such, predictably, was the outcome. Faced with this eloquent reminder of the ideal of Roman citizen law (*ius civile*), Priscus' opponent broke down in tears: 'the laws were indeed noble and the Roman constitution good, and it was the magistrates (*archontes*) who failed to match those of long ago and undermined its reputation'. The fault, in other words, lay, not with the system of law itself, but with those who administered it.

Priscus and his friend were not alone in their idealisation of the Roman *politeia*. Writing in the early third century, Ulpian argued that law was virtually a religion and that legal experts, like himself, were its priests; 'For we serve the needs of justice and advance knowledge of the good and the just, distinguishing the just from the unjust, separating the legal from the illegal, seeking to make men good not only through fear of punishment but through the incentive of rewards, practising, if I am not mistaken, no fake philosophy but a true one.'[4] Idealism of a different kind was expressed by a former enemy of Rome. In the early fifth century, the Spanish historian, Orosius, heard tell that a citizen of Narbonne had had conversations with the Goth Athaulf, who had succeeded his brother Alaric as leader of the Goths a few months after the Sack of Rome in 410.

---

[3] This view contrasts with that of Ulpian, *Dig.* 1.3.31 (from *Lex Julia et Papia*). Princeps legibus solutus est (as was the empress), but for expression of imperial subjection to law, see *CJ* 1. 14. 4 (429, west), 'maius imperio est submittere legibus principatum'. It was, of course, in the interests of the powerful block of lawyers in the administration that the emperor be subject to law.

[4] *Dig.* 1.1.1 (from Ulpian, *Institutes* 1), iustitiam namque colimus et boni et aequi notitiam profitemur, aequum ab iniquo separantes, licitum ab illicito discernentes, bonos non solum metu poenarum, verum etiam praemiorum quoque exhortatione efficere cupientes, veram, nisi fallor, philosophiam, non simulatam affectantes. Cf. Honoré (1978) on the legal profession as 'a body of initiates, conscious of its moral worth, with a continuous history from the pontifical college of the republic to Tribonian's commission'. For a further encomium, with a sting in the tail, see Gregory Thaumaturge, *Address to Origen* 7, on 'these admirable laws of ours, by which the affairs of all men under Roman rule are governed and which were neither composed nor can be mastered without effort, being themselves wise, precise, varied, wonderful and, in short, – very Hellenic'. Gregory had chosen to drop out of his legal education.

After being at first hostile to Rome, Athaulf had come round to believing that laws were a pre-requisite for both civilisation (as opposed to barbarism) and statehood. Having seen, all too often, that the Goths were unable to obey laws because of their 'unrestrained barbarity', Athaulf further concluded that laws could not be banned from a state (*respublica*) because without laws a state could not be a state at all, therefore he would amalgamate his Gothic strength with the 'Roman name'.[5] This interpretation is not far removed from that of Priscus, in that both connected law and the state, but, while Priscus, the Roman citizen, saw law as being envisaged by the founders of the Roman constitution as an integral part of the state, Athaulf, the outsider, saw it as a precondition for having a state in the first place. However, the outsiders, Athaulf and Priscus' opponent, who had the advantage of surveying the Roman system from the standpoint of competing systems, those of the Huns and the Goths, also differed in one important respect; the former subject of the Empire was disaffected because of the unjust operation of law, while the Germanic observer set the issue of operation to one side, in the belief that, without any system of law, there could exist neither order nor a state.

Despite their differences, all the contemporaries thus far discussed subscribed to the existence of the ideal constitution or system of laws (*nomoi*) which, if observed, should guarantee order and justice. Priscus and his Greek-speaking acquaintance also both believed that this ideal system could be subverted by those who ran it, resulting in injustice. This simple opposition between the law, as a set of inviolable rules requiring to be obeyed, and extraneous factors, such as the exertion of arbitrary power by litigants through wealth or influence, or the susceptibility to extra-legal pressures of judges, tax-collectors or other officials,was one subscribed to by contemporaries, including emperors, and offers, at first sight, a convenient explanation for the malfunctioning, if not the decline, of the Later Roman Empire. It is the contention of much of this book that analysis of law and society based on a supposed conflict between the law (or rules) and power is simplistic and inappropriate. Instead, late Roman society must be viewed in terms of a multiplicity of relationships, in which the law was used as a tool of enforcement, an expression of power, or a pawn in the endless games played out between emperor and citizen, centre and periphery, rich and poor.

Confusion and ambiguities? The legal heritage

Not all were content to ascribe the failings of the legal system only to those who ran it. The law itself was regarded by some as being riddled

---

[5] Oros. *Historia adversus paganos*, 7.43.

with confusion, making it impossible to know what the law was. In the late 360s, an anonymous petitioner concluded a small treatise on military machines and other matters with a plea to the emperors to 'cast light on the muddled and contradictory rulings of the laws, throwing out unprincipled litigation, by the judgement of your imperial opinion'.[6] Although slow to take action, emperors, once convinced of the merit of systematising the law, took credit to themselves for addressing the problem. Launching his collection of imperial constitutions, the Theodosian Code, in 438, Theodosius II blamed the chronic shortage of legal experts on there being too many books, forms of bringing suit and heaps of imperial constitutions, which concealed knowledge of the law in a thick, dark fog.[7] This state of affairs (he claimed) was exploited by self-styled experts in the law to conceal their own ignorance and overawe their clients.[8] Nearly a century later, the emperor Justinian found the 'way of the law' in so confused a state that it appeared to be stretching ahead with no end in sight,[9] a situation which his *Digest*, a compilation of extracts from juristic writings, was designed to remedy.

Codifications of law had obvious attractions for emperors as prestige projects. It would have been less clear that the more the law was defined, the less scope there might be for emperors to exert discretionary powers as patrons. The confusion and ambiguities in the system so much deplored by the imperial codifiers had in fact given them greater scope to exercise discretion as patrons and innovators.[10] By contrast, given that rationalisation of law limited imperial discretion, codification should have worked to diminish imperial power. Yet neither Theodosius II nor Justinian seem to have regarded this as a problem. Perhaps they believed that adequate scope for patronage remained. More important would have been the conviction that the creation of a law-code incorporating the laws of predecessors set the codifier on a higher level than the legislators who had gone before him. Despite the rhetoric, emperors' reasons for authorising prestige projects like the codification of law were not wholly

---

[6] *De Rebus Bellicis* 21, ut confusas legum contrariasque sententias, improbitatis reiecto litigio, augustae dignationis illumines.

[7] *NTh.* 1.1 pr., quod ne a quoquam ulterius sedula ambiguitate tractetur si copia immensa librorum, si actionum diversitas difficultatesque causarum animis nostris occurrat, si denique moles constitutionum divalium principum, quae velut sub crassa demersae caligine obscuritatis valde sui notitiam humanis ingeniis interclusit.

[8] Id., ne iurisperitorum ulterius severitate mentita dissimulata inscientia velut ab ipsis adytis expectarentur formidanda responsa...

[9] *Const. Deo auctore* 1, repperimus autem omnem legum tramitem, qui ab urbe Roma condita et Romuleis descendit temporibus, ita esse confusum, ut in infinitum extendatur et nullius humanae naturae capacitate concludatur. See Note on abbreviations, p. 217.

[10] For imperial interest in maintaining confusion, see C. M. Kelly (1994).

based on an altruistic yearning for clarity or a reduction in the legal costs incurred by Roman citizens.[11]

What forms of law, then, combined to create this system? By the time of Justinian, what mattered, and what was therefore codified, was the *ius civile*, the citizen-law of the Romans. But, from early in the development of their law, Roman jurists were aware of the influence of external factors, and other, broader systems, with which the citizen-law would be required constantly to interact. As the small Republic gradually extended its dominance over its neighbours, it was forced to find ways of conducting legal dealings with people who were not Romans, but whose laws could have something in common with Roman law. The imperial jurists distinguished the *ius civile*, the law of the *civitas* from the *ius gentium*, law of peoples, and the *ius naturale*, the law of nature. The *ius gentium* did not refer to anything approximating to international law, but rather to the things that the Roman *ius civile* had in common with the usages of other peoples. Gaius, in the second century, assimilated the law of peoples to the law of nature, writing that the 'naturalis ratio' was observed equally among all peoples and was therefore called the law of peoples as all nations used it.[12] Ulpian, however, perhaps with Gaius' *Institutes* in mind, insisted that the law of nature was that which applied to creatures of the land and sea and to birds, as well as to man, citing procreation and the rearing of young as an example; the *ius gentium*, on the other hand, applied to men only, not to animals, and, as an illustration of this, slavery originated from the *ius gentium* and clearly could not be part of the *ius naturale*, under which all men were born free.[13] Although these contradictory statements, both later included in Justinian's *Digest*, indicate some uncertainty over the definitions, they had in common one important limitation: they were statements of fact, in juristic terms, not a moral prescription, that men ought to be equal, or on a level. The law of nature was, usually, the actual (and flawed) common practice of living creatures, not the divine law.[14] Not that there was agreement about this either. Some

---

[11] For Theodosius' political motives with regard to the West, see Matthews (1993) and below, pp. 37 and 64. For Justinian's justification for imposing his law (as the sovereign legislator) on ancient texts, see *Const. Deo auctore* 7.

[12] Gaius, *Inst.* 1. 1, quod vero naturalis ratio inter omnes honines constituit, id apud omnes populos peraeque custoditur, vocaturque ius gentium, quasi quo iure omnes gentes utuntur.

[13] *Dig.* 1.1.1. 4 (Ulpian), ius gentium est quo gentes humanae utuntur. Quod a naturali recedere facile intellegere licet, quia illud omnibus animalibus, hoc solis hominibus inter se commune sit. Also id. 1.1.4, that slavery originates from the *ius gentium*, 'utpote cum iure naturali omnes liberi nascerentur'.

[14] Contrast Cicero, *De Officiis* 3.5.23, arguing, from Greek philosophy, that men would not cheat, or be acquisitive at another's expense, if they obeyed the law of nature: Atque hoc multo magis efficit ipsa naturae ratio, quae est lex divina et humana: cui parere qui velit – omnes autem parebunt, qui secundum naturam volunt vivere – numquam committet ut alienum appetat . . .

jurists, notably Paulus, did see the *ius naturale* as an expression of what was 'always' good and fair, while the *ius civile* was designed to benefit all, or the majority, of the citizens of a city or state.[15] The universal principles of what was good and 'fair' were therefore set against the strict law of the citizen body, and the importation into the citizen-law of the social attitudes defining the concept of 'fairness' or *aequitas*, at any given time was legitimised. Even, therefore, on the most fundamental level, law would be influenced by contemporary morality,[16] no less (and perhaps more) than by strictly legal principles.

Writing under Septimius Severus, Papinian, perhaps the authority on law most respected in late antiquity, listed the sources of the *ius civile* as statutes (*leges*), popular resolutions (*plebiscita*), senatorial enactments (*senatusconsulta*), decrees of emperors (*decreta principum*) and the authoritative pronouncements of men learned in law, the jurists (*auctoritas prudentium*).[17] To these was added the *ius honorarium*, the law contained in the Edict of the praetor, who, under the Republic and Early Empire administered law in Rome; this form of law derived its name from the praetor's magistracy (*honos*) and was held to 'assist, supplement or amend' the *ius civile*.[18] This accumulation of diverse forms of legal pronouncement had its roots in the length of time over which Roman law had developed. In the 530s, Justinian complained that his codification of Roman law had to sort out confusions stretching back over 1400 years[19] – to, on his calculation, *c.*870 BC. Others, less ambitiously, took the Law of the Twelve Tables of 450 BC as their starting point. In 380, Theodosius I insisted that the law of the Twelve Tables be enforced, alongside the Praetorian Edict, in cases of succession to the property of condemned criminals,[20] and, in 392, the same emperor derived the law's authority to refer to arbitration boundary disputes over strips of land less than five feet wide from 'the ancient law', meaning, again, the Twelve Tables.[21]

Thanks to the Roman disinclination to break any tie that bound them to the past, all forms of past legal enactment were still, technically, valid, although, as we shall see, laws could also cease to be valid, if they fell into desuetude.[22] Under the Republic, statutes (*leges*) were passed by the popular assemblies, who, being sovereign, had the right to enact legislation binding on the whole state. Centuries later, in Late Antiquity, some of these

---

[15] *Dig.* I.I.II (Paulus, *Sabinus* 14). Ius pluribus modis dicitur: uno modo, cum id quod semper aequum ac bonum est ius dicitur, ut est ius naturale, altero modo, quod omnibus aut pluribus in quaque civitate utile est, ut est ius civile.

[16] For a stimulating, if dated, discussion of *ius naturale*, see Maine (1861) chs. 3 and 4.

[17] *Dig.* I.I.7 (Papinian, *Definitiones* 2).

[18] *Dig.* I.I.7.I (Papinian), ius praetorium est, quod praetores introduxerunt adiuvandi vel supplendi vel corigendi iuris civilis gratia, propter utilitatem publicam.

[19] Justinian, *Const.Deo auctore* 5, totum ius antequam per millesimum et quadringentesimum paene annum confusum.   [20] *CT* 9.42.9 pr. and 3.   [21] *CT* 2.26.5.

[22] *Dig.* I.3.32–40, discussed below, pp. 33–4.

statutes still made their ghostly presence felt. Citations in the legal enactments of emperors in the fourth century included reference to the Lex
Laetoria of 200 BC for the protection of minors,[23] and the Lex Cincia of the
same period, both cited by Constantine,[24] to the *stipulatio Aquilia*, from the
early but undated Lex Aquilia on wrongful damage to property[25] and the
Lex Falcidia on legacies of 40 BC.[26] Nor were the powers of the Senate as
legislator ignored. Resolutions of the Senate (*senatusconsulta*) had acquired
greater authority under the Early Empire, as the legislative powers of the
popular assemblies fell into disuse, and favoured points of reference for late
antique lawyers were the SC Claudianum on the marriage of free women
with slaves[27] and the SC Tertullianum, from the reign of Hadrian, allowing
mothers to inherit from their children.[28]

The criminal law owed much to the reforms of two past lawgivers, the
proto-emperor, L. Cornelius Sulla (dictator and consul, 81–80 BC), and
the emperor Augustus. Sulla established a number of courts (*quaestiones*)
to try various criminal offences, such as murder and poisoning (or use of
charms), or forgery; in the statutes he would have defined the crime and
the penalty. In other areas of criminal law, the framework supplied for
later developments by the Leges Iuliae, the legislation of Augustus,
predominates, with whole sections of the imperial law-codes devoted to
imperial enactments relevant to the Julian laws on adulteries, corrupt
solicitation (*ambitus*), extortion (*repetundae*), treason (*maiestas*) and on
violence.[29]

As the jury-courts fell out of use under the Early Empire, to be replaced
by hearings before a single magistrate or judge, the courts established by
the criminal statutes ceased to operate, but the statutes themselves remained, as they specified offence and punishment. People prosecuted for
murder, poisoning, or other relevant offences were still prosecuted under
Sulla's law and liable to its penalties. Since his time, the definition of the
offences had been progressively refined by juristic interpretations and
imperial enactments. Liability under the Lex Cornelia on forgery, for
example, was extended to the malicious giving of false witness, the taking

---

[23] *CT* 8.12.2 (316).
[24] *CT* 8.12.4 (319) see also *Fragmenta Vaticana* (hereafter *FV*) 260–316.
[25] *CT* 2.9.2 (Theodosius I, 381).   [26] *CT* 9.14.3.2 and 5 (Arcadius, 397).
[27] *CT* 4.12. Ad Senatus Consultum Claudianum, contains some seven constitutions rel-
    evant to the SC., which is also cited by Gratian at *CT* 10.20.10 and by Honorius at *CT*
    12.1.179 (415), 'confirming the authority' of the SC. Juristic commentaries were also
    compiled, on *senatusconsulta* in general (Pomponius, 5 books; Paulus, 1 book), and single
    books by Paulus on the SCs Orfitianum, Tertullianum, Silanianum, Velleianum and
    Libonianum/Claudianum.
[28] *CT* 3.8.2.1 (Theodosius I, 381), referring only to a 'decree of the Senate'.
[29] *CT* 9.7 = *CJ* 9.9 (adulteries); *CT* and *CJ* 9.26 (corruption); *CT* and *CJ* 9.27 (extortion);
    CT 9.5 and *CJ* 9.8 (treason); *CT* 9.10 and *CJ* 9.12 (violence).

of money for giving or withholding evidence, the corruption of a judge, falsification of records, opening the will of a person who was still alive,[30] destruction of a will in order to claim intestacy[31]or selling the same thing as a whole twice to two different people.[32] Jurists writing on *falsum* (forgery) cited the precedent of an edict of Claudius, making those who wrote legacies to themselves in another's will liable as if he had offended against the Lex Cornelia;[33] other precedents for revision of definitions came from rescripts of Hadrian, Pius, Marcus and Commodus, and Severus Alexander,[34] along with Septimius Severus' condemnation of the Prefect of Egypt for forgery of public records.[35] In addition, the *Codex Justinianus* contained twenty rescripts relating to types of offences counting as forgery, plus four imperial 'general laws'. The expansion of the criminal law and the effective creation of new criminal offences by including more actions under the provisions of the criminal statutes must have been hard to keep track of, before the authoritative imperial codifications, which catalogued the modifications under the heading of the statute itself, 'Ad Legem'. Such knowledge was necessary for proper procedure as a man accused of a crime covered by a criminal statute would be prosecuted as a 'reus' (defendant) under that statute, and be liable to its penalty.[36] In that, limited, sense, the statutes of Sulla and Augustus were still living law.

None of this is evidence for the existence in Late Antiquity of libraries or of private collections featuring the complete texts of Republican or even Augustan statutes. Many of the references to the past in late antique texts are in fact formulaic; lawyers knew, for example, the basics of the requirements of the Lex Cincia on gift-giving, without having to go back to a text now some six hundred years old, and the 'quarta Falcidia', the minimum portion of an inheritance to be left to an *heres* (heir and executor), was accepted common usage, at least among lawyers, as were the testamentary restrictions imposed on the childless by the Lex Iulia et Papia.[37] Nor could the texts themselves have remained immune from the ravages of the centuries, from emendation, or copyists' errors. The continuance of procedures or provisions deriving, or claiming to derive, from ancient statutes provides no proof of the survival of their texts, indepen-

---

[30] *Dig.* 48. 10. 1 (Marcian, *Institutes* 14).   [31] *Dig.* 48. 10. 26.   [32] *Dig.* 48. 10. 21.
[33] *Dig.* 48.10. 15 (Callistratus, *Quaestiones*) cf. *CJ* 9. 23. 3 (223).
[34] *Dig.* 48. 10. 1. 7; 21; 29; 31–2.   [35] *Dig.* 48. 10. 1. 4.
[36] *CT* 9.14 = *CJ* 9.16 (murder); *CT* 9.19 = *CJ* 9.22 (forgery). See esp. *CJ* 9. 16. 5, si quis te reum Corneliae legis de sicariis fecerit, and 6, Is, qui cum telo ambulaverit hominis necandi causa ... legis Corneliae de sicariis poena coercetur. Compare refs. to Lex Fabia on kidnapping at *CJ* 9. 20 2 (213), legis Fabiae crimen ... persequi potes; 3(224) Ut legis Fabiae poena debeatur ...; 5(259) legis eum Fabiae ... reum debes postulare; 9(293) Fabiae legis crimine teneri non est incerti iuris.
[37] *CT* 13.5.7 (Constantine, 334) exempting shipowners.

dently of the use of extracts in commentaries by the jurists writing in the first to the third centuries.[38] However, past statute law retained one important function. By exploitation of these ancient and respected points of reference, lawyers were able to fit later legal enactments or texts into convenient and accessible categories, while reference to laws enacted in the distant past had the further, reassuring effect of asserting the length and continuity of the legal tradition and its roots in Roman imperial history.

Hadrian and the jurists

The Praetorian Edict, codified by Salvius Julianus on the orders of Hadrian, probably in the 130s, had considerably more impact on the shape of private law in late antiquity than did the ancient statutes. The intrinsic value of its quaintly archaic text[39] was limited, except as a reaffirmation of continuity with the ancient past, and its contents had been superseded, for practical purposes, by later legal commentaries and imperial enactments. However, the Edict, known from the Severan period onwards as the Edictum Perpetuum[40] was uniquely influential in the field of private law in two important respects. One was that the order of its books and clauses, which shaped two major legal commentaries by Hadrianic jurists, the *Digesta* of Salvius Julianus and Celsus, was followed by the creators of the structure of later imperial codifications of law. The imperial law-codes of Theodosius II in 438 and Justinian (529, revised 534) had distinct beginnings,[41] but then both proceeded to arrange their extracts from imperial constitutions in a structure generally shadowing that of the Edict.[42]

The second was that, in the light of later events, Hadrian achieved an extraordinary status as being, in some respects, the first late-antique imperial lawgiver.[43] This was not only due to his initiative in authorising

---

[38] When Theodosius II planned his definitive Code of Roman Law in 429, he had no intention of including the texts of Republican or Augustan statutes; as Justinian was to do in 529–34, he envisaged law in terms only of imperial enactments (constitutions) and juristic writings.

[39] The Praetorian Edict (or Edictum Perpetuum) was partially reconstructed by Lenel (1927), largely from citations of the text in the juristic commentaries. For the text as reconstructed, see also *FIRA* I (2nd ed.): 335–89. For its construction, see Guarino (1980).

[40] See Pringsheim (1931/61) for collected references to Edictum as 'perpetuum', or 'praetorium' in the jurists and imperial constitutions.

[41] The *Codex Justinianus* begins with Christian legislation, a topic postponed by Theodosius' lawyers to their final book.

[42] For the Edict and the Theodosian Code, see Mommsen (1905).

[43] If the anonymous author of the *Historia Augusta* was, as suggested by Honoré (1987), a lawyer, his beginning his biographies of emperors with Hadrian becomes a further

the codification of part of Roman law through the Edict and thus providing a model for future imperial codifiers. Even more important, perhaps,
from the emperors' standpoint, was that he arrogated to himself (and
therefore removed from the Praetor) the sole right to modify the *ius
honorarium*, the law of the Praetorian Edict, by means of imperial enactments. Consequently, from Hadrian onwards, the updating and modification of much of private law was expressed through imperial law, thus
creating a new, distinct category of involvement on the part of the
emperor with the law of the Empire. However, there was no mechanism
for integrating imperial law into the Edict. Instead, imperial enactments,
specifically rescripts, were treated as a continuation of the Edict. Therefore when, in the 290s, one Gregorius decided to codify imperial rescripts, he naturally began with Hadrian, and collected rescripts from
Hadrian to Diocletian in the *Codex Gregorianus*.[44] His code was in turn
continued by Hermogenianus, almost certainly one of Diocletian's lawyers and their identification of Hadrian as a starting point fed through
into Justinian's codification of imperial law which merged the Diocletianic codes with that of Theodosius II. Moreover, Justinian used
Hadrian's insistence that the praetor's law could be changed only through
imperial constitutions as precedent and justification of his own extension
of imperial legislative authority to cover the writings of the jurists, collected in extracts in his *Digest*. Henceforward, he asserted, there would be
no more juristic commentaries as all changes to law would be the emperor's responsibility.[45]

Despite, then, the attachment of late antiquity to the legal tradition,
past law was used mainly as a framework for the living law, which took
two forms, the writings of past experts on the law, the jurists, some of
whom had achieved canonical status, and the legal enactments of emperors, whose authority surpassed every other source of law. Under the
Republic, the jurist was an aristocratic amateur, whose expertise in law
was a kind of hobby co-existing with more important career obligations.
According to Pomponius,[46] writing under Hadrian and Antoninus Pius,
the founders of the *ius civile* were the jurists of the second century BC,
P. Mucius Scaevola, M. Junius Brutus and M. Manilius, all of whom
compiled collections of legal opinions. A generation later, Q. Mucius

expression of the special status of that emperor in the eyes of lawyers.
[44] On Gregorius, Hermogenian and Diocletian, see Corcoran (1996).
[45] *Const. Deo auctore* 12, nullis iuris peritis in posterum audentibus commentarios illi
applicare et verbositate sua supra dicti codicis compendium confundere; *Const. Tanta* 18
citing Salvius Julianus (and Hadrian) that deficiencies in the Edictum Perpetuum should
be supplied by imperial fiat ('ab imperiali sanctione').
[46] *Dig.* 1.2.2.39, from Pomponius' *Enchiridion*, or 'Handbook'. On Pomponius in general,
see Nörr (1976).

Scaevola, the son of Publius wrote a book on the definitions of terms in law, which was influenced by Greek treatises, not on law but on knowledge, which drew attention to techniques for inferring the general from the particular. These jurists of the late Republic were men active in public life who were free to discuss matters of law and express divergent opinions. Their eminence derived partly from their social and political status as leading men in the senate, and partly from the fact that there was no separate legal 'profession' in Rome. The judges to whom the praetor delegated the hearing of cases, once he had established the form of the action, were non-experts whose job was simply to establish the facts in a case. Advocates could, and did, master the details of law, as Cicero demonstrated in a number of show-trials, but it was a matter of debate as to whether too much legal learning might not be detrimental to a client's interests.[47]

Already in Cicero's lifetime, however, changes, which foreshadowed what was to come, were making themselves felt. Caesar as Dictator in the 40s BC had in his entourage legal advisers, whose status depended on his patronage and whose assistance he may have intended to use in his projected codification of Roman law.[48] Under the Early Empire, many jurists, such as Neratius Priscus, Cervidius Scaevola, Salvius Julianus, Paulus and Ulpian, were to be found serving on the emperor's *consilium*, either as 'friends' (*amici*) of the princeps, without formal responsibilities, or as holders of office; both Papinian and Ulpian rose to the Praetorian Prefecture under the Severi. They were recruited not only from Italy and the Latin West but increasingly from the Greek and, under the Severans, the Semitic, East; Papinian was allegedly related to Julia Domna, from Emesa and Ulpian came from Tyre, which fondly preserved his memory into the fourth century For ambitious men, seeking to make their mark, the emperor's service was the best avenue for advancement. Conversely, the dependence of many jurists on his patronage gave enterprising emperors openings to expand their personal control of Roman law. In his short history of Roman jurisprudence, Pomponius ascribed to Augustus a reform which granted to a few favoured jurists the right to give opinions (*ius respondendi*) which carried with them the emperor's *auctoritas*, the alleged aim being to enhance the authority of the law;[49] other jurists could give opinions too, but they would carry less weight. Although it was characteristic of Augustus both to take an interest in expressions of

---

[47] Discussed by 'Crassus' and 'Antonius' in Cicero's *De oratore* I, a fictitious dialogue set in 91 BC. In the *Pro Murena*, of 63 BC, Cicero also mocked the distinguished but dull jurist, Servius Sulpicius Rufus, for his forensic ineffectiveness.

[48] Suetonius, *Divus Julius* 23. For jurists under the Republic, and discussion of the significance of Caesar, see Frier (1985), and for the intellectual background, Rawson (1985) 211–14.   [49] *Dig.* 1.2.2.49, ut maior iuris auctoritas haberetur.

auctoritas and to expand the range of his own patronage and control, there is no contemporary attestation for this innovation and the power to designate favoured jurists does not appear to have been exploited by his successors;[50] there remains, therefore, the possibility that Pomponius innocently reproduced a Hadrianic version of the past, justifying a similar innovation by that energetic emperor[51] by reference to an imaginary Augustan precedent. Hadrian's own interest in asserting himself in the field of law (as elsewhere), which we have seen in action with reference to the Edict, also showed itself in a declaration that, in trials, unanimity of view among a group of approved jurists could count 'as if it were law' and that, where they differed, a judge could choose freely between them.[52] However, Hadrian's endorsement of an imperially chosen juristic elite was little more than a ratification of existing acceptance of officially sponsored jurists as, in effect, lawmakers; thus the shadowy second-century jurist, Gaius, defined the 'opinions of jurists' (*responsa pruden-tium*) as the 'decisions and opinions of those *to whom it is permitted* to lay down the law'.[53] What is not clear, however, is whether Gaius himself was ever one of the favoured few and, if he were not, how his writings came to be copied (and presumably read) in Egypt by the late second or third century.[54]

Selection of authorities had a second motive; it helped to regulate and restrict the volume of authoritative material liable to be cited in court. By the late empire it was clear that such restrictions were inadequate. When Justinian's legal team, led by his legal officer, or quaestor, Tribonian, turned their energies to the *Digest* of juristic writings, they found themselves faced with the task of reading some 3,000,000 lines of writings by no less than 38 jurists (and others may have been excluded from the final version). Among them were several ominously prolific authors: Salvius Julianus had 101 books, including his *Digest* (90 books); Pomponius had 129 books, Cervidius Scaevola 72, Gaius, 86 (including 32 on the Provincial Edict), Papinian an elegant 61 books, Ulpian, 242, of which 83

---

[50] Reform accepted as Augustan by e.g. Schulz (1946) 113. For a brief summary of the state of the question see Tellegen-Couperus (1990, tr. 1993) 95–7.

[51] Honoré (1962) 82–5 on *Dig.* 1.2.2.49, expounds a punning reply given by Hadrian to a group of *viri praetorii* foolish enough to request Hadrian 'that they might have permission to reply'. Playing on the meaning of 'praestari' as either 'to be granted' or 'to make good, perform', Hadrian replies 'hoc non peti sed praestari solere', either that this is a favour granted, not asked, or that this is something you do, not something you ask to do.

[52] Gaius, *Institutes* 1.7, legis vicem. Crook (1955) 58 n.2 suggests that this was to alleviate the workload of emperor and *consilium*.

[53] Id. sententiae et opiniones eorum quibus permissum est iura condere.

[54] Parts of *Institutes* 4 survive in *P. Oxy.* 2103. Honoré (1962) suggests that the clarity of the *Institutes* won Gaius a wide readership, as the 'teacher of the Roman Empire', although he was not listed among the canonical jurists before *CT* 1.4.3 (426).

comprised his commentary on the Praetorian Edict, and Paulus 296, including 80 books also on the Edict and no less than 71 different titles; finally the third-century jurist, Modestinus, clocked in with a mere 64. Little wonder, then, as Theodosius II observed in 438, few had the learning to master the law, despite the great rewards available to its practitioners.

Students of law in late antiquity would have been confronted with a bewildering variety of authorities on civil, criminal and, increasingly, administrative law. Some books were on subjects which needed specialised treatment; trusts, *fideicommissa*, for example, generated treatises by Pomponius (5 books), Valens (7 books), Maecian (16 books), Gaius (2 books), Ulpian (6 books), Paulus (3 books) and Modestinus (one book, on Legacies and Trusts). Jurists also formulated their thoughts in terms of controversies, through works entitled *Quaestiones* (Questions) and *Responsa* (Replies); Papinian's surviving work consists mainly of 37 books of *Quaestiones* and 19 of *Responsa*. Attempts were also made to provide analyses of law in the form of *Digesta*, which were both comprehensive and comprehensible; Salvius Julianus' reputation rested mainly on his *Digest* of 90 books, along with his codification of the Edict. Jurists also seem to have understood the need to make their subject accessible by going back to first principles; five jurists, in addition to Gaius, composed *Institutes*, without perhaps appreciating that a proliferation of basic explanations might confuse rather than clarify the subject.[55] From the late second century onwards, in a development significant for the self-definition of 'law', jurists wrote treatises about the duties of officials. Most influential of these was Ulpian's 10-book work, *De Officio Proconsulis* (On the Duties of a Provincial Governor),[56] although three other jurists also contributed briefer treatments.[57] Under the Severi, the administration of the city of Rome still exerted a fascination over his provincial-born jurists and short works were compiled on the City Prefect (Papinian, Paulus, Ulpian), the Praefectus Vigilum, and the Praetor Tutelaris (Paulus and Ulpian), with further discussions by Ulpian (who ended his days prematurely as Praetorian Prefect), on the consul, and, reverting to a less Rome-centred focus, the curator rei publicae. Finally, a century later, Arcadius Charisius responded to Diocletian's administrative overhaul of the Roman Empire with a treatise on the new-style Praetorian Prefect. These encroachments on administrative law created a

---

[55] Florentinus (12 books), Ulpian (2 books), Paulus (2 books), Callistratus (3 books), Marcian (16 books).

[56] *AE* 1966 from Ephesus (3rd c), 436, discussed by Millar (1986) 279, is a letter, probably from the proconsul of Asia, urging the city to present evidence for its privileges compiled from the 'ancient *nomoi* in the *De Officio* of Ulpian', imperial constitutions, and senatus-consulta.   [57] Venuleius Saturninus (4 books), Paulus(2 books), Macer (2 books).

precedent for the sections on officials, which were to be prominent in Justinian's *Digest* and the codifications of imperial law.

Although it suited the imperial codifiers to make much of the confusions they sought to rectify, in practice citations of jurists in courts were limited to a few authorities who were generally read, perhaps excerpted in anthologies, like the so-called *Fragmenta Vaticana* from the early fourth century, and sometimes endorsed by imperial fiat. In the early 320s, Constantine, with characteristic contempt for 'interminable controversies', withdrew official sanction from the so-called notes of Ulpian and Paulus on Papinian, because their interpretations of Papinian were wrong[58] but, a few years later, granted formal approval to Paulus' *Sententiae*, (which were not by Paulus)[59] as being clear, well expressed and legally sound.[60] A century later, in a long communication to the Roman Senate (*oratio*), Valentinian III and Theodosius II continued the long-established imperial practice of nominating authorities.[61] This time, they confirmed the writings of Papinian, Paulus, Gaius, Ulpian and Modestinus, laying especial emphasis on Gaius as equal to the rest. Authority was given to their works in their entirety, and to others whose treatises had been incorporated into the works of the big five, such as Cervidius Scaevola, Sabinus, Julianus and Marcellus, – provided that the manuscript texts were checked first, 'because of the uncertainty of antiquity'. When conflicting opinions were cited, the majority were to prevail; if there was a tie, Papinian's view was to take precedence. To purists, this reads like a deplorable abdication of responsibility; the opinions of 'authorities' were to prevail, to the exclusion of creative legal argument. But, as we have seen from the practice of Augustus, perhaps, and certainly Hadrian, the nomination of jurists with *auctoritas*, whose opinions were expected to be adhered to, would have come as a welcome relief to hard-pressed judges and was not a phenomenon peculiar to late antiquity.

Constitutions: the emperor and the law

Alongside the jurists, imperial constitutions, described by their authors as '*leges*', formed the living law of the Later Empire. Gaius had defined a '*constitutio principis*' as what the emperor decided through decree, edict or letter[62] and had no doubt that this counted as '*lex*' because the emperor had received his *imperium* as a magistrate by virtue of a '*lex*', which

---

[58] *CT* 1.4.1 (321/4).
[59] Liebs (1989) argues that the *Sententiae* were not by Paulus but originated in Africa sometime before 300.   [60] *CT* 1.4.2 (327/8).
[61] *CT* 1.4.3 (426), of which many other extracts are preserved in the *CT* and *CJ*.
[62] Gaius, *Inst.* 1.5.

reflected the will of the sovereign *populus*, a view also developed by Ulpian.[63] In discussing the form taken by what 'we call, in common parlance, constitutions', Ulpian, influenced perhaps by his own experience in the imperial law offices, distinguished between pronouncements by letter or subscript, decrees issued as judicial decisions, interlocutory decisions and instructions promulgated as edicts.[64]

More significantly for the relationship of the emperor to the law, Ulpian also perceived the necessity of differentiating imperial acts of patronage, shown in the granting of favours (or especially bad treatment) to individuals, from laws which established precedents.[65] This differentiation went to the heart of the emperor's relationship with the law of the empire. No one could challenge his right to act as a patron, and exercise his power in a discretionary fashion, as and when he chose. What Ulpian attempted to do was to limit the impact of the emperor's activities as patron on the operation of the general law, by which the empire was governed. The emperor could, of course, make deliberate changes to Roman general law, as and when he chose, and the constitutions of the Later Empire show the reformer's hand constantly at work. What was not desirable was that changes should be made through the creation of precedents by casual infringements of the rules. The resultant tension between the emperor's urge to exhibit power through the conferring of favours, *beneficia*, and his subjection to the law as it stood emerges even in Justinian's own discussion of the constitutions of emperors. On the one hand, the '*beneficium imperatoris*' was to be interpreted as generously as possible.[66] On the other, he was subject to the law; if, wrote Ulpian in a different context, law which had been regarded as just for a long time was to be reformed, there had better be good reason for the change.[67]

In late antiquity, imperial constitutions took three main forms, edicts, issued to the People or Provincials or some other generalised recipients, along with *orationes* to the Senate, official letters, *epistulae*, sent to heads of bureaux or provincial administrators, and rescripts, sent to private indi-

---

[63] *Dig.* 1.4.1 (Ulp., *Institutes* 1). Quod principi placuit, legis habet vigorem: utpote cum lege regia, quae de imperio eius lata est, populus ei et in eum omne suum imperium et potestatem conferat.

[64] *Dig.* 1.4.1.1. Quodcumque igitur imperator per epistulam et subscriptionem statuit, vel cognoscens decrevit, vel de plano interlocutus est vel edicto praecepit, haec sunt quas volgo constitutiones appellamus.

[65] *Dig.* 1.4.1.2. Plane ex his quaedam sunt personales nec ad exemplum trahuntur; nam quae princeps alicui ob merita indulsit vel si quam poenam irrogavit vel si cui sine exemplo subvenit, personam non egreditur.

[66] *Dig.* 1.4.3 (Iavolenus). Beneficium imperatoris, quod a divina scilicet eius indulgentia proficiscitur, quam plenissime interpretari debemus.

[67] *Dig.* 1.4.2 (Ulpian, *De Fideicommissis*). In rebus novis constituendis evidens esse utilitas debet, ut recedatur ab eo iure, quod diu aequum visum est. The emperor's subjection to the law was acknowledged at *CJ* 1. 14. 4 (429).

viduals. A problem of terminology should be acknowledged here. Because a 'rescript' is literally something 'written back', it is also possible to label *epistulae* as rescripts.[68] However, between the 290s, when Gregorius and Hermogenianus issued their codification of imperial rescripts, with the intention that they should have universal validity,[69] and the issue of the Theodosian Code in 438, new ideas about the forms in which laws should be expressed came to the fore. Edicts, *orationes* and letters came to be the form in which were couched 'general laws', *leges generales*, while rescripts were issued to private individuals, for specific purposes. The use of the word rescript, therefore, will be confined to the brief documents on both law and status issued to private individuals from the late third century onwards by the imperial bureaux. It should also be noted that brief answers to petitions added to their text were also known as subscriptions; as many apparent 'rescripts' survive independently of the petitions to which they responded, the precise status of some as 'rescripts' or 'subscripts' is unknowable, but has little significance for their legal importance.[70]

The means by which imperial law has survived the centuries place further pitfalls in the path of its students. Important inscriptions record the whole or substantial sections of some original texts, notably edicts from the reigns of Diocletian and Constantine, such as Diocletian's Edict on Maximum Prices and Constantine's On Accusations.[71] Private anthologies, such as the *Fragmenta Vaticana*, a collection of extracts from jurists and imperial constitutions dating from the early fourth century; an eccentric compilation mostly[72] dating from the same period, known as the *Collatio Legum Mosaicarum et Romanarum*; or the so-called *Constitutiones Sirmondianae*, a collection of laws about the Church,[73] preserve the full texts of laws known otherwise only in part or not at all. However, most of what we think of as imperial laws survive in the form of extracts, made from substantially longer texts by the lawyers of Theodosius II, who created the Theodosian Code and their successors under Justinian, who used and adapted the work of the lawyers of both Diocletian and Theodosius to create the more rigorously structured Justinianic Code of imperial law as the first step in their creation of the *Corpus Iuris Civilis*.

Although the compilers of the Theodosian Code described their undertaking as being 'like' the Diocletianic Codes of Gregorius and Her-

---

[68] See e.g. Watson (1995b).   [69] See Corcoran (1996) 25–42.

[70] On subscripts and petitions, see Turpin (1991).

[71] Listed by Corcoran (1996) 170–203.

[72] The *Collatio* contains a copy of a law against homosexuals from 390, posted 'in atrio Minervae' but many put the main text in *c.* 320, because of references to laws of 315 as 'novellae constitutiones'. There can, as yet, be no certainty as to date. For refs. to recent discussions, see Corcoran (1996).   [73] Discussed by Vessey (1993).

mogenianus, the project of 429 probably had stronger official backing and tighter controls than its predecessor. In 429, when the 'first commission' of nine experts, headed by the elder Antiochus, was set up,[74] it was envisaged that there would be a Code of imperial law from Constantine to Theodosius II, a collection of juristic writings, and a final code, which would be an amalgamation of the Diocletianic Codes, and the other two, to create a definitive statement of Roman law. In the event, only the first part of the great design was realised, but the project as a whole was never officially abandoned.[75] In 429, the ground rules for the undertaking of the first code were laid down. It would contain extracts from laws, conveying their legal substance, but omitting the surrounding rhetoric, from the time of Constantine to the present. Although there was a case for limiting the contents of the Code to valid laws, nevertheless the preference of the 'diligentiores', experts in legal history, for recording laws 'valid only for their own time' was also to be catered for. As laws would be dated by consular year, it would be possible to arrange them chronologically under subject-headings, with the later entries accorded greater validity. Thus it could be used both in the courts and as a form of potted legal history.

Whether the Code actually contained every law illustrating the development of imperial legal decisions is uncertain. It is true that some laws were included which were no longer in force. A simple example is the fate of the festival of the Maiuma, which was dealt with by two laws, the first allowing it to continue, provided decorum was preserved, the second abolishing the celebrations, on the grounds that the conditions set out in the first law had not been honoured.[76] Another example concerns lawless monks who, in a law of 390, were kept away from urban centres, but who, in 392, were allowed to return.[77] However, if all laws relevant to the evolution of existing law were eligible for inclusion, it is not clear what criteria were used, if any, for leaving laws out. In 438, Theodosius explicitly excluded all previous imperial constitutions not included in the Code from having any validity in the courts, implying that vagrant, and now non-authorised, constitutions were still at large. If all constitutions unearthed by the compilers were included – and if the extant text of the Theodosian Code were complete, which it is not – we would reach an average rate of production of imperial constitutions per annum of twenty-one. Even allowing for fallow years, disrupted by wars, usurpations or wrangles with the Church, this seems a low rate of output. It must

---

[74] *CT* 1. 1. 5 (26 March 429).
[75] In the *Gesta Senatus* of 25 December 438, when the Theodosian Code was formally received by the Senate at Rome, the constitution of 429 was read out as still operative. See Honoré (1986), Matthews (1993).   [76] *CT* 15. 6. 1 (396); 2 (399).
[77] *CT* 16. 3. 1 and 2, both eastern, but the first given by Theodosius I at Verona, when temporarily resident in the West.

therefore be concluded that some constitutions were excluded, but perhaps fewer than might be expected.

Between the setting up of the first commission and a second law on the Code in 435, the movements and policy of the compilers are uncertain. On one view, they travelled over much of the Empire visiting official archives and private collections, in order to accumulate as much material as possible. This activity would of course have included not only centres such as Rome, Ravenna and Carthage, along with, perhaps, other African towns, but also research in the archives at Constantinople itself. An alternative interpretation of the gap is that the compilers spent most of their time in Constantinople itself, that they did not travel and that the relatively few constitutions which could not have derived from the central archive were extracted from private collections.[78] Six years seems a long time for the job of collection, but the interval did see various distractions, not least the events surrounding the controversial Council of Ephesus in 431, and progress may have been further impeded by the deaths of some of the members of the commission. By 435, when a second commission was set up, consisting this time of sixteen people, the elder Antiochus had left the scene and his place as head of the group was taken by his son, Antiochus 'Chuzon', who as quaestor, had drafted the initial law of 429. The job of the new commission was to arrange the material collected under headings, as specified in 429, remove superfluous verbiage and make the minor stylistic adjustments required by the excerpting process. What they were not entitled to do was to create new law.

The editing process launched by the constitution of 435 did not represent a departure from the initial project, rather a refinement of its first stage. The work of arrangement was not to take long. In October 437, Valentinian III was married to Theodosius' daughter at Constantinople and the senior Augustus took the opportunity to present completed copies of the Code for official launch in East and West, to come into effect on 1 January 439, and, as he declared in February 438, 'to be called by our name'.

Theodosius' agreement to name the 'first code' after himself may denote a private cooling of enthusiasm for the larger project initially envisaged. It also signalled a greater personal involvement on the part of the emperor with legal codification; the Diocletianic codes had been called after their authors. Moreover, the text itself was given greater protection than had been the case with Gregorius and Hermogenian, whose codes were continued with additions well into the reign of Constantine and, less systematically, down to the mid-fourth century. Special

---

[78] Matthews (1993) for the view that compilers travelled, versus Sirks (1993) championing near-exclusive use of central archive.

officials, called *constitutionarii*, were entrusted with the task of making reliable copies of the text, which would be kept safe in the offices of named administrators. Any constitution excluded from the Code would have no validity in law, a provision which, in effect, repealed all previous laws not, for whatever reason, made part of the Code.

In the late 520s, Justinian took steps to succeed, where Theodosius II had failed. His Codex Justinianus brought together the Diocletianic Codes, the Theodosian Code and subsequent *novellae* (new laws) of emperors, which were, of course, excerpted, as previous laws had been. The commission to see to this was set up on 13 February, worked with great speed and produced the first recension of the Justinianic Code on 7 April 529. On 15 December 530, a second commission was set up, chaired by the quaestor, Tribonian,[79] for the compilation of the *Digest* in fifty books, which, with Justinian's new *Institutes*, would form the basic texts for legal education thereafter. This great project was completed late in 533, and the whole was rounded off with a new edition of the Justinianic Code, incorporating recent new laws, which appeared in 534 and superseded its predecessor.[80] Whereas Theodosius II had allowed for the inclusion of material for its historical interest and condoned some repetition, Justinian's lawyers were more rigorous in their exclusion of what they regarded as redundant, and, on occasion, fused together the texts of more than one constitution, from different dates, to make the statement of law more coherent. Like Theodosius' project, Justinian's codification had a political dimension. Victorious in war, the emperor turned to law as the supreme art of peace, defining his roles as general and legislator.[81] While this may seem banal, it is worth recollecting that rule 'through law' is one of several options available to a ruler, that many fields of human activity of interest to rulers lay (and lie) outside the scope of law, and that questions of more or less regulation are part of current public debate in Britain, as they were not in late antiquity.

Two dangers threaten the unwary historian who ventures into the minefield of codified imperial law. One is that the Theodosian compilers in 438 were obliged to impose their concept of 'general law' on imperial enactments going back to Constantine, and emperors who had not em-

---

[79] For his career, see Honoré (1978) 40–69.

[80] *P. Oxy* 1814 contains a list of titles from the first *CJ*. Of particular interest is the section 'de legibus et constitutionibus principum et edictis', which retains *CT* 1. 4. 3, the famous 'Law of Citations', extracted from a long *oratio* issued to the Roman Senate in 426. This was excluded from the final *CJ*. The first *CJ* had, however, already dropped *CT* 1. 4. 1 and 2, the rule being better expressed in *CJ* 1. 17. 1. 6.

[81] *Const. Imperatoriam* prooemium; Imperatoriam maiestatem non solum armis decoratam, sed etiam legibus oportet esse armatam, ut utrumque tempus, et bellorum et pacis, recte possit gubernari. For similar sentiment of Theodosius' propaganda, see *Gesta Senatus* 2: ornamentis pacis instruit, quos bellorum sorte defendit. cf. Simon (1994): 1–12.

ployed that term. Consequently, they had to fit their heterogeneous documentation preserved from more than a century previously, into a system for which the originals were not designed. The result of this was that the final production glossed over the diverse and curious ways in which earlier emperors went about disseminating their legislation. Official letters, *epistulae*, for example, as complete samples from Constantine or Julian show, might or might not contain what the Theodosian lawyers chose to regard as a 'general law'. This lack of distinction between a law-letter and a general policy pronouncement, such as Constantine's declarations to Eastern cities about Christianity, which contained no laws, does not seem to have bothered emperors and, as we shall see, is important for appreciating what they thought they were doing when they did issue 'laws'. But it did (and does) worry lawyers.

The second problem for the historian lies in the form taken by the imperial codifications. The imperial lawyers' exclusion of what they viewed as 'superfluous verbiage' has consequences for understanding what imperial laws were really about. Robbed of their context, many 'laws' in the Codes are silent on the things we need to know. How did a particular law come into being? What was the background, the specific situation that evoked it? What else was in the law, which might affect our interpretation of what we have? Did the compilers extract from the now irrecoverable complete text the bit that really mattered? How was the law justified by the legislator? How effective a response was it to the problem it was designed to address? Many of these questions can be partially answered by reference to the complete texts of laws, especially the Novellae, which survive independently, or from fuller extracts in the Codes themselves. But, in using the laws as documents for late antique history, we must be aware of what we do not, and cannot know. The Theodosian Code (which does not survive intact) and, to a different degree, the Code of Justinian are, for the historian, a net full of holes.

Late Antiquity, then, was an autocracy, but an autocracy founded on accumulated tradition, which was required to pay at least lip-service to the rule of law. It was part of the emperor's image that his authority rested on popular consent, on the 'consensus universorum'. The language of constitutionality survived. Ammianus praised the 'venerated city', Rome, for handing over the regulation of her heritage to the Caesars 'as to her children'; the tribal and centuriate assemblies were no more but the stability of Numa's reign had returned.[82] Constantius II on his visit to Rome in 357 exchanged witty pleasantries with the plebs in the Circus; the crowd did not presume on their position, commented the historian,

---

[82] Amm. Marc. 14.6. 5–6.

nor 'were they sparing in expressing their traditional freedom of speech'.[83] The ceremonial of imperial *adventus* or the expression of the popular will through acclamation were designed to give public legitimation to the rulers, but the rulers had also to give something in return. Flagrant abuses of power invited criticism. When Constantius II violated the conventions of a 'civile iustumque imperium', an empire governed by law and justice, by acting 'more cruelly than in the manner of a citizen' ('acrius quam civiliter'), he undermined both the human rights of the citizen and his own position.[84] Nor should an emperor display excessive pleasure in the execution even of traitors, 'lest his people are perceived as subject to the arbitrary rule of a despot, not lawful power'.[85] This is more than the hopeful rhetoric of a subject trusting to the frail weapon of language against the emperor's power to enforce his arbitrary will. Behind Ammianus and others who insisted on the principle that the emperor was indeed subject to the constraints of law was the full strength of the Roman legal tradition, which, although protective of the legal privilege of the rich, nevertheless also consistently affirmed, as the jurists had done, the ideal of *aequitas*, fairness and justice. The emperor was not the only constitution the empire had.

Rescripts as law

Rescripts were issued by the various legal secretariats to apply in individual cases only and were of two kinds. One was the special grant to an individual, usually in letter form, of, perhaps, honorary status or some other privilege. This was a method of exercising imperial patronage through the conferment of *beneficia*, which could prove controversial if either the validity of the grant (which could have been improperly elicited or a forgery) or its implications in terms of other privileges (such as exemption from public duties) were challenged. Controversies over grants could result from corrupt activity, or possible administrative incompetence (to which emperors were reluctant to admit). In *c*.341, Fl. Abinnaeus produced his imperial letter of appointment as a minor military commander in Egypt, only to find that 'other men have deposited letters of this kind'.[86] Abinnaeus had therefore to petition the emperors to confirm his job and sack the other claimants 'who had won promotion to the camp by patronage (*suffragium*)'. We have no means of assessing the

---

[83] Amm. Marc. 16.10.3.   [84] Amm. Marc. 12.16.8.
[85] Amm. Marc. 19.12.18, see Matthews (1989) 251–2. A.'s rhetoric could be perceived as part of the general emphasis of the Greek cultured elite on constitutionality, used as a means of curbing what was in fact total despotic power. But the persistence of this language proves that the emperor felt obliged to respond, to maintain his own position.
[86] *P. Abinn.* 1. 11–12.

strength of the rivals' claims, but the Prefect of Egypt seems to have favoured one of them, and succeeded in replacing Abinnaeus, for a short time, in 344. This time, Abinnaeus had to visit Constantinople in person, before he was finally reinstated.[87] Challenges could be provoked also by the consequences of a grant, in particular if it brought with it exemption from municipal duties. One Plutarch, the recipient of the rank of *vir egregius* from the emperors was obliged to petition the *strategos* of the Oxyrhynchite nome, protesting against his nomination in his absence to the *decemprimatus*, the board of ten tax-collectors. He enclosed copies of proceedings, in which his advocate asserted that the nomination 'ignored his acquisition of a superior rank, which presumably releases him from municipal offices'.[88] Plutarch's self-assertion is not that of the desperate victim, but that of an ambitious man who had improved his status and intended to benefit from the consequences.[89]

The other kind, which was of central importance for the evolution of private law, was the rescript, which established the legal position in a given case, in response to claims set out in a petition and might also refer the hearing of the dispute to a judge. These did not make judgements on whether the facts as represented were true or not, but gave rulings on the basis of the facts as presented, and authorised the taking of a case before an appropriate judge (*iudex*), who would establish the facts.[90] This procedure took account of administrators' ignorance of whether the facts really were as presented; petitioners' versions of events, as the papyri show, were often one-sided and selective and to accept the story of one side without hearing the other would inevitably result in miscarriages of justice. This was therefore pre-empted often by a formulation along the lines of 'if X is as represented, then the consequence is Y'. For example, a law of Valentinian I[91] addressed to Sextus Petronius Probus about claims for runaway slaves, explained that masters who obtained a rescript giving them ownership of a disputed slave did not win their case automatically; they had to take it to court, reveal the name of their informant and submit to an investigation by the governor. If the governor found out something which contravened the assumptions on which the rescript had been issued, he had the power to set it aside.

Rescripts issued by one office might contravene the priorities of another. The fact that a judge empowered to hear a case might be referred to

[87] *P. Abinn.* 58 refers to his visit to Constantinople. [88] *P. Oxy.* 1204.
[89] Contra MacMullen (1988) 46 who cites *P. Oxy.* 1204 in support of his view that 'the life – their elite – was being crushed out of them by the weight of the demands laid on them. Nothing else explains the insistent urge of decurions to get out of their curiae.'
[90] Including cases on appeal or referred to a higher court, cf. Symm. *Relat.* 26.2, cum apud me ex rescripto, quod Cyriades v.c. impetravit, recidiva cognitione confligerent.
[91] *CT* 10. 12. 2.

in general terms, or he might be named,[92] could bear on an issue of some importance to litigants, the *praescriptio fori*, the specification of a court where a case might be heard.[93] Blanket recommendations of 'appropriate judges' could create problems for *iudices* if too many rescripts were issued by the imperial bureaux; Constantine wrote to an Italian official reassuring him that he need not take cases better handled by the governors, but should handle only those referred to him from the governors or cases in which a more powerful person might oppress a judge of inferior status.[94] Conversely, rescripts might point litigants in the direction of inconvenient judges, and Constantine had to rule that, 'not even by our rescript' should *navicularii*, shipmasters, be required to attend extraordinary courts.[95] Even in so apparently routine an area, therefore, as the specification of a judge there was scope for confusion – and consequent allegations of corrupt dealings.

Because rescripts provided a provisional legal ruling and empowered a litigant to approach a judge, they counted as one method of launching a case, or taking it forward to the next stage,[96] but they were not in themselves the last word. They had to be 'legally impetrated', obtained by proper means, and the suits themselves had to be conducted between people legally qualified to act.[97] Failure to establish either of these points could lead to the failure of a case, regardless of the contents of the rescript. Moreover an alleged rescript produced after the initial stage (*denuntiatio*) but before the actual hearing (*litis contestatio*) was regarded as suspect and 'frivolous' and could not be used to extend the time limits, within which a hearing had to take place and be concluded.[98] Doubts about both the accuracy and authenticity of rescripts, which could appear to contradict each other, surfaced at the highest senatorial level. Sym-

[92] E.g. *FV* 32. Aditus competens iudex considerato tutelae iudicio eam curabit ferre sententiam, quam agnitam legibus esse providerit; *FV* 33, Quare iudicem competentem adire par est, qui in liberali ea faciet compleri, quae in hiusce modi contentionbisu ordinari consuerunt, secundum iudiciariam disciplinam partibus audientiam praebiturus; and, for a named judge, *FV* 273, Quare Vettium Rufinum, clarissimum virum praefectum urbi amicum nostrum, cuius notio est, adire non prohiberis, qui partium allegationibus examinatis petitioni tuae secundum iuris providebit iustitiam.

[93] For general laws on rescripts, see *CT* 1.7. 4; 1.15. 1; 13.5.7; *CJ* 3.23.2 – all refer to *praescriptio fori*.   [94] *CT* 1.15.1 (325).

[95] *CT* 13.5.7 (334). For other general rulings on *praescriptio fori*, prescribed locations of trials, involving rescripts, see *CT* 1.7.4 (414) and *CJ* 3.23.2 (440).

[96] E.g. Symm. *Rel.* 19.5–6.

[97] *CT* 2.4.4 (385) Post celebratam denuntiationem seu edicto seu editione rescripti, quod tamen iure sit impetratum, lis exordium auspicatur inter iustas videlicet legitimasque personas. The 'edictum' referred to as the alternative to the rescript was a general response to the prosecutor's libellus, containing his charge or complaint. On this see Paulus, *Sententiae* 5.5a.6.

[98] *CT* 2.4.4.1. On 'procedure by rescript' see Maggio (1995).

machus, as City Prefect in 384, although acting as judge under delegated authority from the emperor, preferred to appeal for an imperial ruling in all cases of doubt, rather than sort out confusions for himself.[99] Such prudence was understandable, on political grounds; Symmachus had powerful enemies at court. But his caution also reflects the problems of combining autocracy with even a semblance of independence on the part of the judiciary.

In rare cases a rescript giving a decision backed by the authority of the magistrate could be challenged by a competing source of authority. Late in the fourth century, a claimant authorised by a rescript tried to uplift a widow's savings left on deposit with the bishop of Pavia. When the bishop, in Ambrose's words 'asserted the authority of the Church', the local *honorati* and mediators insisted the emperor's orders could not be opposed, the rescript was read out, along with supporting material from the *magister officiorum*, the head of the civil service, who had presumably scrutinised the merits of the case.[100] Although an imperial agent was expected at any moment, the bishop, with Ambrose's support, stood firm and, after a further standoff, the emperor backed down.

This incident, in which imperial authority based on the full judicial process was openly defied, may be unusual; few bishops dared behave as did the bishop of the imperial capital. But the dubious reputation acquired by rescripts by the late fourth century, as evidenced in the growing interest in 'general' legislation, may have lent some superficial plausibility to Ambrose's challenge to the legal rightness of the decision.

Rescripts as legal decisions, then, could have a hypothetical character; they were a response to facts as presented by a petitioner, but the facts themselves could be challenged.[101] But as rulings on particular situations, rescripts could acquire a *de facto* general relevance for other analogous situations. The jurists of the second and third centuries cited imperial rescripts as having general and binding force in support of their own interpretations of law and acceptance of rescripts as being general in practice would have justified the collection as a 'Code' of rescripts from Hadrian to Diocletian by Gregorius in the 290s, and the continuation of the collection by the *magister libellorum*, Hermogenianus. As Hermogenianus, at least, was one of the emperors' principal legal advisers, his

---

[99] See below, pp. 114–17.
[100] Ambr. *De Officiis* 2. 29. 150–1. Honorati quoque et intercessores dati non posse praeceptis imperatoris obviari ferbant: legebatur rescripti forma directior, magistri officiorum statuta. The episode is discussed by McLynn (1994) 286, referring to the attempt on the widow's hoard as 'a perfectly legitimate claim'.
[101] Cf. Symm. *Rel.* 34, challenging a rescript based on 'letters' of Constantius II, on the grounds that he has other evidence.

reading of rescripts as being of general validity must reflect the emperors' own view of how their legislation could be used.[102]

However, the increasing complexity of imperial administration made the control of both the issuing and the content of rescripts harder. Rescripts of both kinds, the special grant and the legal decision, became vulnerable to the charge that they were 'obtained contrary to law' or 'surreptitiously' and emperors issued regular denunciations of rescripts which, for one reason or another, were to be dismissed as invalid.[103] Checking the authenticity of rescripts was virtually impossible and the use of one allegedly employed in an analogous case was also hard to verify. By the late fourth century, reform was in the air. The author of the unreliable imperial biographies, written probably in the 390s and known as the *Historia Augusta*, had an interest in law.[104] He inserted into his inventive biography of Macrinus (217–18) some fanciful reflections on that emperor:

'He was no fool in matters of law, and therefore even decided to repeal all the rescripts of former emperors, so that decisions could be made on the basis of law, not rescripts. He said that it was wicked that the caprices (*voluntates*) of Commodus and Caracalla and unskilled amateurs should be regarded as laws (*leges*), when Trajan avoided giving responses to petitions (*libelli*) in order that rulings clearly given out of favour (*gratia*) should not be applied in other cases.'[105]

Concern about the abuse of the rescript system fuelled the thinking at the court of Arcadius on the importance of 'general law', which could be more easily controlled. Therefore, in 398 the emperor and his advisers in Constantinople resolved that one form of rescript could no longer count as 'general'; 'Rescripts sent out or to be sent out in response to legal queries (*consultationes*) are in future to apply only to those cases for which they shall be proved to have been issued.'[106] This did not allay suspicions but contributed to a legislative climate which increasingly favoured imperial use of 'general legislation' as a means of controlling arbitrary rulings. In the Roman Senate's reception of the Theodosian Code in December 438, support was vociferously given to the principle that general laws should not be promulgated in response to petitions (*preces*),[107] a practice which caused the law to be thrown into confusion and damaged the interests of the landowners.[108] The perceived inadequacy of

---

[102] See Honoré (1994) 41 on rescripts for an earlier period but still applicable to the fourth century; 'They did not purport to make new law, although in practice they could not wholly avoid doing so . . . In this they were unlike edicts, which were used for legislation in the modern sense and so could openly innovate. As an element in the development of law, rescripts amounted to a form of authoritative interpretation.'

[103] E.g. *CT* 1.2.9; 11.30.1; 11.12.4; 14.15.3; 15.1.22; 15.2.8; *NTh.* 8.1; *NVal.* 4.1; 19.1.

[104] Honoré (1987).   [105] *SHA Macrinus* 13.   [106] *CT* 1.2.11 (December 398).

[107] *Gesta Senatus* 6 (repeated 21 times).

rescripts as law may also have had a political dimension and it may be no coincidence that rejection of rescript-law as 'general' and the resultant diminution of the office of the *libelli* coincided with the establishment of the quaestor as the legislative supremo on the consistory, the man who 'dictated' *leges*.

All this had its effect also on how the law was perceived in retrospect. When, in 429, the compilers of the Theodosian Code began their task of collecting general laws issued from Constantine onwards, they not only imposed fifth-century classifications on material produced by a different system more than a century old, but also excluded much rescript material, which Gregorius or Hermogenianus would have regarded as genuine 'law'. Apart from chance survivals, such as a few rescripts of Valentinian and Valens preserved by the fifth or sixth-century *Consultatio veteris cuiusdam iurisconsulti*,[109] the historian of late antique law is deprived of numerous case-decisions, whose comparatively restrained style and close focus on the legal point at issue would have acted as a corrective to modern perceptions of late Roman law as sloppy and rhetorical. More important, we have to recognise the existence of a major gap in the legal history of the period. Although developments, particularly in private law, which originated in the operation of rescript-law, would have filtered through into the general law of emperors (such as the moral legislation of Constantine and others), it is hard to trace with any certainty the path along which rescript-law must also have continued to evolve as it had done in the second and third centuries. Thanks to the lawyers of Arcadius and Theodosius, what may have been an important area of late Roman legal evolution is a virtual blank.[110]

Custom and desuetude

By Late Antiquity, custom, *consuetudo*, was a somewhat hybrid concept. It referred to law which was usually unwritten and which was agreed to by 'tacit consent'.[111] As it operated within Roman law, the concept was unproblematic: usages grew up and either became part of what everybody did by general consent, or were incorporated formally into law. But as the

[108] Id. (repeated 17 times).
[109] See, briefly, Schultz (1946) 323–4, rejecting the hypothesis that the author used the *Breviarium* of Alaric (AD 506).
[110] But note the view of Watson (1995a) that evolution of some areas of law covered by jurists had come to a full stop, because every problem had been thought about. This view, if true, would affect the importance of (lost) rescripts for the evolution of private law.
[111] E.g. Gaius, *Inst.* 3.82 on forms of succession to property not catered for by the Twelve Tables or the Edict, 'sed eo iure, quod tacito consensu receptum est, introductae sunt'; also id. 4.26.

Roman Empire expanded, so too did the range and variety of both formal laws and 'customary' law practised in the cities under its rule. Of course, many relationships between Rome and individual cities, especially in the Greek East, had been established by treaties, which safeguarded the validity of local laws. However, the expansion of Roman citizenship, and with it, the authority of the *ius civile*, progressively undermined local systems of jurisdiction and regulation; in the cities of Baetica, for example, in the late first century, Roman law came largely to supplant local law, even for non-citizens.[112]

This would have had comparatively little effect on the operation of local customary law based on 'tacit consent', provided that open conflict with the law as observed in the courts was avoided.[113] In the late third or early fourth century, Menander Rhetor, in a treatise offering templates for panegyrics of cities, observed that 'the topic of laws' was of no help, because all cities conducted public affairs under the laws of the Romans. However, 'different cities have different customs', and the cities could win praise for those.[114] Some systems of *nomoi* (laws) may still have existed, independently of Rome. In the early fourth century the sophist Innocentius of Sardis was credited with 'holding the power of a "nomothete"', lawgiver, having been granted it by the emperors,[115] although it is not clear where he held it or whether it applied specifically to Sardis: if it did, Innocentius' 'lawgiving' probably amounted to no more than a systematisation of local regulations. Becoming a Roman citizen, and therefore subject to Roman law, would not entail abandonment overnight of previously accepted customary behaviour. This can be illustrated by the fact that a perception of Roman law as containing a quality of 'otherness' survived Caracalla's Edict of universal citizenship of 212 by several generations; in the early fourth century, when women in court in Roman Egypt asserted their right of self-representation, because they had three children and therefore the *ius trium liberorum*, they referred to their right as existing 'according to the laws of the Romans'.[116]

The Roman jurists, like modern anthropologists, understood that custom could be more binding than formal regulation, because it was founded on common consent. As Hermogenianus, codifier of imperial rescript-law under Diocletian, wrote, people kept to customary law 'as

[112] As demonstrated by the municipal law of Irni (AD 91), esp. ch. 93. For full text and discussion, see Gonzalez (1986).
[113] The contentious topic of the relationship of 'Volksrecht' and 'Staatsrecht', as developed by L. Mitteis and others, is beyond the scope of this book.
[114] Menander Rhetor, I, 363, trans. D.A. Russell and N.G. Wilson, Oxford 1981, 67.
[115] Eunapius, *Vitae Sophistarum* 23. I. 3–4; *PLRE* i Innocentius I, p. 457, described him as 'legal adviser to the emperors'.   [116] E.g. *P. Berl. Möller*, I (AD 300).

being a tacit agreement of the citizens' ('tacita civium conventio'),[117] and Paulus, writing before 212, ascribed to custom even greater strength than to written law, because it was so universally approved that there had been no need to set it down in writing.[118] It followed that what was established by common consent could also be, in effect, abrogated by the same authority. Thus if laws ceased to be invoked or observed by common consent, they ceased to count as law at all. This doctrine was most magisterially set out by Salvius Julianus:

In situations where we do not use written law, what is sanctioned by habit and custom should be upheld; and if there is anything lacking in this area, then what is nearest and compatible with it; if even this fails, then the law (*ius*) which the city of Rome uses should be followed. Ancient custom is upheld in place of law not without reason, and it too is law which is said to be founded on habit. For seeing that the statutes themselves have authority over us for no reason other than that they were passed by the verdict of the People, it is right that those laws too which the People endorsed in unwritten form will have universal authority. For what difference does it make whether the People declares its will by vote or by the things it does and the facts? Therefore it is very right and proper that it should follow that laws may be abrogated not only by the decision of the legislator but also through desuetude, by the consent of all, expressed without words.[119]

What Julianus observed, and assimilated into a coherent legal and constitutional doctrine on custom and desuetude, has a direct bearing on the operation of late Roman law. Although many ancient statutes had never been formally abrogated, they were no longer consulted. More recent legal rulings had taken their place and some authorities were widely used while others were ignored. The process of natural selection also made the jurists more manageable. Despite the large number available, not all past legal commentators were in practice cited in court. The thirty-eight jurists whose works were to be found in the library of Tribonian and contributed to the *Digest* were an exceptionally large number. A clearer guide to the number generally used in court by the early fifth century is the 'Law of Citations' of 426, which must have reflected contemporary practice when it effectively debarred from citation all but the Big Five,

[117] *Dig.* 1.3.35 (Hermogenian, *Epitome iuris*).   [118] *Dig.* 1.3.36 (Paulus, *Ad Sabinum* 7).
[119] *Dig.* 1.3.32 (Julianus, *Digesta* 84). De quibus causis scriptis legibus non utimur, id custodiri oportet, quod moribus et consuetudine: et si qua in re hoc deficeret, tunc quod proximum et consequens ei est; si nec id quidem appareat, tunc ius, quo urbs Roma utitur, servari oportet. Inveterata consuetudo pro lege non inmerito custoditur, et hoc est ius quod dicitur moribus constitutum. Nam cum ipsae leges nulla alia ex causa nos teneant, quam quod iudicio populi receptae sunt, merito et ea, quae sine ullo scripto populus probavit, tenebunt omnes: nam quid interest suffragio populus voluntatem suam declaret an rebus ipsis et factis? Quare rectissime etiam illud receptum est, ut leges non solum suffragio legis latoris, sed etiam tacito consensu omnium per desuetudinem abrogentur.

Gaius, Paulus, Papinian, Ulpian and Modestinus. Thus for all the emperors' and others' complaints about confusion and ambiguity, the situation with regard to the jurists was, to some extent, simplified by a 'tacit agreement' to limit operations to a few canonical texts. One may even speculate that the 'Law of Citations', by sorting out and simplifying the problem of citation of the jurists for the time being, ultimately postponed the need for a *Digest* of their works for a further hundred years.[120]

Custom also influenced the interpretation of statutes. Paulus commented that if a question arose over the interpretation of a statute, the first thing to find out was how the *civitas* had interpreted the law in previous cases, 'for custom is the best interpreter of the statutes',[121] while Paulus' contemporary, Callistratus, recorded that Septimius Severus had ruled that in cases of doubt arising from the statutes, custom or the authority of an unbroken series of judicial rulings should have the 'force of statute'.[122] However, the authority of custom was not to be accepted blindly; an unreasonable precedent, created in error and sanctioned by the passage of time, was not valid in analogous cases.[123] Thus 'custom' could always be challenged as erroneous and unreasonable. Nevertheless, the role of custom as interpreter of statute was crucial to the nature of imperial legislation. As many imperial constitutions were issued in response to requests to clarify statutes, they themselves had a certain 'interpretative' quality and were thus also liable to be influenced by custom, as well as other considerations. 'Consuetudo', for better or worse, was inevitably part of late Roman law. However, despite the jurists' comments on the authority of 'tacit' popular consent, custom could never prevail, in legal contexts, against the power of the 'lex scripta', the written law. Constantine, in an enactment which reveals in a few words a sophisticated awareness of *lex* and *ratio* as the roots of law, acknowledged that the authority of ancient custom was far from despicable but declared, probably for purposes of court proceedings, that custom could not prevail over 'reason or statute',[124] thus definitively establishing the primacy of Roman law and legal thinking over other means of adjudication.

'Consuetudo', therefore, could both simplify existing practices and

---

[120] The compilers of the Theodosian Code envisaged a second stage, consisting of a Digest of juristic works, on which see *CT* 1.1.5 (26 March 429) and below, p. 64 but it was never implemented.

[121] *Dig.* 1.3.37 (Paulus, *Quaestiones*), optima enim est legum interpres consuetudo.

[122] *Dig.* 1.3.38 (Callistratus, *Quaestiones* 1) (Severus), rescripsit ... consuetudinem aut rerum perpetuo similiter iudicatarum auctoritatem vim legis obtinere debere.

[123] *Dig.* 1.3.39 (Celsus).

[124] *CJ* 8.52.2 (319), consuetudinis ususque longaevi non vilis auctoritas est, verum non usque adeo sui valitura momento, ut aut rationem vincat aut legem.

creatively influence the content of law. What it could not do was remove the muddles in the legal system, which occasioned so much complaint, although it should be conceded that most complex legal systems are liable to confusion and ambiguities. It is true that the jurists contradicted each other, but they were probably not the main source of confusion. That responsibility rested with the emperor, whose constitutions were issued at will, diligently published, haphazardly collected into public archives and private collections, and, as we shall see, erratically cited thereafter, depending on the access available. He, or his legal officers, were the sole source of new law in Late Antiquity and we should now see how he carried out his task.

2   Making the law

Although dirigiste in its language, imperial general law was in fact more often negotiated than imposed. No law was formulated in a political or juristic vacuum. Its content was determined by precedent, current policy, the state of the information available and pressures from interest groups with access to the consistory. Although laws were advertised as intended to endure 'in perpetuity', in practice they could be, and were, modified in the light of experience and further representations from those who operated the law or were affected by it.

To whom was any given law to apply? When, in November 426, the emperors Theodosius II and Valentinian III (then aged 5) addressed their *oratio* to the Roman Senate setting out some principles of government and law, they discussed what 'general laws' (*leges generales*) were, how they were brought into being and how they were to be recognised. Laws could be created either by the emperor's own initiative ('spontaneus motus') or in response to a plea or request (*precatio*), a report or referral (*relatio*), or a legal controversy arising from a lawsuit (*lis mota*). They were 'general' if addressed to the Senate as an *oratio* or labelled as an edict. As they were like edicts they would be publicised throughout the Empire through the offices of the governors, and they would be 'general' also if the emperors declared explicitly that the decision taken on a particular matter would also apply in analogous cases – or, of course, if they were called 'leges generales' and made applicable to all.[1] By contrast, two categories of imperial pronouncement, namely decisions taken in response to referrals or reports, or proposals from provincial *iudices* forwarded to the court by means of *consultationes* (queries on specific points of law), and special grants to bodies, provinces, cities or city councils, would be valid and

---

[1] *CJ* 1.14.3, leges ut generales ab omnibus aequabiliter in posterum observentur, quae vel missa ad venerabilem coetum oratione conduntur vel inserto edicti vocabulo nuncupantur, sive eas nobis spontaneus motus ingesserit sive precatio vel relatio vel lis mota legis occasionem postulaverit. Nam satis est edicti eas nuncupatione censeri vel per omnes populos iudicum programmate divulgari vel expressius contineri, quod principes censuerunt ea, quae in certis negotiis statuta sunt, similium quoque causarum fata componere. Sed si generalis lex vocata est vel ad omnes iussa est pertinere, vim obtineat edicti.

must be upheld and not got round, but would not count as 'general laws'.[2]

The political context of the *oratio* of November 426 is significant. A year earlier, the child Valentinian III had been restored to the western throne by his cousin, Theodosius II, some of whose ministers may still have been an active presence at the court at Ravenna. Both as a means of providing an impressive start for the new reign, and as a form of assertion of political superiority, the easterners may have seized their chance to import into, and impose on, the west, ideas on the systematising of law already current among the ministers of Arcadius[3] and Theodosius II. Certainly, there is almost[4] no evidence, apart from this, that western emperors or their administrations took any interest in the questions of analysing and systematising the law, which came increasingly to preoccupy the ministers of Theodosius II and which were to result in the inception of the Theodosian Code project in March 429 and its promulgation in 438. The idea that the restoration of legitimate government could be appropriately celebrated by the issue of a virtual mini-code clearly springs from the 'spontaneus motus' recorded by the authors of the *oratio* as a trigger for legislation, but it was surely more than that. To codify the law, even in a small way, was also to assert the authority of the codifiers, as exponents and champions of law, against those who would exercise power arbitrarily, be they usurpers or, as the sources of special grants and patronage, even the emperors themselves.

However, such bureaucratic self-assertion was not necessarily detrimental to imperial authority as such, although it may have curtailed the actions of individual emperors. By the mid-fifth century, law, as we shall see, was a product of a lengthy process of consultation within the palace administration, a process which allowed for the voicing of competing views. At its worst, this could, of course, degenerate into factional squabbling but the emphasis on collective decision-making also allowed for a more sophisticated formulation of the policies which could affect the content of legislation. Consequently, although laws were perhaps more

[2] *CJ* 1.14.2. Quae ex relationibus vel suggestionibus iudicantium per consultationem in commune florentissimum sacri nostri palatii procerum auditorium introducto negotio statuimus vel quibuslibet corporibus aut legatis aut provinciae vel civitati vel curiae donavimus, nec generalia iura sint, sed leges fiunt his dumtaxat negotiis atque personis, pro quibus fuerint promulgata, nec ab aliqo retractentur...
[3] *CT* 1.2.11 (398, Arcadius), declares that rescripts issued in response to *consultationes* shall be valid only for those cases for which they are issued, and may mark an early stage in eastern attempts to define 'generality'. All rescripts were to be excluded from the Theodosian Code.
[4] *CJ* 1.14.4, a western law addressed to Volusianus, prefect of Italy, in June 429, states the emperor's subjection to the laws as a constitutional doctrine, but lack of a broader context prevents assessment of its real significance for legal or constitutional thinking (if any).

frequently evoked by external approaches, often from interest-groups with their own strategies for influencing the outcome, the resultant general legislation could go well beyond a simple response to the issue raised.

In consistory

In the fifth century, the imperial council, known since the time of Constantius II as the consistory, was the main forum for the debating and framing of legislation. As a council of advisers, it had a long history. Under the Roman Republic, heads of households consulted with their family councils and magistrates relied on a *consilium* of 'friends' for expert guidance. From Augustus onwards, the *consilium principis* was a consistently influential source of advice and expertise,[5] although its membership varied, while provincial governors and judges continued to rely on advice tendered by *consilia* or, in trials, bodies of legally trained assessors. In late antiquity,[6] the emperors' generals and ministers continued to assemble to carry out their time-honoured function of providing support and advice. In one important respect, however, the *consistorium* differed from its early imperial counterpart, and that was that it largely consisted of palace departmental and provincial supremos, who represented not only themselves but their areas of responsibility. Although the emperor could in theory control its membership, in practice by the fifth century, the consistory was based round the praetorian prefects as heads of the provincial administrations, the master of the offices (*magister officiorum*), the head of the palace administration, the two counts of the treasuries (the public, *sacrae largitiones*, and the personal property of the emperor, the *res privata*), the imperial quaestor, who drafted laws and, uniquely, had no office (*officium*) and various 'counts of the consistory' (*comites consistoriani*), who were advisers without fixed responsibilities.

While in public, the emperor might appear aloof, even godlike, in the more intimate environment of the consistory, freedom of speech was not discouraged. One reason for a continued tradition of informality was that at least some consistory sessions were held in public as late as the reigns of Diocletian and Maximian, when the not always helpful public reactions were also read into the consistory minutes. On one occasion, the emperors' quite proper decision that sons of decurions found guilty of some crime should not be thrown to the wild beasts, was greeted with howls of protest from the disappointed crowd. The emperors reacted with contempt: 'The vain outcries of the people should not be listened to; no weight should be attached to their shouting, when they want either the

[5] For changes in its function and membership under the Early Empire, see Crook (1955).
[6] For important stages in its evolution under Constantius II, see Vogler (1979) 216–20.

acquittal of a guilty man or the condemnation of an innocent'.[7] Two general rules could be inferred from these proceedings. One was that decurions' sons were still a protected group. Secondly, despite the attention professedly paid by emperors to acclamations and other demonstrations of popular opinion, justice was not to be determined by the mob. In this case, imperial contempt for lynch-law would have been further buttressed by the emperors' need to safeguard the privileges of the elite.

The consistory also acted as adjudicator in disputes, thus generating further decisions of general application. A case about exemptions from *munera*, civic obligations, was brought before Diocletian's consistory, in the presence of two named individuals and the leading men of Antioch, whose probable representative, Sabinus, made a speech, which does not survive. The imperial ruling was that former *praepositi* and *protectores* were exempt from public *munera*. Clearly, the situation was one which was repeated over and over again in hearings before emperors and governors, a conflict between the city council and members of it claiming non-liability to duties or contributions. Here, exemption was being sought by former holders of the two named positions, perhaps the two named individuals. This would have been resisted by the leaders of the Antiochene council, who stood to lose out, if the resources of their council were depleted by a grant, which could subsequently be extended to all former office-holders of this type. Nor could this be isolated as a one-off exercise in imperial generosity. The inclusion of this extract in the Codes of Gregorius and Hermogenian, from which it passed into the Codex Justinianus, elevated it to a statement of general principle, to be followed and exploited by others in similar cases, and extracts from the *acta consistorii* of later emperors were to be accepted, where appropriate, as 'general laws' by the compilers of the Theodosian Code.

As the fourth century progressed, consistory business may have been conducted increasingly behind closed doors. Extracts from the *acta consistorii* of Julian and Theodosius I[8] show emperors in consistory giving rulings on, respectively, written documentation, the role of bishops as witnesses and the cession of goods, but no indication as to whether the cases were discussed in public. That some still may have been, especially when the consistory acted as a court, is suggested by the known fact that Julian, for one, did give judgements in public and that emperors, who exerted some pressure on their *iudices* to conduct legal hearings in public, could not themselves have been seen to set a bad example of secrecy. However, some confidential consistory business must always have been handled in private and, by the late fourth century, Theodosius I was

---

[7] *CJ* 9.47.12.   [8] *CT* 11.39.5(362); 11.39.8(381); 4.20.3(386).

moved to insist that the confidentiality of consistory proceedings be strictly preserved.[9]

Properly used, consistory hearings and discussions allowed the emperor to become better informed and acted as a restraining force on arbitrary government – provided that the emperor would listen. An incident in 369–70, recounted by Ammianus, reveals both the failings of the system and how they could be rectified. Having received a report from Rome that senators were engaged in murderous and magical practices, Valentinian I flew into a rage and issued a general ruling which assimilated these crimes 'arbitrarily' ('arroganter') to that of treason, thus making all classes of suspect people liable to torture; in Ammianus' paraphrase of the new law, 'All whom the justice of the ancient law and the decisions of previous emperors had exempted from interrogation under torture should, if the investigation demanded, be liable to torments.'[10] This was a serious violation of the civil rights of those who counted most in society, the senatorial elite, and the result was a bloodbath in Rome. In desperation, the Senate mobilised its collective *auctoritas* and appointed a delegation of three senators, representing the three ranks of *illustris, spectabilis* and *clarissimus*, and led by the highly respected senator, Vettius Agorius Praetextatus. They approached Valentinian with two requests, that the punishment inflicted should fit the crime, and that no senator should be subject to torture. Valentinian was shocked. He had never made such a ruling (he said) and was being falsely accused. At this point, Eupraxius, the first imperial quaestor known also to have exerted authority in consistory on a legal matter, intervened to tell the emperor he was wrong. Valentinian accepted the correction and the decree was rescinded.[11]

The incident shows that, when faced with an emperor notoriously prone to losing his temper, a fine balance had to be struck. The senatorial delegation was able to gain access in the first place because that was the Senate's privilege, but the success of its petition depended on the goodwill, expertise and courage of the quaestor Eupraxius. Conversely, Eupraxius, who, as quaestor from 367, had been party to the original wrong decision but had failed to do anything to reverse it, needed the help of the Senate to get his way. Success in negotiating with wilful emperors – and contradicting them, if need be – depended to a great extent on tact, as Eupraxius showed on another occasion when he intervened to protect decurions from execution, by persuading the irate emperor that they would be honoured as martyrs.[12] Similar verbal adroitness was displayed by the Gallic Praetorian Prefect, Florentius, who, when confronted with

[9] Ambrose, *Ep.* 74.   [10] Amm. Marc. 28.1.11.   [11] Amm. Marc. 28.1.24.
[12] Amm. Marc. 27.7.6.

an imperial order, again from Valentinian, to execute three decurions per city, suggested, facetiously, that some cities might not possess as many as three decurions and that there should be a rider added, 'provided the city has them'.[13] However, quick thinking, free speech and the opportune arrival of friendly delegations were resources not always available for consistory members hoping to check the excesses of angry emperors. Although decurions had connections, and therefore could hope for help from the likes of Eupraxius and Florentius, Ammianus, who himself came from the curial or office-holding class, believed that such interventions had only a limited effect on Valentinian's policies, because, like other proud rulers, he was not open to advice and denied his *amici* the opportunity to dissuade him from unjust designs or actions, while also terrifying his opponents into silence.[14] Thus while pressure on emperors, from friend and foe alike, acted to check the arbitariness of imperial rule, the success of the consistory as a means of control still depended on the qualities and rapid responses of individuals, rather than on any obligation on the part of the emperor to listen to its counsel.

By the mid-fifth century, consistory procedure for the making of general legislation in Constantinople had become formalised. The role of the emperor's council was defined as an integral part of the consultative process.[15] A proposed new measure was first discussed by 'all' the leading men (*proceres*) of the palace and by the Senate at Constantinople. If the emperor and all consulted agreed, a draft was drawn up, probably by the imperial quaestor, whose job it was to draft legislation. 'Everyone' then assembled and looked at it again and when 'everyone' had assented, it was formally presented in the 'sacred consistory of our divinity', and, finally, with universal assent, the new law was validated by the imperial authority, through the affixing of the emperor's subscription.

The emphasis on consultation and universal agreement was standard rhetoric. It was essential to the emperor's own representation of himself to his Empire that his actions commanded wide support. In this case, Theodosius was able to list the steps taken to ensure that support was forthcoming. But the law entailed more than just paying lip-service to public opinion. Consensus precluded arbitrary decisions by the ruler, and guaranteed constitutional behaviour and the legitimacy of the emperors' rule. Emperors had to live up to their own professions, to some extent, and the formalising through a written law of procedures which allowed a wide range of views to be taken into account made him accountable to the laws in a way which Valentinian had not been. Probably, the procedure would have been too cumbersome to use in routine cases, when the

---

[13] Amm. Marc. 27.7.7.   [14] Amm. Marc. 27.7.9.
[15] *CJ* 1.14.8 (17 October 446), discussed by Honoré (1986) 136–7, Harries (1988) 165–6.

consistory would have done no more than rubber-stamp a formal response to a report or proposal. What the law did was to establish a procedure and specify the parties who had a right to be consulted, ensuring space for negotiations on contentious matters, before laws were issued.

The causes of the formalisation of consultative procedures may be traced in this, as in other areas of legal activity, to the growing collective influence of the administration of the East. A largely stationary court, based in Constantinople, a stable and increasingly self-confident bureaucracy staffed by gifted and ambitious careerists, drawn from the governing classes of the Greek East, a general sense of peace and prosperity, and a personally unassertive emperor, Theodosius II, encouraged the evolution of a governing class, with a confident sense of its own identity, and a willingness to tackle long-term problems, not least those arising from the unregulated relationship of the absolutist emperor with Roman law. As we shall see, the greatest achievement of the Theodosian lawyers, the Theodosian Code, offered no explicit challenge to the theory of absolutism and indeed the *Gesta Senatus* of December 438, when the Code was presented to the Roman Senate, reaffirmed imperial supremacy. Nevertheless, the act of codification was in fact one of several by which the imperial bureaucracy asserted the rule of law over the rule of the emperor.

Making the text: the imperial quaestor

Imperial general laws from late antiquity often fail to convey the impression of being laws at all. Instead, their lengthy preambles feature virtuoso displays of eloquence, which extend into the parts of the text containing the 'legal content' or *ius*. The apparent preference of some drafters of laws for rhetorical fireworks rather than legal precision inevitably raises questions about the validity of the entire law-making process. If accuracy in terminology was sacrificed to an obsession with language, conceptual integrity and the philosophy of law might also be put at risk.

Recent studies of the language of imperial constitutions[16] and the role of their main authors, the imperial quaestors, reveal a more complex picture.[17] Even using the relatively brief fragments of longer constitutions preserved in the Theodosian Code, it is possible, as Tony Honoré has shown, to discern a number of different styles and approaches to legislation, comprising the legal, the bureaucratic and the plain rhetorical, the last exemplified by Gratian's former tutor and quaestor in 376, the poet

---

[16] See esp. Voss (1982).
[17] Honoré (1986); (1993); (1998); Harries (1988). On the language, see Voss (1982).

Ausonius. Although the legal grasp of some quaestors (such as Ausonius) was weak,[18] on the whole the language of imperial laws did not seriously undermine their legal content. This was partly because, by the early fifth century, eastern quaestors had considerable personal knowledge of law, but also because law-making was, as we have seen, often a collective exercise, which allowed men who did understand law to formulate the concepts, which were then dressed up in appropriately dignified language by the quaestor.

The prime responsibility of the quaestor for the language of the laws derived from his original function, which he never lost, as imperial spokesman.[19] By the time the great civil and military service list, the *Notitia Dignitatum*, was put together in the late fourth century, the imperial quaestor had the main responsibility for drafting the text of laws,[20] eaning that he was responsible for their language, but not their content. Thus, although, in the East, the quaestor increasingly took on the role of the emperor's chief legal officer, the initial requirement for the job was not legal expertise but skill with words, *eloquentia*, a qualification with a long history.[21] The original and primary role of the imperial quaestor of late antiquity as no more (or less) than a spokesman of the emperor evolved out of the *quaestor candidatus*[22] of the Early Empire, who was charged with reading out the emperor's words to the Roman Senate. Emperors were supposed to address their subjects in their own words. In the reign of Constantine, the convention that the emperor himself still wrote some of his own laws and speeches survived: according to his biographer, Eusebius of Caesarea, Constantine wrote a letter on the errors of paganism in his own hand, orations in Latin, which were translated into Greek, and theological discussions, delivered to large captive audiences.[23]

Constantine's personal touch in matters religious also provided a precedent for that most individual of imperial authors, Julian. Whether or not he personally drafted all his official enactments, the texts reflect an idiosyncratic and distinctive approach, suggesting that Julian at least strongly influenced what was written in his name. For example, his laws show an unusual disregard for predecessors, especially Constantine, whose laws he delighted to abrogate. He also on occasion yielded to the

---

[18] See Honoré (1984); (1986) 207–10; Harries (1988) 166–9.
[19] For 6th C. examples in East and West, see *Anth. Pal.* 16.48, referring to Proclus as 'the mouth of the king', and Cassiodorus, *Var.* 6.5., the king addressing his quaestor, 'quaesturam toto corde recipimus, quam nostrae linguae vocem esse censemus'.
[20] *ND Or* 12 and *Occ* 10, leges dictandae, preces. For more detailed analyses of the quaestorship and quaestors, see Harries (1988); Honoré (1986); (1993); (1998).
[21] Purcell (1986) 589. [22] Talbert (1984) 163–84; Ulpian at *Dig.* 1.13.2 and 4.
[23] Eus. *Vita Constantini* 4.8; 4.32; 4.29.2; 2.47; Millar (1977) 205–6.

temptation to score debating points at the expense of Christians; in a letter to the citizens of Bostra, which exhorted Christians to renounce violence, Julian exploited the reports sent by their own bishop to undermine their case,[24] while the Christians of Edessa, who had to endure the sight of their church being stripped of its wealth to pay soldiers, also were consoled by the apostate emperor with the thought that they should be grateful for their chance to practise Christian poverty 'and not lose that heavenly kingdom, for which they still hope'.[25]

Julian, although peculiarly vehement, was perhaps less eccentric than might appear. The use of official letters as a means of advertising the emperor's personal convictions was not new: Constantine's support of his favoured religion in his official letters to eastern recipients had been equally fervent.[26] Moreover, the letter-form as a means of conveying legal pronouncements was, in the early fourth century, perhaps too flexible a medium of communication, in that an official *epistula* could contain what would be later recognised as 'general law' but might also be no more than a manifesto on some policy matter, like religion, of which the emperor wished his subjects to become aware. He would also have appreciated that subjects' perceptions of his wishes might in turn influence their requests to him. Thus the persecuting emperor, Maximinus Daia, went to some lengths in showing hostility to Christians in order to encourage cities to win his favour by requesting permission to persecute Christians.[27] A similar calculation would have been made by the citizens of Orcistus in Phrygia, when they petitioned Constantine in 331 for full city-status, because of ancient usage, magistrates, population, site, water-supply – and because they were all 'followers of the most holy religion'.[28] In the light of this precedent, Julian's verbose attempts at self-justification should not be analysed only in terms of an unprecedented personal compulsion to communicate.[29] Like his predecessors, he used the official 'open' letter both as a proclamation of policy, perhaps reinforced by a legal enactment, and as a straightforward rhetorical exercise in imperial propaganda, which might generate convenient responses in interested sections of the population.

Whether or not emperors continued to use their own words for some

---

[24] Julian, *Ep.* 41, 437D.   [25] Julian, *Ep.* 40, 425A.
[26] E.g. in letters reproduced at Eus. *Vita Constantini* 2.47–50.
[27] Eusebius' account in *HE* 9. is confirmed by inscriptional evidence analysed by Mitchell (1988).
[28] For the Orcistus dossier, see *FIRA* 1.463–5. This contained Constantine's letter to Ablabius, giving his reasons for the grant, a copy of the petition of the Orcistians, and the formal 'rescript' (*praesens rescriptio*) of Constantine Augustus and the two Caesars, Constantine and Constantius, granting independent *civitas* status.
[29] On Julian's use of traditional methods of communication, see Gleason (1986), on the *Misopogon*.

purposes, many legal pronouncements had long been drafted by others in the imperial secretariats. In the fourth century, the quaestor's role as imperial spokesman took on increasing significance, perhaps to the detriment of the principal legal bureaux of the *memoria, epistulae,* and *libelli*. The Byzantine historian, Zosimus, writing in the early sixth century, believed that Constantine was the first to appoint quaestors 'to communicate the emperor's decisions',[30] and imperial quaestors are found negotiating with foreign powers and advising Caesars under Constantius II.[31] One of Julian's most prominent supporters, the pagan Saturninus Secundus Salutius, served as his quaestor and was simultaneously a member of the consistorium.[32] Although only of the second rank, as *viri spectabiles*, in the 370s,[33] by the time of the *Notitia Dignitatum*, they were *illustres*.[34] Unusually, they had no office-staff of their own (and therefore, in theory, no private interest to represent);[35] instead, they used assistance from the secretariats, the *scrinia*.[36]

Their career patterns were diverse and, by the fifth century, a clear division emerged between the quaestors of East and West. On the whole, quaestors in the fourth century rose through the palace bureaucracy, especially the secretariats, but some, like Nicomachus Flavianus in 389, were drawn from the senatorial aristocracy. Their backgrounds inevitably affected the qualities they brought to the job. Many incumbents, although perhaps more prominent for their eloquence, would have had some legal knowledge but Eupraxius (Western quaestor 367–70) is one of the few whose legal expertise is emphasised in the sources. By the early fifth century, the quaestorship in the East had, on the whole, become more legally professionalised than its western counterpart. While the quaestors of Arcadius and Theodosius II worked towards the creation of a system of imperial law, no such urge can be detected in the western court, except in the late 420s, when eastern influence was strong in Ravenna, following the restoration of Valentinian III. The few western quaestors recorded for the fifth century, such as Victor and Fulgentius, the associ-

[30] Zos. *Historia Nova* 5.32 (of 408).
[31] Amm. Marc. 14.11.14 (Fl. Taurus' mission to Armenia); 14.7.12–18 (Montius, quaestor, lynched by soldiers of Gallus the Caesar); 20.9.4 (Nebridius and Leonas negotiate with Julian as Caesar on behalf of Constantius II).
[32] *CIL* 6.1764 = *ILS* 1255, item comes ordinis primi intra consistorium et quaestor. For Iovius as quaestor in the consistory under Julian, see *CT* 11.39.5, adstante Iovio viro clarissimo quaestore.   [33] *CT* 6.9.1 (372), on quaestors' precedence over proconsuls.
[34] Insignia of quaestor are described in the *Not. Dig.* as belonging to the 'viri illustris quaestoris'.
[35] Usually true, but note the quaestors' struggle for control of the *laterculum minus*, or roll of lesser offices, recorded at *CT* 1.8.1–3.
[36] *Not. Dig. Or.* 12, officium non habet sed adiutores de scriniis quos voluerit, with *Occ.* 10, habet subaudientes adiutores memoriales de scriniis diversis.

ates of Sidonius Apollinaris, are praised for their eloquence, rather than their knowledge of law. The same contrast between East and West survived into the sixth century: in Italy, the eloquent Cassiodorus devoted his linguistic skills to composing the letters of the Ostrogothic kings, while, in the East a little later, Tribonian created for Justinian the massive *Corpus Iuris Civilis*.

While quaestors may generally be credited with responsibility for the language of imperial law, their role in the creation of the content of the text was diluted by the input of the original proponent of the legislation and the various discussions with interested parties, formalised for the East in the law of 446. Moreover, the texts preserved in the Codes are often in the form of the *epistulae* sent out by the secretariat. By the late fourth century, these were listed in the *Notitia Dignitatum* as the offices of the *memoria*, or records, who 'dictated all *annotationes* and sent them out';[37] the *epistulae*, who 'handled embassies from cities and requests for legal advice (*consultationes*)';[38] and the *libelli*, who dealt with trials (*cognitiones*),[39] probably over procedural matters. All three also responded to petitions (*preces*). What the *Notitia* omitted was the role of the *magister memoriae* as the draftsman of non-legal imperial communications to the Senate, for which there is some evidence in the late 370s.[40] Also, from the 390s, comes evidence from the eccentric biographer of emperors, the author of the *Historia Augusta*, that the *memoria* could plausibly be represented as drafting letters for emperors: claiming that Claudius Gothicus had dictated an imperial, (but fictitious), letter himself, the 'scriptor' claimed loftily that 'I have no need for the words of the *magister memoriae*'[41] . From the drafting of non-legal pronouncements, it was a short step to the formulation of laws; a request to one Benivolus, *magister memoriae*, in the 380s, to write out a law, which he refused because of its pro-Arian content,[42] may not have been atypical. Certainly, the quaestor could not always have been present when required, or there may have times when the office was vacant. In such circumstances, the head of the *memoria*, the senior of the three secretarial *magistri*, was the obvious deputy.[43]

By the fifth century, the quaestorship was an office of great power and influence, held by the highest in the land, who often went on to hold one of the great praetorian prefectures. Once tenure of the office was com-

---

[37] *Not. Dig. Or.* 19.6–7.   [38] Id. 8–9.   [39] Id. 10–11.

[40] Harries (1988) 160–1 on Symm. *Epp.* 1.95 and 3.17, with reference to an *oratio* to the Senate drafted by the probable *mag. mem.*, Proculus Gregorius.

[41] SHA *Claudius Gothicus* 7.1–2. See also *Carus* 8.4 on an invented letter from a *mag. mem.* 'proving' that Carus died naturally.   [42] Harries (1988) 162–3.

[43] It therefore follows that stylistic analysis of some 'quaestors', especially those with apparently short terms or standing in for short periods, may in fact apply to laws drafted by *magistri memoriae*.

bined, in the East, with a solid understanding of the law itself, the position became one in which the incumbent could not only draft the laws elegantly, but could also impose his expertise on the content. But, as we have seen, the production of complex or contentious legislation was not likely to be due to one individual, be he emperor or quaestor. In reality, the content of imperial law was the result of the interplay of personalities in the consistory, of interest groups within and outside the imperial councils, of imperial policy and the perceived needs of the empire, of legal tradition, precedent and custom. Whenever emperors turned to legislation, whether due to 'spontaneus motus' or promptings from outside, the resultant text was, by the fifth century, no longer 'his' personally, but the creation of a collective legal and administrative culture. In the Constantinople of Arcadius and Theodosius II, the vagaries of the emperor were no longer important in the formulation of law; he was not a personality, he was an institution.

Suggestio

General laws were issued at the emperor's own initiative or in response to promptings from officials at court and others in the provinces, who in turn might be responding to pressures from below.[44] Inevitably his administration was battered by a constant stream of requests, reports and petitions. Where these were not routine, they could take the form of a proposal, usually referred to as a *suggestio*, backed often by a report from the parties concerned.[45] The importance of *suggestio* procedure for the overall character of imperial law-making was that the procedure triggered a response. However, it did not dictate what that response was, and therefore its prevalence does not in itself establish that imperial government was 'passive'. The nature of the response was, as we have seen, determined by the individual emperor's will, precedent, advice and the existing framework of the law, which the emperor had the power to modify but to which he was also subject.[46]

The extracts of laws preserved in the Theodosian Code often refer to the emperor having 'learned' of a particular situation, which required him to act.[47] Here the existence of a report or *suggestio* may be inferred, but in other places it is made explicit that the law is issued in response to a

[44] See Panciera (1971).   [45] See Honoré (1986); Harries (1993).
[46] *CJ* 1.14.4 (429, West) and above, pp. 36–7.
[47] E.g. *CT* 2.14.1 (400), 'animadvertimus'; 6.1.17. (397), 'adfirmatur'; 6.29.12 (415), 'compertum est'; 7.4.3 (357), 'dicitur'; 7.4.12 (364), Ursicini comitis suggestione cognovimus; 8.1.15 ex insinuatione magnificentiae tuae cognitis his . . .

proposal.[48] By the time of Constantius II a filtering process was in place, which channelled *suggestiones* and *relationes* (which could be reports or referrals of cases to a higher court) from the provinces through the *vicarii*.[49] This did not preclude direct communication between an emperor and a lesser official on a matter raised by him: Constantius II, for example, addressed a ruling on the recruitment of civil servants into the army to the *dux* of Mesopotamia, although the initial report had come from the *vicarius* in charge of the area.[50] Similarly, in 397, a warning against abuse of the public post system was dispatched directly by Arcadius to the *dux* of Armenia;[51] this could have been a response to information emanating from a source independent of, and perhaps hostile to, the offending *dux*, and is an illustration of how the Roman government held its officials to account, by using information submitted by others against them.

Suggestio was an essential part of the imperial information system. Provincial governors and commanders, along with palatine ministers, submitted reports and proposals on military, administrative and juridical topics, some of which merely required rubber-stamping by the consistory.[52] Others were contentious, and one means by which the channels of communication were kept open was competition between officials to aggrandise themselves and undermine opponents. The stakes were high, as the result might be publicly proclaimed in a general law. An official with a grievance had every incentive to bring it to the emperor's attention and victory or defeat might have more important effects on the individual's *dignitas* than the original subject of dispute. The Prefects of the City in both Rome and Constantinople, for example, were especially alert in defence of their privileges. Symmachus the Elder successfully upheld his right to hear appeals from the *vicarius Romae*[53] and, in 423, the Roman Senate fought off attempts to favour military jurisdiction in the City at the expense of the Prefect.[54] In Constantinople, under Theodosius I, the Prefect extended his jurisdiction over Bithynia, Paphlagonia and Phrygia Salutaris[55] and encroachments by others were successfully resisted: in 391, the Count of the Sacred Largesses was severely and publicly reprimanded for assaulting and fining merchants without sanction from the Prefect, and the right of the Prefect to adjudicate in tax cases was confirmed;[56] in 393, the over-zealous Addeus, Master of the Soldiers, was warned that the punishment of governors, even when justified, was not his responsibility but that of the Prefect.[57] Others also extended their

---

[48] E.g. *CT* 6.30.8 (385), placuit iusta et ... profutura suggestio; 7.8.8 secuti suggestionem tuam.   [49] *CT* 1.15.3 (352).   [50] *CT* 8.4.4 (349).   [51] *CT* 8.5.57.
[52] E.g.*CT* 6.27.23 (430) to Paulinus, *magister officiorum*, accepting regulations for staff in secret service.
[53] *CT* 1.6.2 and 3, addressed, respectively to Symmachus, as Prefect, and Severus, the vicar, of the City in June 364.   [54] *CT* 1.6.11.   [55] *CT* 1.6.10 (385).   [56] *CT* 1.5.10.

personal fiefdoms where they could. The proconsul of Asia scored a coup in 396, when the administration of the Hellespont was transferred to his authority from that of the *vicarius Asiae*, in response to complaints from the office-staff, who appeared to have resorted to an appeal to a rival patron, in order to benefit both him and themselves.[58] Closer to the emperor, a nine-year battle between the imperial quaestors and the Master of the Offices, the head of the civil service, for control of the 'lesser register' (*Laterculum Minus*), which conferred patronage in minor appointments, ended in victory for the quaestor.[59]

Competition within the palace administration could be expressed through *suggestiones*, which had as their main purpose the making of laws that would undermine a rival department. In June 440, Valentinian III agreed to a proposal from his praetorian prefect, the future emperor Petronius Maximus, which in effect made him the last court of appeal on taxation matters.[60] Palace tax-collectors were forbidden to collect more than was specified in the lists and provincials who felt oppressed could appeal to the counts of the treasuries, who would be liable for failures to Maximus himself, or to their own governors, who in turn could also refer such cases to Maximus, while the jurisdiction of the counts of the treasuries over provincial tax-collection was also handed over to the office of the praetorian prefect. It may be safely assumed that the law embodies the *suggestio* of the main beneficiary, Petronius Maximus, whose reform subsumed the hitherto separate offices of the treasury under the wing of the praetorian prefecture. Although the alleged justification was to control extortion by the tax-collectors, the issue at stake was not reform, but power. This reform did not last. Two years later, Maximus had left office and the new prefect, the less impressive Paterius, had to report that, due to the restrictions of the previous law, the counts of the treasuries were unable (they said) to collect taxes at all. Unable to resist pressures from his financial officers, backed by the new prefect, Valentinian gave way; 'we restore to the aforesaid Illustrious Men (the counts) every right which they have had for a long time now'.[61] The *novella* did not add that there were other reasons for problems with tax-collections in some areas, due to Vandal raids on the coasts of Italy, which made it the more imperative that Valentinian collected such revenues as he could.

Laws of emperors framed in response to the requests of subjects inevitably reflected the diversity of the empire itself. As under the Early Empire, the imperial court acted as a magnet for representations from all kinds of interest-groups, including cities, guilds and provincial councils,

[57] *CT* 1.7.2.   [58] *CT* 1.12.5.   [59] *CT* 1.8.1–3.   [60] *NVal.* 7.1.
[61] *NVal.* 7.2 (September 442). See *NVal.* 9 (24 June 440) for advice on self-help against the Vandals in Italy.

who used political clout or patronage to catch the emperor's ear.[62] From Constantine onwards, these were joined by bishops, whose representations to the emperor could carry the added authority of independent adjudication on matters of doctrine and in the episcopal hearings. As one of the main requirements of a successful embassy was cheap and comfortable travel, it was worth seeking free access to the *cursus publicus*, on which there are an impressive sixty-six entries in the relevant section of the Theodosian Code.[63] Ammianus accused Constantius II of cluttering up the whole public post system with bishops 'rushing about to and fro' to attend Church Councils.[64] Even the Senate asserted its rights to a free ride; in 371, Valentinian conceded to a worried Senate that senators as well as provincials were entitled to use the public post when on embassies to him.[65]

The Senate at Rome reasserted its influence in the fourth century[66]and was among the most influential and articulate pressure groups to deal with the imperial authority in the West. Custom prescribed a special format for imperial communications with that august body, the *oratio*, which could deal with matters of law, as did the mini-code of 426, which covered the nature of law, jurisdiction and the law of succession.[67] The Senate itself was chaired by the Prefect of the City and channelled some of its opinions to the imperial court through the medium of the Prefects' official state papers, or *Relationes*.[68] On occasions, there could be controversy as to whether a Prefect's representations were in fact representative of the whole of senatorial opinion: Symmachus found himself in difficulties over matters religious, notoriously in his presentation to Valentinian II of a 'senatorial' request for the restoration of the altar of Victory to the Senate-house as if it had majority support.[69] Although much was done by correspondence and the exchange of official documents, which were duly filed, business was also conducted in person, through embassies. Missions of congratulation on imperial victories were routine (as were the announcements of the victories to the Senate in formal *orationes*), but delegations were also dispatched to deal with matters of especial concern, such as the pogrom of senators carried out in Rome in *c.* 370.[70]

Dealing with the Senate allowed for complex negotiations before a law came into being, and shows clearly that the texts of many laws that have

---

[62] At *CT* 1.16.2 (317), Constantine tried to ensure that approaches from provincial councils were first vetted by governors. This is re-enacted among other laws in the contents of *CT* 12.12.   [63] *CT* 8.5.   [64] Amm. Marc. 21.16.18.   [65] *CT* 8.5.32.

[66] Matthews (1975) passim.   [67] *CJ* 1.14.2 and 3; *CT* 1.4.3; *CJ* 1.2.13; 1.19.7; 1.22.5.

[68] On Symmachus' *Relationes*, see Barrow (1973); Vera (1981).

[69] Symm. *Rel.* 3, opposed by Ambrose, *Epp.* 17 and 18, a controversy revisited by Prudentius, *Contra Symmachum* II in *c.* 402.

[70] For the mission of Vettius Agorius Praetextatus and two others on this, see above, p. 40.

come down to us have no single creator. In 384, Symmachus, as Prefect of the City, sent a formal letter of thanks for an imperial *oratio*, which limited senatorial expenditure on games and restored precedence in making speeches in the Senate to present and former holders of high office. The senate had debated the proposals set out in the *oratio* (which could itself have been couched in terms agreed after consultation with senators), and had passed their resolution about it 'with no dissenting voice'. This resolution defined in detail the liability for the giving of public entertainments, the limits on, and apportioning of, expenditure on gladiatorial games and stage plays and the fines to be imposed on absentees.[71] The emperor was now requested to confirm by an imperial *lex* the resolution of the Senate, which could thus be expected to feature largely in the final binding enactment.

Complex, however, as this set of exchanges might appear, expenditure on games was a comparatively uncontroversial matter of direct concern to senators, who, in this case, were best qualified to assess their own needs, without excessive outside interference. This was not always the case. Despite the ornate courtesy shown in the style of Symmachus' official communications and the public emphasis on 'unanimous decisions', neither Prefect nor Senate would passively acquiesce in decisions contrary to its interests. Symmachus himself criticised Valentinian II for not appointing suitable men to junior administrative positions, an act of defiance which may have elicited a formal public rebuke.[72] Perhaps the most notorious demonstration of senatorial independence (or narrow self-interest) occurred in 397, when the Empire was confronted with a dangerous revolt in Africa. While happy to reassert its ancient privilege of declaring the rebel, Gildo, a public enemy, senators refused to provide recruits from their estates, proposing instead to substitute for each recruit a cash payment of 25 solidi. The emperor agreed. Nine years later, after several years of insecurity and devastation in some regions of Italy, the Senate loyally voted for war against Alaric and his Goths, but denied to Honorius and his general, Stilicho, the resources to fight it. The emperor then demanded that they fund a payment of 4,000 pounds of gold, which was reluctantly conceded, although one senator spoke out against the deal, referring to it as being not peace but a compact of slavery.[73] Such freedom of speech is partly a reflection of imperial weakness at the time; Valentinian II and Honorius lacked the force of character to impose themselves on the seasoned politicians of the Roman scene. But it was also a feature of dealings between emperor and subjects in general. Outspokenness on the part of (some) senators, ministers and bishops,

[71] Symm. *Rel.* 8.3.   [72] Symm. *Rel.* 17; Matthews (1986) 165–6; *CT* 1.6.9.
[73] Zosimus, *New History* 5.29.6–9.

both within and beyond the consistory, co-existed with the ceremonial formality of the emperor's public role and counteracted the isolation of the imperial figure-head.

Consultation had one further consequence. Laws made with or without promptings from outside could require to be changed or modified in the light of experience. The mandate given to the compilers of the Theodosian Code allowed for the inclusion of outmoded legislation, with the proviso that the more recent of contradictory constitutions was the valid one. This allowed the imperial lawyers to indulge their fondness for legal history by inserting into the record how some legislation had evolved, especially, but not exclusively, in the relatively unfamiliar area of Christianity. Sweeping reforms of criminal legislation were especially risky because of the seriousness of the consequences, if the innocent were unintentionally implicated. Among the less well-known initiatives of Constantine was an attempt to tighten the law on forgery. In 318, owners of farms and houses used as bases for counterfeiting coinage were made liable to deportation (perpetual exile) to an island and loss of all property, but, if he was ignorant, his loss was limited to the place of the crime. He escaped punishment only if he informed of the offence, once he knew about it.[74] Several years later, perhaps due to test cases in the courts, the excessive harshness of the law had become apparent, and Constantine refined the conditions, basing liability to punishment on access to knowledge, gender, and legal capacity. If the owner lived a long way off (and so could not have known) he was free of blame, as was a widow owner, provided she was ignorant, and a ward, as a minor would not understand what he saw; a tutor, on the other hand, if resident locally, would be penalised (out of his own property, not that of his ward), as he should have known what was happening on the property of his charge.[75]

Laws could also be modified in the light of pressures from groups whose interests had, initially, been ignored. Theodosius II responded in 416 to the 'unhelpful claims' of a delegation from the city council of Alexandria by laying out regulations about *parabalani*, religious nurses of the sick, whose numbers were to be limited to five hundred, and whose names were to be reported to the *Praefectus Augustalis*, the governor of Egypt, and, through him, to the Praetorian Prefect.[76] Probably this provoked further representations from Alexandria and, just over a year later, a new law was issued, raising the number to six hundred and making their recruitment the responsibility of the bishop, a clear victory for the somewhat turbulent ecclesiastical establishment of that divided city.[77] Whether this entailed a real improvement in the situation rather than the

---

[74] *CT* 9.21.2.4.   [75] *CT* 9.21.4 (326).   [76] *CT* 16.2.42 (5 October 416).
[77] *CT* 16.2.43 (3 February 418).

victory of one pressure group over another may be doubted. Consultation was not an unmixed blessing, in that it created perhaps unnecessary contradictions in the law. However, it was the price to be paid for the emperors' responsiveness to the needs of those they governed.[78]

Judges and courts

Those who adjudicated in the courts between disputants or condemned and sentenced criminals were often recipients of imperial legal rulings, which they had themselves requested to avoid the embarrassment, or worse, of being found to be wrong on appeal. Such referrals were a major spur to imperial legislation, which clarified the law in relation to situations which had actually arisen in the course of court hearings. The problem of assessing how far *iudices* could themselves create new law through their interpretation of existing law is perhaps insoluble. We may speculate, however, that, because what survives are the imperial pronouncements issued to those *iudices* who did ask for guidance (or were seen to require it on other grounds), we run the risk of under-estimating the extent to which *iudices* did make the law, if only on matters of detail. It may be doubted that any legal system is or was so comprehensive as to exclude all scope for interpretation of doubtful points on the part of the judiciary, and it was in those areas that Roman *iudices* may have offered *ad hoc* solutions, which may have come to have local validity as precedents – provided they did not obviously conflict with imperial rulings. However, whereas in modern Britain, there is a convention that judges keep their distance from the political arena, and, conversely, that politicians do not interfere with the workings or decisions of the judiciary,[79] in Late Antiquity, not only were all judges in fact political appointments, but also the emperor was the supreme judge, as well as the supreme lawgiver, who could not only define the offence but also, if he wished, specify the exact penalty.[80]

Frequent, and often critical references were made in imperial laws to *iudices*. Usually the judges in question were the provincial governors, the *praesides*, proconsuls or *consulares*, whose main function, after Diocletian's reorganisation of the provinces into smaller units, was to preside

---

[78] Cf. MacMullen (1988) 263 n. 64, citing the contradiction of *CT* 16.5.25 (March 390) by 16.5.27 (June/Dec. 395) and 11.22.2 (385) reversed by 3 (387). Reference to this as 'legislative tergiversation' underrates the flexibility of imperial responses to changing situations or improved information.

[79] A convention somewhat strained in recent years. See Rozenberg (1997) 1–78.

[80] Contrast the opposition of judges in the House of Lords to the setting, by statute, of minimum sentences in the Crime (Sentences) Act 1997, on which see, briefly, Rozenberg (1997) 62–7.

over the courts of first resort. While many cases involving small claims seem to have reached their courts, such judges were also entitled to delegate hearings to deputies. Although such delegation may have reduced the governor-judge's workload, it may also have had a secondary purpose of diverting disputes between neighbours into the less confrontational modes of arbitration or negotiation.[81] Lesser judges, at least in Egypt, might use their closer links with local communities to broker a settlement to more effect than their distant Alexandrine counterparts.

The functioning in practice of the lesser judge as adjudicator of local disputes created the context in which evolved the early version of the *defensor civitatis* (Greek *syndikos* or *ekdikos*) in Egypt in the first part of the fourth century.[82] These early *defensores* were a response to a perceived need for effective and, to a point, disinterested representation on the part of cities or individuals and came into being without, apparently, the assistance of imperial legislation.[83] When Valentinian I came to legislate on the matter in the late 360s, he laid heavy emphasis on the duty of his new-style *defensor* to act in the interests of the 'innocent and peaceful country-folk' against the corruption of the courts and the abuses of the powerful.[84] His *defensores* were to act as advocates (*patroni*) of the less well-off, and should be men of good character, drawn from retired governors, barristers or various branches of the palatine service, including the spy network, the *agentes in rebus*. Their job as deputy-judges was to handle cases involving small amounts of money or property, including small debts, runaway slaves or over-exaction of taxes, but more important cases were to be referred to the governor, who might also be appealed to from the *defensor* anyway. As was perhaps inevitable, controversies arose about how *defensores* were to be selected and the extent of their powers. In 387, a Praetorian Prefect was reminded that *defensores* were to be appointed by decrees of the cities and improperly appointed *defensores* were threatened with a fine of five pounds of gold.[85] Five years later, the *defensores* were admonished that they could not levy fines, still less subject people to the *quaestio*, judicial examination under torture.[86] Evidence of

---

[81] For formal litigation, or the threat thereof as part of wider strategies for dispute-handling and settlement, see below, ch. 9.

[82] *P. Oxy.* 1426 (332); 901 (336); SB 8246 (as judge, 340). For the office in Egypt, see Rees (1952).

[83] For the *syndikos* as the legal representative of the municipium see *Dig.* 50. 4. 1. 2 (Hermogenian), defensio civitatis, id est ut syndicus fiat, and *Dig.* 50. 4. 18. 13 (Arcadius Charisius), defensores, quos Graeci syndicos appellant.

[84] *CT* I. 29. 5 (370) 'innocens et quieta rusticitas'. For the legislation as a whole, see *CT* I. 29 passim. The addressee of Valentinian's law of 368, introducing *defensores* to Illyricum (1. 29. 3) was the Praetorian Prefect, Sex. Petronius Probus, a man not noted for the integrity of his government, nor for compassion for the weak.   [85] *CT* I. 29. 6.

[86] *CT* I. 29. 7.

such malfunctions in the system does not indicate, in itself, a general or serious breakdown of Valentinian's system; 'general' laws do not, as we shall see in Chapter 4, indicate 'general' problems. But it was perhaps inevitable that the supposed *patroni* of the poor, drawn as they were from the ranks of the powerful, the *potentes*, might, on occasion, behave like bad *potentes* themselves.

All judicial decisions of governors were subject to appeal to a higher ranking provincial official, a fact which acted as a potent means of holding the governor-judges to account. Where cases went after the court of first resort, that of the governor, varied. This was because, despite Diocletian's reorganisation of the provinces (under *praesides* and the rest) and dioceses (groups of provinces, under *vicarii*, who were deputies of the praetorian prefects), there remained considerable anomalies. For example, proconsuls were both judges of first instance and recipients of appeals, and the proconsul of Africa Proconsularis heard appeals from other African provinces as well. Constantine, after some experimentation, established a framework for judges *vice sacra iudicantes*, who heard appeals 'in the emperor's stead' and were therefore, in effect, able to exercise delegated powers of appellate jurisdiction, as if they were emperors. After 331, appeals were allowed from the lesser appeal courts, namely those of the proconsuls, *comites* of provinces and *vicarii*, but not from the praetorian prefects[87] or the urban prefect of Rome (later joined by his counterpart in Constantinople).[88] The Praetorian and Urban Prefects therefore became the last courts of appeal, or so the legislator hoped. However, some cases were too difficult, or delicate, even for them and, by the middle of the century, cases were referred upwards, even from the Prefectures, to the emperor himself. The emperor's attempts to lighten his own workload, by subscribing to the fiction that his judicial powers could be fully delegated to a subordinate, were bound to have only limited success. As the ultimate authority in the interpretation, as well as the making of law, his role as the judge in the court of last resort was a responsibility he could not escape.

---

[87] For suggestions that there was a fifth 'regional' prefecture of Africa, which are relevant to the jurisdiction of the proconsul envisaged by Constantine, see Barnes (1992), but, against his view, Salway (1994).

[88] *CT* 11. 30. 16; Jones (1964) 481, n. 23. Arcadius Charisius (*Dig.* 1. 11. 1) commented that people had appealed from the prefects before but that this was forbidden by a later law, 'postea publice senetentia principali lecta appellandi facultas interdicta est'. He also supplied the justification, not present in *CT* 11. 30. 16, that men who reached high office, having proved their loyalty (*fides*) and seriousness (*gravitas*), could be expected to judge, just as the emperor in his shining wisdom would have done. Although Charisius' comments are often linked to the law of 331, it should be noted that Honoré (1994) believes Charisius' work to be Diocletianic.

3   The construction of authority

In 370, the local senate at Oxyrhynchus assembled to debate a routine matter.[1] After 'the acclamations' (*euphemiai*), they turned to business. One of their number had lodged a complaint against his appointment as administrator of soldiers' woollen clothing, on the grounds that, as one of the twenty-four chief decurions, he was exempt, by a regulation of 'our lord, the most illustrious Tatianus', Praetorian Prefect of the East. The surviving minutes of the meeting record each casting his vote in turn in favour of their colleague, excusing the nomination on grounds of ignorance, and indulging in extravagant assertions of the rightness of the laws. Having affirmed in unison the validity of the tablet of law, statements were offered by individuals, evoking the authority of Tatianus and the whole senate, then Tatianus, plus his referral of the matter to the emperors and the Praetorian Prefecture, then, finally, 'what has been approved by the masters of the world and by the lords, the most illustrious prefects'.

The written record was designed to stand as proof, if proof were needed, of the loyalty of this relatively insignificant Egyptian council to its rulers. The effect of the language used in the meeting, which would have been employed regularly, with variations, on such occasions, was to create a tie between the councillors and the far-off emperor, whose attention could be claimed even by so minor a matter as soldiers' woollens. By invoking the authority (*auctoritas*) of the emperor, the council gave legitimacy to its own proceedings. It also reminded itself of the power of a ruler most would never see in person and thus served to reinforce the invisible authority of the central power over even its most peripheral citizens.[2]

Auctoritas reinforced and was essential to effectiveness. The first Augustus had based his rule on an *auctoritas*, a quasi-moral authority,

---

[1] *P. Oxy.* 17: 2110; cf. *P. Oxy* 41; 1305; 1413–16.
[2] But ties of 'peripheral' people with emperors should not be underestimated. Cf. Abinnaeus' journey to Constantinople in the 340s (*P. Abinn.* 1; 2; 58) and the patronage of Dioscuros of Aphrodito by the empress Theodora in the sixth century (MacCoull 1988).

superior to that of other magistrates, to which obedience was owed. In the day-to-day operations of government, little could be achieved over the long-term through the crude exercise of physical coercion or tenure of high office as such. Powerful though the machinery of central government had become, the size of both bureaucracy and army was inadequate to control the Roman Empire, had its subjects refused *en masse* to allow them to do so. Effective power therefore depended on its acceptance by the citizens at large as legitimate, and a complex social apparatus was put in place, with the connivance of the elite among the governed, to ensure that imperial authority was continually asserted. Although the ceremonial trappings of the late antique emperor may appear to have more to do with power in an obvious sense than the more subtle workings of 'authority', in fact Late Roman rulership depended on both.

The authority, as well as the power, of the emperor was reinforced by ceremonial, an increasingly hierarchical elite, and his self-representation through his laws. In addition, as we have seen at Oxyrhynchus, formal structures were imposed on what was seen, spoken, written and read in public contexts to maximise the *auctoritas* of what was done. Through the recording of the formal proceedings, including acclamations, the legit-imacy of what took place was established beyond doubt.[3] Such tech-niques were not confined to the affirming of the authority of emperors. In an increasingly Christian Empire, the authority of any individual im-plicated in ecclesiastical controversy, could be confirmed or undermined by close, even obsessive attention to the creation of a written record at the time of a debate or Council, and the exploitation of written records of past proceedings. Moreover, what was written could also be read, and thus, in the words of the imperial laws, 'brought to the knowledge of all'.[4] The creation of a Code of written law by an emperor may seem far removed from the recording of, say, the *acta* of a theological dispute in a small African town, but in fact the two are both products of a culture in which much weight was ascribed to the authority of the official written word, be it imperial laws, the *acta publica* of cities and magistrates, or the *acta* of Church councils and public theological debates.

The authority of the imperial *lex scripta* was constantly reinforced by

[3] For court records, taken down verbatim from time of Diocletian, see Coles (1966); on *notarii* and tachygraphy, Teitler (1985) 16–26; 95–103.
[4] The Theodosian Novellae end with variations on the formula, 'edictis propositis, in omnium populorum in omnium provinciarum notitiam scita maiestatis nostrae faciat pervenire', cf. *NTh.* 4.3; 5.1.5; 5.2.2; 5.3.2; 7.1.3; 7.2.3; 7.3.2; 7.4.10; 8.1.3; 9.5; 10.1; 11.4.12 (publicari); 13; 14; 15.2.4; 16; 19; 20. Extra variants include further reinforcement after the order to publish, e.g. *NTh.* 17.1.5. Valentinian III was more inclined to vary the formula and to supplement the order to publish with additional exhortations, e.g. *NVal.* 2.4.; 3; 6.1.4; 7.1.5; 10.4; 11.2; 13.16; 21.7; 22; 23.9; 25.10; 27; 35.20; also *CT* 2. 27 (421), per omnem hunc annum pendere iubemus edictum.

the language of constitutions. Through the rhetoric of legislation, a moral universe was created, headed by a caring emperor, responsive to problems, but stern with evildoers, in particular his own servants. But imperial laws were far more than an exercise in marketing the emperor; they were also a form of communication, through which the autocrat conferred *beneficia* on the governed. Analogous values were expressed through the ceremony of *adoratio*, which encapsulated the connection between the assertion of supreme power and the conferment of favour or reassurance; when an emperor wished to assure a courtier that he was (still) in favour, he gave the man his purple robe to kiss,[5] and the conferral of this mark of confidence could be adduced by the recipient, if his privileges were later challenged.[6] Likewise, the rhetoric of the laws, especially when drafted by practised wordsmiths, like Ausonius, acted as a reassurance to the literate that they and the emperor inhabited the same moral world and that the autocrat, whose rhetoric demonstrated that he shared the values of the elite, would also respect the laws. Thus the morality of imperial legislation enabled its values to be played back by petitioners and others hoping for redress.[7] Not that anyone was necessarily deceived into the belief that emperors were anything but autocratic and unaccountable. But the emperor, of his own volition, allowed the moral undertakings expressed in the language of constitutions to be a form of hostage for his good behaviour as a ruler. Just as shared *paideia* enabled communication between rulers and ruled,[8] so laws served both to communicate and to reassure.

The laws of emperors were designed to fit into a wider pattern of communication and response. Late Roman imperial government rested on a peculiar blend of a highly stylised autocracy with an insistence that the legitimacy of government depended on the consent of everybody, the 'consensus universorum'. Although the emperor was seldom confronted with the experience of having the 'consensus' denied him,[9] it was still essential for his acts to appear to have popular support, whether expressed through acclamation or a less high-profile process of formal consultation. Moreover, acclamation should not be analysed only from the imperial perspective. As we shall see, while emperors could usually count on carefully orchestrated demonstrations of support, the same crowds that might greet an emperor's triumphal progress could also turn against unpopular figures or use a church service to engage in their own

---

[5] For discussion of this in Ammianus, see Matthews (1989) 244–9.
[6] As by Abinnaeus, in his petition to Constantius II and Constans, requesting that his appointment as praefectus alae be honoured, (*P. Abinn.* 1. v. 8), 'me e ducenario divinitas vestra venerandam purpuram suam adorare iussit'.   [7] See below, ch. 9 'Petitions'.
[8] Brown (1992).
[9] But see Symm. *Rel.* 14. 1 on the possibility of hostile demonstrations at Rome, 'ne librationem clementiae vestrae querela publica praeveniret'.

individualistic responses to whatever their bishop was doing at the time. The vulnerability of public officials to demonstrations of popular feeling was exploited by Constantine who ordered that he be informed of acclamations, or the reverse, to ensure gubernatorial accountability to the governed, while Libanius, who appears not to have known about Constantine's law, complained of the governor, Tisamenos, that he paid far too much attention to acclamations, thus becoming the tool of the people instead of their master.[10]

The authority of the laws therefore depended on the self-assertion of the emperor over the governed, expressed in the language of power, and also of permanence, the latter expressed through routine claims that laws should endure 'in perpetuity', accompanied, sometimes, by instructions that they be given permanent physical form as well.[11] Linguistic hyperbole is, especially to a first-time reader, the most obvious aspect of imperial constitutions. But a consideration of the high-profile launch of the Theodosian Code reveals that the authority of the emperor's laws was backed in less obvious ways by a complex strategy of material and literary symbolism, central to which was the interaction, however contrived, between ruler and ruled.

'Magisterium vitae': the Theodosian Code

On 15 February 438, Theodosius II issued the first of his 'new constitutions' validating the *auctoritas* of the Theodosian Code. It began by constructing a history of the project. The emperor had been, he said, long 'puzzled' by the fact that, although aspirants to culture in general were richly rewarded, few men had complete knowledge of the *ius civile*, and that at the price of long hours of nocturnal study.[12] The emperor therefore thought it right that the limitless numbers of law-books, legal actions, difficult cases and mass of imperial constitutions, 'which close off from human understanding a knowledge of themselves by a wall, as though they were swallowed up in a thick cloud of obscurity'[13] should be dealt with, 'so that the problem should not be further discussed by anyone with

---

[10] *CT* 1. 16. 6. 1 (law of Constantine); Lib. *Or.* 33.11.

[11] For instructions to engrave laws on bronze, see *CT* 12.5.2; 14.4.4; and, for the use of bronze, wax tablets and linen sheets 11.27.1, 'aereis tabulis vel cerussatis aut linteis mappis scribta per omnes civitates Italiae proponatur lex'. For laws on bronze in general, see Williamson (1987).

[12] *NTh* 1.pr. Saepe nostra clementia dubitavit, quae causa faceret ut tantis propositis praemiis quibus artes et studia nutriuntur, tam pauci rarique extiterint, qui plene iuris civilis scientia ditarentur, et in tanto lucubrationum tristi pallore vix unus aut alter receperit soliditatem perfectae doctrinae.

[13] Id. 1, quae velut sub crassa demersae caligine obscuritatis vallo sui notitiam humanis ingeniis interclusit.

enthusiastic ambiguity' ('sedula ambiguitate').[14] The Novella deals in the language of contrasts, light and dark, clarity and mist, simplicity and confusion, brevity and prolixity. Darkness was to be scattered and the 'light of brevity' shed on the laws by means of a 'compendium'.[15] The imperial achievement was to dispel mist and darkness and shed light; processes of civil law, once obscure, were brought out into the open and the clear light by the 'shining radiance' of the imperial name.[16] All the books, which explained nothing and on which so many lives had been wasted were to be swept away.[17]

What the emperor sought, therefore, was the ending of what he called 'obscurity', the abbreviation (and therefore the simplification) of large and unmanageable bodies of material, and the creation of certainty, which should put an end to interminable (but eagerly pursued) discussions. The programme was designed to be attractive to those, like the author of the *De Rebus Bellicis* in the previous century, who complained about confusions in the laws, but it contained two drawbacks. One is that abbreviation could entail simplification without removing 'ambiguity', thus subverting the purpose of the Code at the outset. Secondly, it attempted to substitute the 'authority' of the Code for the discussions of legal principle and precedent, which had been the foundation of the science of jurisprudence in the past.

Theodosius, however, did not see those features of his Code as drawbacks. On the contrary, the aim throughout his law of validation was to establish the authority of his Code, basing it on its monopoly position as the sole source of valid imperial law, his own power as emperor, the eminence of his advisers, 'loyal and learned men, trained in public office', and the accumulated authority of the past emperors, from Constantine onwards, whose general laws were included and preserved. Thus the authority of the Code as law was to supersede all other sources of imperial legislation. After I January 439, no litigant was to cite an imperial law in court, or other legal transactions, unless it was included in the Theodosian Code. The creation of the Code was not to redound to the discredit of previous emperors, as the name of each imperial lawgiver was preserved in the heading of the laws, which, although modified for the sake of

[14] Id. 'Quod ne a quoquam ulterius sedula ambiguitate tractetur.' Cf. *CT* 1.1.5 on the ultimate Code, never completed, which envisaged that 'noster erit alius qui nullum errorem, nullas patietur ambages, qui ... sequenda omnibus vitandaque monstrabit'; and for discussion of the connection of this suppression of divergent opinions with other contemporary attempts to impose unanimity, see Lim (1995) 217–29.

[15] Id. pr. and 1.

[16] Id. 1. Quae singula prudentium detecta vigiliis in apertum lucemque deducta sunt nominis nostri radiante splendore.

[17] Id. 3. Quamobrem detersa nube voluminum, in quibus multorum nihil explicantium aetates adtritae sunt...

clarity, nevertheless still belonged to their authors, which were 'joined' to Theodosius by 'august association' and whose memory would last forever. The modest claim of the 'inaugurator' of the Code was to have illuminated the past laws by the 'light of brevity' and rescued the laws of his imperial 'ancestors' from obscurity.[18]

Theodosius then turned to the future. Knowing that confusion[19] could arise when laws were issued in one part of the Empire, unknown to the other, Theodosius ruled that in future no laws issued in the West could be cited as valid, unless the Eastern court was informed, and the same was to apply in reverse. Exceptions were made, however, for military regulations and public accounts. While the aim was clearly to avoid the confusions that could arise when contradictory laws ostensibly from the same imperial college were cited, the effect was also further to assert central control of the law-making procedure. However, this took for granted that the Empire would continue to function as a unity and that the impetus for law reform would not end with the promulgation of the Theodosian Code. As neither condition was fulfilled, it was inevitable that the attempt to standardise new law across the Empire was not to work in practice. Over nine years passed before Theodosius attempted to revive the regulation by despatching a package of his own *Novellae* to Valentinian III, requesting that he publish Theodosius' laws and transmit to Constantinople all general constitutions issued by him in the interval. Although Valentinian complied with the first part of the request,[20] there were to be no further attempts to standardise the laws. Two years later, Theodosius was dead; in 455, Valentinian was assassinated and his successors had other things, not least the defence of the western empire, as well as their own security, on their minds.[21]

Although Theodosius had issued two constitutions prior to 438, setting out the nature of the Code, how it was to be compiled and who was to do it,[22] the Novella of 438 was the first full public statement of its purpose on

---

[18] Id. 3 and 4, immo lucis gratia mutati claritudine consultorum augusta nobiscum societate iunguntur. Manet igitur manebitque perpetuo elimata gloria conditorum nec in nostrum titulum demigravit nisi lux sola brevitatis ... Nobis ad fructum bonae conscientiae satis abundeque sufficiet revelatis legibus inventa maiorum obscuritatis iniuria vindicasse.

[19] Important if the *CT* was designed to be used in courts, as implied by Theodosius and argued by Turpin (1987).

[20] *NTh.* 1.2 (1 Oct. 447) and *NVal.* 26.1 (3 June 448). He may not have sent his own laws to the East: the Codex Justinianus contains no western law later than 432.

[21] Although Anthemius, eastern in origin but appointed Western Augustus by Leo in 467, took care to issue laws in accordance with laws in the east, on which see *NAnth.* 2.1 and 3.1 (19 March 468), the second a copy of a constitution of Leo preceding one of Anthemius. Anthemius was overthrown by Ricimer in civil war in 472.

[22] *CT* 1.1.5 (26 March 429) and 1.1.6 (20 Dec. 435), see above, pp. 21–3.

completion. It is significant, not only for what it states about the Code as being definitive, exclusive of all else, and a statement of laws resting on the legislation of past emperors 'brought to light' and systematised by the present ruler, but also for what it does not say. Theodosius' Novella never envisages his Code as a statement of the legal rights of the citizen, of protection against the abuse of power, or of access to justice regardless of the influence of an opponent – except in two respects. One was that the concept of 'generality', evolved in the East from the late fourth century, implied the equality of all citizens under the law, in the sense that the law applied equally to all.[23] Secondly, what the Theodosian Code did supply to litigants was the 'right to know'. Although in the Novella this is defined narrowly, in terms of the legal procedures relating to gifts and other civil law processes, unflattering generalised references to the propensity of jurists to exploit the obscurities of the law and frighten their clients, suggest a wider concern. Professional obscurantists were to become redundant – along with books that decided nothing and discussions that got nowhere. By offering knowledge, the lawgiver acted as an educator, an idea hinted at in the description of the 'final' code as, potentially, the 'educator of life', the 'magisterium vitae'. All who needed knowledge of the law (and had access to a copy of the Code) could find out.

Knowledge, brevity, and certainty, then, were the keywords of the new legal era inaugurated by the Theodosian Code, and all these had more to do with imperial power than Roman law. The new Code did provide knowledge of past imperial constitutions, but the vast corpus of juristic writings remained untouched, although, as has been argued above, in practice only an agreed authoritative selection was used by advocates or judges' assessors in the courts. Moreover, it provided no certain knowledge of the future and within weeks of the Code's completion late in 437,[24] Theodosius was issuing Novellae on matters clearly covered within the Code, but which he, his lawyers or his subjects, felt required elucidation. Although his Novellae, like those of Valentinian III and later emperors survive because they were collected, no provision was made by the Theodosian codifiers for regular revision or updating. Without this, the Code ran the risk of becoming out of date within a few years, and the law of becoming as confused and ambiguous as ever.[25] The enjoyment of the benefits of knowledge and brevity were therefore likely to be brief. Nor could certainty be guaranteed. Even if the law as it stood was unambiguous, it was not immune from the pressures of social change, or from the

---

[23] Cf. Simon (1994) 6.
[24] *NTh.* 3.1 (31 Jan. 438); 4.1 (25 Feb. 438); 5.1 (9 May 438); 6.1 (4 Nov. 438).
[25] Hence Leo in 468 (*NAnth.* 3.1. pr.) observed that it was (still) the job of emperors to interpret ambiguities in the laws.

chance that a new emperor might take a different view on a contentious matter from his precedessor.

By the early fifth century, drafters of imperial law understood that 'generality' also conveyed authority. Over the years before the formal inception of the Code project in March 429, the legal concept of 'generality' that was to determine the shape of the 'compendium' had been progressively refined. Pressure for the systematisation of the laws had grown in the reigns of Arcadius and Theodosius II in particular, as lawyers worked on the concept of 'general' laws, aiming to contrast enactments of general validity with special grants and rulings designed to apply only to the situations for which they were issued. In 398, rescripts issued in response to *consultationes*, requests for advice from judges, were denied general validity[26] and, in November 426, the Senate at Rome received a long *oratio* from Theodosius II and the newly restored Valentinian III, which set out definitions of 'general' laws and laws with specific application, and which jurists' writings could be cited in court.[27] Even from the fragments of the constitution which survive, it is clear that the jurists of, probably, Theodosius,[28] were engaged in a fundamental re-examination of how their laws should work, with the aim of removing ambiguity about which imperial enactments were generally valid, and which were not. The Theodosian Code, therefore, did not spring fully-formed from an intellectual vacuum; by 426, the stage was already set.

Laws, both individually and in codified form, derived their authority, in part, from their place in the continuous process of legal evolution. In March 429, his ambitious attempt to impose a system on all of Roman Law, namely the imperial constitutions and the writings of the jurists was launched by Theodosius in a constitution which, like that of 426, was addressed to the Senate, in this case, the Senate at Constantinople.[29] In the opening sentence he established the general character of the Code and added to its authority by connecting it to a precedent. The collection would be made 'in the likeness of' ('ad similitudinem') the Gregorian and Hermogenian Codes created under Diocletian in the 290s. By connecting his compilation with the Diocletianic codes, Theodosius endowed his undertaking with the authority of precedent, without committing himself as to how accurate that precedent might be. In fact, while the Theodosian

---

[26] *CT* 1.2.11 (6 Dec. 398); see above, p. 30.
[27] *CJ* 1.14.2; 3; *CT* 1.4.3 (the 'Law of Citations'); Archi (1976) 11–21.
[28] Although, technically, Valentinian III had been restored by Theodosius, easterners were still prominent at the western court in 426. However, a western contribution cannot be ruled out; the law which states that the emperor is subject to the laws (*CJ* 1.14.4, 'maius imperio est submittere legibus principatum') is western and dates from 429.
[29] For full discussions of the constitutions of March 429 and Dec. 435 and how the Code project evolved, see Archi (1976) 24–37; Honoré (1986); Matthews (1993); Sirks (1993).

Code was to follow the earlier Codes in its arrangement under headings, there were important differences between the two. Gregorius and Hermogenian collected rescripts, which were to be excluded from Theodosius' Code, their work was issued under their names, not that of Diocletian, and their text was not protected from unauthorised continuations and, potentially, from interpolation and even forgery. Even the widespread perception that the efforts of Gregorius and Hermogenian were, in some sense, 'official' may derive from the privileged position granted retrospectively to their Codes by Theodosius.[30]

Beyond the 'first code' was the prospect of a final, definitive statement of Roman Law, which would have supreme authority, because it would have removed all possibility of any alternatives. The grand design, which was never to reach fruition, was that the Theodosian Code, as we have it, was to be only the first of three compilations. The second, as we have seen, was to consist of extracts from the jurists, and a third would combine the collections of constitutions and jurists into a definitive statement of Roman Law, which would allow no 'error or ambiguity', which would be called 'by Our Name' and which would demonstrate 'what should be followed and what should be avoided by all'. Dirigiste, prescriptive and as insistent on orthodoxy in law as a Christian bishop would be in theology, Theodosius represented an intellectual authoritarianism in law which had parallels elsewhere,[31] but in a form which was to prove impossible to implement.

After some modifications to original instructions,[32] the Theodosian Code was finally ready for its launch in October 437, on the auspicious occasion of the marriage of Valentinian III with Theodosius' daughter, Eudoxia. The occasion chosen was one designed to highlight Theodosius' authority as Senior Augustus and father-in-law of his junior colleague by using the opportunity to advertise his new role as the lawgiver, through his Code, of the whole Empire. In a special ceremony, Theodosius presented a Codex to the two principal praetorian prefects of East and West.[33] The western prefect, Anicius Acilius Glabrio Faustus, was to return with his Codex to the West, and there, in December 438, was to present it to an obsequious – and vociferous – Senate at Rome.

---

[30] See Corcoran (1996) for context of *CG* and *CH*.

[31] See Lim (1995), ch. 7 'The Containment of the Logos'.

[32] *CT* 1.1.6 (20 Dec. 435). Matthews (1993) 23–30 argues that this constitution represents instructions on the final editing procedure, not a change of direction. The reading out of *CT* 1.1.5 at the Roman Senate meeting in December 438 shows that the original grand design was still officially in place.

[33] *Gesta Senatus* 3, Faustus' account of his meeting with Theodosius given to the Roman Senate in December 438.

Acclamation and response

The reception of the Theodosian Code at Rome was the final act in a planned and orchestrated projection to the whole Empire of the power of the lawgiver. More than a year passed between Faustus' reception of the Code at the hands of Theodosius in Constantinople and his presentation of it to the Senate at Rome, and his formal announcement to the Senate took place less than a week before it came into effect on 1 January 439. As Faustus reminded his colleagues, he had left for the East to attend the 'felicitous' nuptials of Valentinian and Eudoxia. While he was there, 'our Lord' Theodosius revealed his Code 'of the rules that must be observed throughout the world, in accordance with the precedents of the laws, which had been collected together in a compendium of sixteen books, . . . consecrated by his most sacred name'. How much of a surprise this was to the new son-in-law and his entourage is unknown, but they could hardly object publicly to Theodosius' unilateral assertion of legislative sovereignty. Instead Valentinian, from a position of weakness, displayed collegiality and *pietas*, approving Theodosius' project 'with the loyalty of a colleague and the affection of a son'.[34]

In a carefully structured ceremony, Faustus made his report to his senatorial colleagues at his house in Rome 'ad Palmas'.[35] As he spoke, he had before him the Codex which he had received from Theodosius personally, and which was the visible symbol of imperial authority. In a sense, the book represented the emperor. The central importance of the text would have been reinforced by the physical presence of the two *constitutionarii*, Anastasius and Martinus, who were responsible for guarding the integrity of the text and reproducing it, under strict conditions. Their role was explained by Faustus towards the end of the proceedings, when he established three keepers of the Codex, namely the office of the praetorian prefecture, which would hold the copy presented by Faustus and received personally from the emperor, the office of the Prefect of the City, and the office of the *constitutionarii*, who would publish the Code 'to the people' and have control of its copyright.[36]

Faustus' report was punctuated throughout by acclamations, all of which were laudatory, but some of which also revealed the characteristic preoccupations of the elite. The first part of Faustus' speech was interrupted by shouts in praise of his eloquence. After describing his reception of the Code, and drawing attention to the presence of the *constitutionarii*, Faustus 'asked permission' to read out the laws which established the

---

[34] *Gest. Sen.* 2.
[35] For an account of the meeting, with a different emphasis, see Matthews (1993) 19–22.
[36] *Gest. Sen.* 7. The *constitutionarii* were also to be instructed to make a copy for Africa.

Code, a permission vociferously granted. Up to this point, however, the shouts had been simple and the numbers of times a sentiment was uttered are not recorded. However, the act of reading the emperor's own laws 'from the first book of the Theodosian Code under the title "De Constitutionibus Principum et Edictis"' in effect brought into the room the imperial presence. The words, not now those of Faustus but of Theodosius himself, evoked a flood of acclamations, which were counted and recorded.[37] All are addressed, not to Faustus, but to the two emperors as a college, as if they were themselves physically present through 'their' laws. They are wished long life and victory, they are hailed as the source of honours, patrimonies (28 times), military strength and laws (20 times), as the suppressors of informers and crooked dealings (28 times), and they had removed the ambiguities of the laws (23 times), providing for lawsuits and the public peace (25 times). Consistent with the oft-repeated fiction that the emperor acted in response to requests from his people, the well-drilled Senate petitioned their emperor to make many (10 times, plus 25 times) copies under seal for the government offices, that the text be authentic (25 times, plus 18 times) and that no annotations be allowed (12 times). However, amid this flood of apparent subservience, other slogans were also to be heard. Competition for office and prestige among senators found expression in shouts of support for Faustus himself and for Paulus and Aëtius, probably from their respective claques. More significant for collective self-assertion by the Senate was the description of the emperors as suppressors of informers, and the request that laws not be promulgated in response to petitions (*preces*), because this confused the rights of landowners (who presumably might find their title challenged by someone claiming the support of an imperial 'law').[38] All this was to be reported to the emperors (20 times). As a guarantee of authenticity, a full written record of the meeting was created, and Faustus 'read into' the record his own reading of the imperial constitutions on the setting up of the Code, which were to be attached to the *Gesta*.

The reception of the Theodosian Code was, of course, a highly stage-managed event, which, on the whole, reinforced the imperial autocracy and the authority of the emperors' laws. But, despite their apparent predictability on this, and many other occasions, acclamations had the important function of establishing for the record the 'consensus universorum' to what was done. In the Eastern cities of the Empire, extensive records of acclamations in different contexts survive,[39] addressed to cities by citizens, and to prominent individuals. Through the act of shouting together, the cohesion of the community was reinforced and the right of

[37] The formal proceedings were preceded by a discussion, which took some time (*Gest. Sen.* 1), and is not recorded. Presumably, if the Senate needed coaching about what to shout, they could have received it then.   [38] *Gest. Sen.* 5.   [39] Roueché (1984); (1989a).

the people as a whole to have a voice in their own future affirmed. Popular self-assertion could even take a constitutional shape derived from the distant past. In parts of Late Roman Italy, some form of assembly of all the citizens with at least notional constitutional powers survived at least down to the 340s and their proceedings were placed, and inscribed, on the record. In Paestum, which preserved the memory of its long history by entitling itself the 'colonia Paestanorum',[40] a crowded assembly voted the status of patrons to a prominent local benefactor and his son and set out the benefits bestowed on the grateful citizens in its resolution.[41] In this case, although public support for the acquisition of a useful patron could be assumed, its formal expression was nonetheless necessary before the local *curia* could pass their own resolution, conferring the bronze *tabula patronatus* on the new official patron. Such orderly proceedings ensured also that the patron was well treated, and therefore well disposed: less formal means of acquiring patrons, and their money, by forcible adlection into the local church were employed by the people of Barcelona in 394, when Paulinus of Nola was ordained a priest,[42] and, a few years later, by Augustine's congregation at Hippo, who sought to do the same by the wealthy aristocrat, Valerius Pinianus.[43] Both attempts failed.

Although canon law was still in its infancy, the records of acclamations included in the proceedings of some Church councils established the legitimacy of what was agreed. Contemporary with the Paestum inscription is the record of an early Council at Carthage in 345/8, presided over by the Bishop of Carthage, Gratus. The record opened with a statement of intent to abide by the law and preserve unity.[44] A series of proposals were then offered, either by Gratus on his own or in response to a question or proposal put forward by another bishop. Some resolutions were backed by reference to Church Council precedent, or to imperial law.[45] After each defining statement from Gratus, 'all' ('universi') ex-

[40] The Roman colony of Paestum was founded on the site of Greek Poseidonia in 273 BCE.
[41] *AE* 1990, 211, pp. 65–7; also Dessau *ILS* 6113, succlamante populo (from Nardo); 6114 'cibes frequentes' (Paestum); *AE* 1962, 184 on the erection of a statue of a patron at Bulla Regia, 'universus populus sinceris suffragiis suis et ordo splendidissimus gravissimo iudicio'. For possible continued involvement of populus in electoral *curiae* in Africa (use uncertain) see Lepelley (1979) vol. 1: 140–5.
[42] Paul. Nol. *Ep.* 1. 10. 2; 3. 4. The ordination did not have the desired effect as he (and his money) removed to Nola the following year.
[43] Aug. *Epp.* 125–6, a distressing experience for the bishop, whose crowd got out of control.
[44] Conc. Carth. 1. pr., quod nec Carthago vigorem legis infringat nec tamen tempore unitatis aliquid durissimum statuamus.
[45] Id. can. 2 (Universi): et lex iubet et sanctitas vestra commonet; can. 4 (Gratus): Etsi infinita sunt quae lege praescripta sunt proficientia disciplinae; can 5 (Gratus): Haec observata res pacem custodit; nam et memini sanctissimi concili Sardicensis similiter statutum..; can. 9 (Gratus, post alia): Quod si in iniuriam constitutionis imperatoriae clericos inquietendos putaverint, et defensio ecclesiastica non deerit et pudor publicus vindicabitur.

pressed their agreement. The brevity of the minutes, compared, for example with the verbatim record of the Council of Carthage in 411, show that this clearly was not a full record of everything that was said at the Council. The minutes were a summary, rather than a verbatim, account of the proceedings. Gratus' *notarii* had therefore the power to slant the record in order to affirm the unity, consensus and concern for law and precedent which should establish the authority of the Council for the future.

The 'consensus universorum' was contractual as well as symbolic. What was agreed to in *acta* must be observed in the future. Even imperial law could be made and in effect ratified by acclamation. In 326,[46] Constantine confronted his loyal but dissatisfied veterans, who, after a few routine acclamations, complained about their lack of special privileges. Constantine produced a platitude about his duty to make veterans happy, and their spokesman then laid a formal complaint about veterans' obligations to perform compulsory public services. When Constantine asked for details, the response was that he already knew, and a formal proclamation of exemptions from the emperor then quickly followed. The inclusion of these proceedings in the Theodosian Code proves that this record counted as law. However, the text of Constantine's proclamation contains a reference to this enactment as an *epistula*, which presumably would have had authority as law once issued, even if it had not been read to the soldiers first. The importance of the record, for Constantine, was that it acted as an advertisement of the emperor's concern for his soldiers, and his responsiveness to their needs.

A very different kind of bargain was struck between bishop and congregation in Africa in the early fifth century.[47] When Augustine resolved to hand over many of his episcopal duties at Hippo to his successor, he convened a public meeting of his priests, clergy and congregation and, after a short meditation on the six Ages of Man (infancy, boyhood, youth, adulthood, maturity and old age), he nominated Eraclius to succeed him, a choice endorsed by acclamations. Augustine then explained to his flock that what he and they were saying was being taken down by the *notarii*, to ensure a public record.[48] The people confirmed the *gesta* and, in response to a further invitation from their bishop, confirmed their 'wish' for Eraclius. A small hitch then occurred, when some enthusiastic spirits urged that Eraclius take the office of bishop; this Augustine refused, explaining that his own tenure of the episcopate in the lifetime of his predecessor had been contrary to the canons of the Council of Nicaea, although he had not realised that at the time. Again, the congregation

---

[46] *CT* 7. 20. 2 (also at *CJ* 12. 46. 1).   [47] See Lepelley (1979): 146–7.
[48] Aug. *Ep.* 213. 2.

agreed. But these agreements were coming too easily. Augustine had to remind his people that their assent was binding. When he had asked to be relieved of his duties on an earlier occasion in order to write more, the *plebs Dei* at Hippo had cheerfully agreed: 'and the record was completed, it was agreed, you acclaimed it; your decision was read out and your acclamations'.[49] But the congregation had not appreciated the import of what it was doing: 'As regards me', said the bishop, 'your decision stood for only a brief time.'

The sophisticated senatorial assembly at Faustus' house in 438 was far removed from the Christian gathering in small-town Africa, just over a decade earlier. However, the nature of 'public' involvement in the proceedings was not dissimilar. What was aimed at by the principal speakers was a formal and binding expression of agreement to what was going on. This would be given permanent form in a written record, which could be referred to later. Although the senatorial reception of the Code reads like, and was, an extended exercise in sycophancy, the ritual also had a deeper meaning; the emperors' book of law had been brought to be received in the home of law, the ancient capital itself. The Senate, which traced its history back to the Twelve Tables and beyond, had a right to its say, and to have it recorded. Without the spoken consent of the audience, the record could not be created. Once it existed, it was also, as Augustine had to explain, a form of contract, binding on both parties. The proceedings and the record together, by establishing the existence of consent, gave authority, in varying degrees, to what was done. But large assemblies of people could not be entirely subject to control, therefore a verbatim record could also be influenced by other agendas.[50] The unpredictability of crowd participation gave space in the *Gesta Senatus* for acclamations of individuals other than the emperors, and some assertion of senatorial self-interest over special grants and the disruption of laws on property, while Augustine had to fend off an attempt to make him resign altogether. Power and accountability were, therefore, as always, uneasy bedfellows, but rituals of acclamation, whether contrived or spontaneous, were indispensable to the powerful, as ratification of their standing and their decisions, and thus gave the governed an element of control, however small, over the actions of their rulers.

[49] Id. 5, et gesta confecta sunt, placuit, adclamastis; recitatur placitum vestrum et adclamationes vestrae. parvo tempore servatum est circa me.

[50] *P. Oxy.* 41 records the acclamations of a crowd at Oxyrhynchus *c.* 300 in favour of a notable reluctant to accept an honour. After refusing to heed his request for postponement to a 'lawful time', the crowd is mollified only by the proposal from the syndikos that it be referred to the Council. Their demonstrations of loyalty to 'the power of the Romans' would indicate a continuing lack of identification with 'Rome', despite the universality of Roman citizenship.

Acta publica: the authority of the written word

The public records contained essential information about property, but they were also archives of legal transactions of every kind and a dossier of promises, complaints and legal hearings. Everything written and stored in the public archives could be referred to by somebody. One function of records of estates and their owners was that they could establish liabilities for taxation. Therefore, if property changed hands through inheritance, sale or gift, it mattered that the transfer be correctly recorded. Regulations on tax-records, who kept them, their copying, and how they were to be authenticated are scattered through the law-codes.[51] The public records were to be amended, when land was transferred as payment for patronage,[52] 'for otherwise such property cannot pass to a new owner or quit former ownership', and validation in the *acta publica* was also required for the transfer of senatorial patrimony.[53] Transfer of land to another could have consequences in other ways, if the land was itself tied to obligations. Therefore decurions were warned that if they put on the official record their intention to desert, or allow others to possess, cultivated (i.e. taxable) lands, their decision could not be reversed later.[54] Conversely, if they were forced to sell their lands, they were to record their reasons and the buyer was to confirm his willingness to take over the land, thus preventing either from backing out at a later stage.[55]

Because of their presumed accuracy, the *acta publica* were also an authoritative point of reference for the resolution of disputes over property. Whatever the actual state of the archives, it was assumed in the imperial constitutions that documents could be safely lodged and recovered at need. The resolution of some disputes depended heavily on archival accuracy and efficient systems of retrieval.[56] Gifts could be especially controversial. Emperors in the early fourth century insisted that gifts could only be valid if entered in the *acta publica*, although an exception was made by Constantine for gifts to an under-age wife at the time of marriage; even if not entered on the record, they could not be

---

[51] E.g. *CT* 5.15.20.1 (fiscus to accept rent of emphyteutic lands, on long-term rentals, up to three times a year, and refusal to be entered on public records); 8.1.9 (368) on registrars; 8.2.2 (370) registrar not to be admitted as decurion without entering his administration on records; 11.1.3 (366) records of taxes paid in Africa; 11.28.13 (422) copying of tax records of Proconsularis; 12.1.173 (409) tax assessments not to start before checked by governor; 12.6.20 (386) tax-collectors to be recorded and confirmed by council meeting; 13.10.8 (383) abolition of exemptions not in records; 13.11.2 (386) changed definition of *capitatio* to be annexed to public records; 13.11.13 (412) impossible taxes to be deleted from records.   [52] *CT* 2.29.2 (394).   [53] *CT* 6.2.18 (397, west).
[54] *CT* 11.24.6.5 (415,east).   [55] *CT* 12.3.1 (386).
[56] For archives in general, see Posner (1972) and, for a dispute over the liturgy of maintaining the public archives, *P. Fam. Tebt.* (1950).

revoked.[57] In the early fifth century, the rules were slightly refined: if a deed of gift were recorded before a marriage, there would be no enquiry as to the date of delivery; the rights of under-age wives were reaffirmed; and registration of gifts worth less than two hundred solidi was no longer required.[58] Further details were laid down as to the formalities required. Constantine explained that deeds of gift were to be publicly executed by the donor or his representative 'with the knowledge of a number of persons', corporeal delivery was to follow, again in front of witnesses and the *acta publica* were to be executed before a *iudex* and appended to the deed of gift, adding later that the deed was to be filed in the donor's place of residence.[59] Towards the end of his reign, Constantine made procedures easier for parents and children by exempting them from the formalities of delivery and *mancipatio*, the act of sale, a law reinforced by his son.[60] In the early fifth century, procedures were tightened up, and would-be donors were told which records office to go to. The law also assured them the place was immaterial, provided corporeal delivery was made.[61]

In fact, the *acta publica* could contain any kind of promise with legal implications. Widows were allowed by Theodosius I to act as guardians of their children, provided they lodged an undertaking with the *acta publica* not to remarry.[62] The position of a widowed father with regard to his son's succession to the *materna bona* was to be read into the public records.[63] Decurions had to record their land transactions, as we have seen, and further, if they wished their illegitimate sons to succeed to their lands and duties, this wish also had to be recorded.[64]

Acta publica could also be used in criminal proceedings to encourage procedural correctness and prevent a rush to judgement. Defendants on criminal charges had certain rights guaranteed (in theory) by resort to the records; Constantine in 326 declared that there must first be a hearing 'apud acta' and the fact of a crime established, then there was to be an interval of incarceration, then a second hearing, also recorded, which would entail a restatement of the whole position (*commemoratio*); the records would thus demonstrate that a hasty conviction had not happened because of the 'anger' of the judge.[65] Towards the end of the fourth

---

[57] *CT* 3.5.1, the general rule; 3.5.3 (330), the exception; 3.5.7 (345), another exception, obscured by corruption of the text, but stipulating that a group of witnesses would suffice to validate the transfer; 3.5.8 (363), no exception for minors.

[58] *CT* 3.5.13 (428, east).   [59] *CT* 8.12.1 (316), re-enacted at 6 (341); 3 (317).

[60] *CT* 8.12.5 (333); 7 (355), reminding that gifts between extraneous persons conditional on mancipation and delivery.   [61] *CT* 8.12.8 (415, east).   [62] *CT* 3.17.4 (390).

[63] *CT* 8.18.8 (407). The *filiusfamilias*, being subject to the *patria potestas* of his father could not own his inheritance from his mother, the *materna bona* in his own right. However, his title to what he was due to inherit from his mother had to be protected for the future.

[64] *NTh* 22.1.1.   [65] *CT* 9.3.2.

century, Theodosius I and his sons allowed a period of grace of thirty days to be allowed for an accused man to settle his affairs, and the municipal records had to show that he had been offered that option.[66] Trial records, and the records made of confessions in the course of the *quaestio* (judicial interrogation, often under torture) were, as we shall see,[67] sources of authority, to be exploited in disputes. Full dossiers, vetted by all concerned, were an essential part of the appeals process, and the date of their forwarding to a higher court was to be officially recorded.[68] If an appeal was renewed, the onus lay on the appellant to deliver notice of this to their adversary, or, if absent to his representative at his house – and enter in the public records that this had been done.[69] Fine detail of this kind demonstrates the reliance of the system on the written record, whenever a dispute over the facts might arise.

Although much was said at the time, and has been since, about the corruption and inefficiency of the Late Roman bureaucratic system, assumptions of incompetence, or distortion of the record, sit uneasily with the well-attested readiness of contemporaries to resort to official documentation as sources of authority to establish the truth of a disputed claim, be it to property or the moral high ground of Christian debate. Conditioned by their traditional exploitation of court records as one form of witness adopted by Christian martyrs and established as true because written by their enemies, Christians accepted the *acta* of court hearings in general as a true acount of what went on and a source of authority in disputes. The same applied to the *acta* of Church Councils or the written record of public debates. Such *scripta*, along with the laws of emperors, provided valuable ammunition for ecclesiastical disputants, who trusted to the authority of the written record to crush dissent on the part of their opponents.

Few are known to have done more, on a regular basis, to politicise the public records than Augustine, whose versatility in the exploitation of what was written and official may have owed much to the unremittingly desperate struggle at close quarters with the Donatists for religious supremacy. Donatist outrages were therefore regularly recorded in the public *acta* , be they acts of violence or offences against the Catholic Church order, such as rebaptism.[70] Later these documents could be exploited; when pleading for Donatists who had confessed under torture to the murder of Catholics, Augustine laid as much emphasis on the

---

[66] *CT* 9.2.3 (380); 6 (409). The latter law was known to Augustine soon after its promulgation and exploited to defend a client; see below, ch. 4, pp. 92–3.   [67] Below, p. 130.
[68] *CT* 11.30.29 (362).   [69] *CT* 11.31.5 (370).
[70] E.g. Aug. *Ep.* 34, the entering of the violence and rebaptism of a young man on the record, opposed by Donatist priest, Victor.

propaganda value of the confessions, which would be reinforced by avoiding excessive harshness in punishment, as he did on the value of clemency.[71] Equally important was the use of the public record to confirm the misdeeds of pagans, hence Augustine's insistence on the recording of a pagan riot at Calama in 408; the Christians' prompt action in putting the pagans' violence onto the record would bolster their case against their assailants – which was to go to the emperor himself.[72]   For Augustine, the existence of the written record of a public debate was almost as important as the debate itself. How it should be composed therefore formed part of preliminary negotiations over the conditions for such a confrontation. When dealing with the Donatist bishop of Hippo via an intermediary, Augustine conceded, as proof of good faith, that his opponent should choose the audience, but insisted that what was said be written down, both to impose some restraint and order on the discussion and to ensure that if anything said 'happened to slip the memory', it could be checked by a reading (*recitatio*) of the *gesta*.[73] These *gesta* could then be read out to the people, or, if the bishop preferred to debate by letter, these too could be read out to the congregations.[74] This negotiation was to come to nothing, but Augustine had rather better success with the elderly Donatist bishop, Fortunius. Accompanied, 'as it happened', by a large following,[75] including his own notaries, Augustine persuaded his opponent to engage in a public debate. Rumour that a show was going on spread, and a large crowd collected, of whom 'very few' were interested in the debate itself. Augustine then asked that the debate be recorded in writing, so that neither side should forget what was said, that the discussion would be soberly conducted, and so that those not present could learn what happened by reading the proceedings later. After some demur, Fortunius conceded the point, but the scribes present 'for some unknown reason' refused to act and Augustine's own scribes were brought in. Augustine's control of the record was, however, to be short-lived; so noisy was the crowd and so excited were the disputants that the scribes were forced to abandon the task as hopeless. The debate, however, continued[76] and Augustine did what he could to rectify matters by producing his own written version in the shape of letters to his friends.

[71] Aug. *Ep.* 133, see below, ch. 6, p. 132.
[72] Aug. *Ep.* 91, discussed below, ch. 4, pp. 88–91.   [73] Aug. *Ep.* 33. 4.
[74] Id., ut postea per nos populus noverit, aut, si per epistulas agi placet, ipsae plebibus recitentur. Reading out letters could be construed as a threat; cf. Aug. *Ep.* 23.3 requesting an explanation of a rebaptism by a Donatist, and warning that his letter would be read 'to our brothers' in Augustine's church.   [75] Aug. *Ep.* 44. 1.
[76] Id. 3–12. The courtesy with which Augustine refers to his opponent throughout and his wish to continue the discussions amicably 'placido et pacato animo' is a reminder that conciliation, it was hoped, would achieve as much against Donatism as force.

While diligently shaping the record of his own doings, Augustine, like his opponents,[77] resorted to the use of past records to strengthen his argument. To establish that the Donatists were indeed schismatics, Augustine referred back to the conciliar records of the beginnings of the controversy under Constantine, and backed up ecclesiastical documentation with the imperial letters of Constantine, which established repeatedly that the Donatists had been found to be in the wrong, and the trial records of the hearings which exonerated Felix of Apthungi from the charge that he was a *traditor*, a hander over of the sacred books to the persecutors,[78] while proving that the Donatist hero, Silvanus, had indeed been implicated in handing over sacred writings and church property at Cirta. The *gesta* on Silvanus, a hearing before the *consularis*, Zenophilus, of Numidia on 8 December 320,[79] had the added attraction of containing records within a record: Augustine could therefore advertise that the case had been proved, not by the one hearing before Zenophilus (whom the Donatists themselves regarded as a persecutor) but by the 'authentic documents, the replies of the witnesses, the reading out of *gesta* and many letters' which had been read into the record of the trial.[80]

Authority, therefore, lay, not in one, but in a multiplicity of testimonies. Any reader of the *Gesta apud Zenophilum*, which was a hearing, but not, apparently, a criminal trial as such,[81] would have found there the familiar confrontation of the interrogating judge with the witness, who would be first asked his name, his 'condicio' and his 'dignitas', job and station in life.[82] Although the defendant, Silvanus, was not present, the prosecutor, the deacon Nundinarius, was allowed to produce his choice of witnesses and documentation. Awkward witnesses would find their resistance broken down by astute questioning[83] and the production of

---

[77] For Donatist use of Julian in support of their legitimacy, see Aug. *Epp.* 93.4.12 and 105. 9–10. Augustine, who could not deny the legality of Julian's acts as emperor, denigrated him as an 'apostate' and associated the return of their churches to heretics with that of the temples to pagans.

[78] For *Acta Purgationis Felicis*, see *CSEL* 26 (ed. C. Ziwsa, 1893), 197–204.

[79] Id. 185–97.

[80] Aug. *Ep.* 53.2.4, quae certis documentis et responsionibus testium et recitatione gestorum et multarum epistularum luce clarius constiterunt.

[81] Although Victor, after repeated evasions, is threatened by Zenophilus with 'sterner' questioning ('simpliciter confitere, ne strictius interrogares'), perhaps a reference to the *quaestio*, interrogation under torture employed in criminal, and occasionally, civil hearings.

[82] Replies to these questions in the *Gesta* indicate that the respondents were not clear as to the precise distinction between 'condicio' and 'dignitas'. While one, Victor, replies to the 'condicio' question that he is a *grammaticus*, and to the 'dignitas' question that he is the son of a decurion, another gives his job as his 'dignitas', while another claims to have no 'dignitas' at all.

[83] Cf. the exposure of the scribe Ingentius as a forger in the *Acta Purgationis Felicis*, *CSEL* 26, p. 200.

written records; thus Victor, the *grammaticus*, who claimed not to know that Silvanus was a *traditor*, because he was not there at the time, was refuted by Nundinarius' production and reading of the *Acta* recording the seizure by Munatius Felix, chief priest and curator, of the sacred books and vessels at Cirta on 19 May 303. Although these showed that Victor was present, the witness continued to deny the evidence of the record and, as his involvement was not the main issue, the point was allowed to lapse.

The *Gesta* also provide proof that the recording of acclamations was no empty formality and that what was affirmed by the people could be cited as having authority in a legal context. Questioned about Silvanus' election as bishop, Victor the *grammaticus* admitted that the people on that occasion had shouted that Silvanus was a *traditor* and, when pressed further by Nundinarius, who cited the acclamation verbatim,[84] conceded also that he and the elders had supported the people's demonstration in favour of an alternative, local candidate.[85] In the light of this, a re-evaluation is due of the significance of the persistent emphasis in imperial propaganda or the *acta* of cities on the importance of popular consent. Assessment of acclamations of emperors cannot be made in isolation from an awareness of the more complex functioning of acclamations in other contexts. It is true that in many, perhaps most, cases where acclamations were organised, consent, and recording of consent, was guaranteed, but, constitutionally, that consent could be withheld. In episcopal elections, the theory was that the bishop had the support of his congregation; that too, as Silvanus found, could be denied, and its denial recorded and produced in evidence against him. If the people consented by acclamation to a course of action, that consent could be held to be contractual, and the people, as Augustine showed, could be reproached for breaking their word.

What was written, read and spoken, therefore, could be deployed in an infinite variety of ways by the elite as sources of authority. But while records could be cited in the course of debate, as Augustine did, they could also be exploited to stifle dissent. In this, control of both the proceedings and the record was all-important. Ambrose of Milan, for example, 'packed' the Council of Aquileia in 381 with his own supporters to crush the challenge to his authority posed by Palladius of Ratiara; thus Palladius was denied his chance to have his case represented fairly at the

---

[84] *Gest. apud Zen.*, vos seniores clamabatis: exaudi deus, civem nostrum volumus, ille traditor est.

[85] Id. (Victor) clamavi et ego et populus. Nos enim civem nostrum petebamus, integrum virum. For discussion of detail of text and date, see Duval (1995).

time or later on the written record.[86] In 411, the Donatists fought bitterly over some two days out of the three allocated to the Council of Carthage to establish their right to a fair hearing in the verbatim record, because they knew it would be exploited by their opponents later (Augustine in fact produced a biassed summary later, for popular consumption). Emperors and elite alike colluded in the sidelining of dissidence. By creating the impression of unity, and by claiming for a particular legal reform or religious stance the 'consensus universorum', the voices of opposition could be silenced.

Moreover, if the elite were to claim 'popular' support for their actions, that support had to be conciliated in ways that could be easily understood, and, if necessary, expressed by the shouting of slogans. Thus official assertions of the virtues of unanimity were reinforced by a widespread distrust, which was not confined to emperors, of the complex or the ambiguous. What was communicated was also 'vulgarised'; the Latin for the communication of imperial laws was 'divulgare'.[87] The cult of 'simplicity' was celebrated in ways as diverse as Constantine's simplification of testamentary and other procedures, the insistence of the *consularis* Zenophilus that suspect witnesses confess 'simpliciter', or the ascription of clarity, simplicity and brevity by Theodosius II (and others) to the codification of law.

Much ingenuity, then, was expended by the powerful in the reinforcement of their authority in competition with each other, and not least by the emperor in establishing the authority of his laws. Moreover, the respect accorded to the written official record suggests that few would dispute the accuracy of the archives or of the courts, and that the citation of such records carried authority in disputes well beyond the boundaries of what was dealt with by law. Yet, despite all this evidence of respect, at least on the part of the elite, for what was 'official', imperial law itself, still stands accused of lacking authority in that it was widely ignored or disobeyed – in which case the ingenuity expended on the construction of authority described above was largely a waste of time. But was it?

---

[86]   See McLynn (1994): 124–37.
[87]   e.g. *NTh.* 2.3. Eas, igitur, domine..., cunctis ex more facias divulgari... *NVal.* 6.1.4, per omnes provinciarum civitates edictis solemnibus divulgabit.

4   The efficacy of law

Emperors, and others, went to great lengths to advertise and strengthen the authority of law. Simultaneously, however, complaints flowed thick and fast from citizens and emperors about the failure of laws to be observed. As a result of such complaints, late Roman law is generally assumed to have been widely disobeyed, ignored or circumvented. Historians of Late Antiquity, following the rhetoric of some imperial legislation, have deplored the subversion of the 'rule of law' by corrupt activities on the part of officials[1] and venal judges[2] and habitual oppression of the poor by the rich, a picture which blends seamlessly with the notions of 'decline' accompanying the political disintegration of the western empire in the fifth century AD.[3]

Probing further, it may be argued that Roman law became the victim of a deep-seated conflict within Roman society between rules, which were universal, and power, which was arbitrary. 'Rules' are not only laws or 'legal rules', written or customary, but also rules of behaviour and accepted normative precepts; the exercise of power, the ability to do things or compel others to act in certain ways, encompasses the pursuit of self-interest, clashes of strength or will, the exertion of patronage, or political factors, such as wealth or influence. The emperor himself was implicated in this conflict, because he was supreme patron as well as legislator. The activity of the patron was, of its nature, arbitrary, in that he sought to benefit those who happened to be his clients, rather than operating universal rules. Thus the emperor's role as legislator and guardian of the laws was constantly liable to subversion by his exercise of 'power' in all its forms.[4] Rules, or laws, were, on this analysis, and despite their allegedly

---

[1] E.g. *CT* 10.1.5 on the Caesarians, refers to the 'habitual fraud with which they customarily violate all regulations'; also Feissel (1995).   [2] See below, ch. 8.

[3] As, notably, MacMullen (1988) 168 'In the upshot, laws were widely ignored, conveying the impression they could be bought off, while of course proving exactly that in many cases.'

[4] For a judicious analysis of this conflict, which it was in emperors' interests to sustain, see C. M. Kelly (1994), esp. 173, 'Emperors were not to be hemmed in by the formulation of inviolable legal maxims or restricted by the strict application of academic rules of construction.'

post-classical (ergo inferior) quality, fundamental to the preservation of the social order and it was their conflict with the arbitrary exercise of extra-legal power by self-interested *potentes*[5] which undermined the efficacy of law and ultimately proved the downfall of Rome.

It will be argued below that the widespread concern voiced about law-breaking or the ignoring of the laws does not in itself establish that laws were ineffective. However, a problem was perceived to exist, and the perception is itself a significant cultural phenomenon, which is indicative, not of the actual scale of law-breaking but the concern on the part of emperors and citizens alike that the laws should be observed, and the ability of the wronged to seek redress, safeguarded.

The traditional interpretation of Late Antiquity as lawless and ungovernable relies on assumptions on the part of historians about how law works which are seldom made explicit. The proliferation of imperial legislation, to which emperors themselves had drawn attention, is interpreted as a sign of weakness, of a central government unable to control the ingenious efforts of subjects to get round legislation combined with a culture of disobedience among both officials, whose activities were severely regulated, and the public at large. Repetition of laws, in particular, is read as reflecting the impotence of emperors: they had to repeat themselves because no-one was listening. And 'disobedience' has often been associated with 'ineffectiveness', as if the purpose of all laws was that they should be 'obeyed'. These assumptions require re-examination.

As a legally oriented society, the Later Roman Empire 'seems, in comparison with one loosely governed by custom, to invite disobedience or social delinquency'.[6] But increased complexity is not necessarily symptomatic of ineffectiveness. Whatever the instinct of the social historian, that of the lawyer is to observe that law has its own rules: 'this apparent weakness is compensated by the specification of remedial procedures, which tend to ensure that defined wrong-doing is established and vindicated, while that conduct which falls outside it constitutes an area of freedom reserved for the citizen'.[7] Thus, if the urge to control characteristic of the emerging late Roman bureaucratic state expressed itself in increased, albeit limited, interference with citizens' 'areas of freedom',

---

[5] Cf. Patlagean (1977) 288–92 affirming that the laws on illicit *patrocinium* of villages at *CT* 11. 24 show that the exercise of such patronage was 'illégitime', as it conflicted directly with the aims of the legislator. Such privatisation of the rural economy could, if widespread, undermine both state revenues and the effectiveness of the law. However, it is unclear how widespread the abuses condemned in the laws were, or the extent to which they undermined the overall aims of the central administration. Nor were illicit rural activities on the part of landowners confined to the later Empire.

[6] Honoré (1978) 35.

[7] Id. Historians have still to take full account of the wisdom of these observations.

laws also contained their own remedies. Their proliferation is an expression of a governmental culture favourable to state intervention, not of the inefficacy of existing law.

More fundamental is the criticism that late Roman law was vulnerable to distortion by the powerful, who escaped justice, helped their friends and generally subverted the system.[8] If it be accepted that rules and power form the basis of social cohesion in any society, then the undermining of the rules of justice and fairness, the 'ars boni et aequi', on which law was based by the arbitrary use of power was bound to be detrimental to the social order as a whole. This analysis, however, contains the flawed assumption that rules are of necessity in competition with power as supports of the social order. Such is not the view taken by legal anthropology. As Simon Roberts observed, 'what purport to be rival explanations of social order in fact rely on different but complementary features found in all societies . . . Consequently, we would do best to start out by seeing the operation of rules and the exercise of power as concurrent features, closely interlinked, of any social life; it is their exact relationship and the precise balance struck between them which deserves further investigation.'[9] Historians might do better, therefore, not to prejudge the position of the 'balance' either by importing inadequately examined assumptions of conflict between rules and power, or by taking at face value the universal denunciations of people who broke or got round the rules, indulged in by imperial legislators. Instead, it must be asked how far the observance of law was assisted, as well as resisted, by the exercise of 'power' through patronage and self-interest.

What of 'obedience' to law, clearly a desideratum in a well-ordered society? Disobedience to laws did worry those who drafted imperial legislation and grandiose tirades against lawbreakers could be sparked off by even minor local incidents. When, for example, a decurion of Emesa exploited his honorary rank as an *illustris*, plus a band of slaves, to intimidate the local governor and tax-collectors, Theodosius II elevated the affair into an occasion for a general complaint about audacious wicked men who were not restrained by fear of the laws or feelings of shame; but for people like this, there would be no need for laws.[10] At about the same time, his cousin, Valentinian III, launched a similar complaint about people who, with 'punishable lawlessness' dodged their obligations on the supply of recruits and the harbouring of deserters, behaviour which obliged him to repeat established laws too often; offend-

---

[8] Actual (as opposed to alleged) miscarriages of justice due to corruption are hard to identify. Note Amm. Marc. 26. 3. 4 on a senator convicted of apprenticing his slave to a worker of magic, who escaped the death penalty by a heavy bribe, 'ut crebrior fama vulgarat'.
[9] Roberts (1979) 168.   [10] *NTh.* 15.2.pr.

ing behaviour, he said, that was not restrained, even by a recent law was indefensible.[11]

Such complaints were, however, inevitable in the context of the issuing of some new legislation, because disobedience to an existing ordinance was one reason, among many, for passing a law in the first place. But law is not simply coercive, and the concept of the 'sovereign' legislator is itself fraught with theoretical difficulties.[12] A law was issued either to clarify and/or supplement existing legislation, or because an existing law was being broken or got round, or in order to reclassify anti-social or inconvenient behaviour as a legal offence. In a sense, therefore, laws existed because they were broken. What is not established by their existence is the scale on which they were broken, not enforced, got round[13] or ignored. The Theodosian Code is not about statistics.

In fact, as is often forgotten, much of Roman law existed, not for purposes of social control, but for the regulation of legal relationships between Roman citizens and it was up to litigants to make use of it as they saw fit. The importance of this large area of law, which was fundamental to the property ownership, transfer, and succession rights of every citizen, and therefore to their families' overall economic well-being, should not be under-estimated. In his Novella confirming the *auctoritas* of his law-code, Theodosius II celebrated the usefulness of his new compilation, 'since it is now clearly evident with what validity a gift may be given, by what action an inheritance may be claimed and by what words a stipulation may be drawn up for the collection of a definite or indefinite debt'.[14] Such was Theodosius' assessment of what really mattered about his completed undertaking, that citizens of the Empire for the first time knew about regulations which defined how their relationships with each other over matters of private law should be conducted. When disputes arose over gifts, inheritances or debts – and if they were brought at the initiative of the disputants themselves into the purview of the law – justice would take its course. By invoking the law, disputants, who now became litigants, accepted the legal (and financial) consequences. If, on the other hand, a family or other group settled a dispute over, say, the division of an

---

[11] *NVal.* 6.1.pr.
[12] For full development of the problems of obedience and the 'coercive' model of law, see Hart (1961, 2nd edn. 1994), ch. 2 (on the coercive model), ch. 3 (the variety of the content, range and origins of laws) and ch. 4 (the concept of sovereignty).
[13] Cf. *Dig.* 1.3.29 (Paulus, *Lex Cincia*), contra legem facit, qui id facit quod lex prohibet, in fraudem vero, qui salvis verbis legis sententiam eius circumvenit. For Theodosius II's complaints about decurions getting round the law on leases by exploiting verbal loopholes, see *NTh* 9.1 (439).
[14] *NTh.* 1.1.1. For gifts, see esp. *CT* 3.5–7; 8.12; actions on inheritances 2.22.1; 4.4.7; 5.1; debts 2.4.3 and 6.

inheritance without going to court, through negotiation, mediation or informal arbitration, the law neither knew nor cared.

Thus, when sorting out many matters of private law, a Roman citizen did not choose to 'obey' or 'disobey' the relevant laws, but whether or not to invoke them in his or her own self-interest. This was a category of activity associated with law totally distinct from the imperial attempts at social engineering or the control of alleged corruption, which usually underlie scholarly discussions of whether or not the law was obeyed and the empire 'governable'.[15] The premise, however, that many laws had to be activated voluntarily by someone other than a government agent, is common to many areas of law-related activity, hence the insistence by imperial legislators that laws 'be brought to the knowledge of all'. Whether or not the law was put into effect, therefore, depended on its activation either by a potential litigant, or by a government official or other concerned party; it could also be enforced because of imperial insistence that it should be (and terror of the consequences if it were not), although this, as we shall see, could never have more than a temporary effect. A law could be obeyed, invoked, enforced, disobeyed, or ignored.

Even when ending up on the wrong side of the law, either through law-breaking or loss of a suit, had consequences, different attitudes to non-compliance were built into Roman concepts of law. The word *poena*, penalty, itself carried a range of meanings, from the death penalty to the forfeit exacted for non-adherence to an arbitration agreement. Those convicted for criminal acts automatically incurred punishment – the death penalty, deportation (permanent exile), sentencing to the mines, loss of property and civil rights. However, the empire had no state prosecution service and crimes had to be brought to the attention of the authorities by private citizens, before justice could take its course. The same applied to official misconduct, which included laziness, negligence, corruption, failing to advise the governor properly and non-enforcement of the emperor's 'salutary laws'; this also was punishable, usually by fines. Another category of laws, such as those on legal marriage (*iustum matri-monium*), did not entail any punitive consequences if they were flouted; the situation was simply that the couple were not legally married and their children would therefore count in the eyes of the law as illegitimate. A third type includes such enactments as those seeking to regulate social mobility, in particular the extensive number of laws restricting the migra-tion of individuals, such as decurions or members of guilds, from the status (and obligations) to which they were born. Infringement of these did not result in a punishment at all, apart from the return of the

---

[15] E.g. by MacMullen (1988).

delinquent to his original status (which, to some, might seem punishment enough, but would hardly deter those prepared to take their chance of not being caught).

It is clear, then, that Roman law itself contained a variety of responses to infringement or non-compliance. When, therefore, the 'ineffectiveness' of law is discussed, or 'disobedience' to imperial instructions, what is usually meant is failure on the part of officials to behave as they should, or of citizens to co-operate over fulfilling their obligations, such as carrying out hereditary duties, providing recruits – or even, as imperial involvement with ecclesiastical orthodoxy and the suppression of pagan rites increased, believing in the Christian God.

Repetition: law and time

High on the charge-sheet of imperial legislative failure is the fact that laws were repeated, showing, we are told,[16] that previous enactments had been ineffective, ignored or forgotten about. A well-known instance already referred to was the migration of decurions, guildsmen and others into occupations other than those to which they were born, which was widespread, despite regular promulgations of imperial laws to the contrary.[17] Worse, the government's priorities in this area of social engineering were inconsistent with each other. While emperors sought repeatedly to protect the governing classes of the cities, on whom they depended for tax revenues, their own administrations were avidly recruiting talent from precisely those social groups, particularly into the burgeoning new bureaucracy establishing itself at Constantinople.[18] We know, therefore, that attempts at social engineering with regard to hereditary occupations and social mobility[19] were, overall, a failure.

However, there is a real difficulty of methodology here. It does not follow from the coincidence of an independently attested social trend with repetition of a number of laws aimed at preventing that trend, that laws were repeated because ineffective. The specific laws known to us may all have succeeded in their purpose at the time of issue among the people to whom they were addressed. The fact that many laws were issued in response to approaches from provincials, either directly or through the

[16] E.g. by Jones (1964) 741, 'Repeated constitutions prove that the imperial government was quite incapable of controlling these abuses,' and 752, 'The constant reiteration of the laws shows that they were only spasmodically enforced and constantly evaded.'
[17] See especially *CT* 12. 1 passim.   [18] See Heather (1994).
[19] Hopkins (1961) on the upward mobility of Ausonius' family takes them from slave status to a consulship in three generations. It was made easier by Ausonius' professorship at Bordeaux, a civic contribution regarded as exempting some holders from liturgical obligations.

offices of the governors and prefects, meant, not only that laws were requested in the expectation that they would assist the self-interest of the petitioner, but also that laws would be repeatedly asked for, because enforcement was likely to prove more effective when backed by a recent law, which could not be challenged on grounds of obsolescence or a change of emperor. When, for example, the people of Byzacium received a law of Valentinian I assuring them that decurions seeking ordination must find a substitute or cede their property to the curia, and that wealthy plebeians could not become clerics,[20] the hard-pressed local councillors gained, by virtue of the new law, the necessary authority to assert their control over the assets of their former colleagues; a comparable ruling to the Moors of Sitifis a few years later on the liability of the grandsons of decurions guaranteed the municipal services of one more doubtful category of person.[21] In both these sample cases, the real initiators of the laws were almost certainly the addressees, decurions of a particular locality with a problem over colleagues seeking to evade their statutory obligations. In a further constitution, of 383, the original source is made explicit; Theodosius I conceded 'to the decurions of the province of Mysia' that rich plebeians could be enrolled in the town councils and 'in response to the petition of the aforesaid decurions', he added the further provision that decurions by birth who had joined the governors' office-staffs in the previous twenty years were to be recalled to the councils.[22]

As Valentinian III observed in 440, it was worse to disobey a recent law. This was a statement based on experience; a new or recent constitution was more effective than an old one. The reasons for this were partly that this was how things worked in practice, but there were also conceptual difficulties, deriving from the peculiarities of the Roman system of creating laws. Although the rhetoric of *leges generales* regularly advertised the permanence in perpetuity of a new regulation, there remained underlying conceptual difficulties over the shelf-life of imperial constitutions, which were rooted in the history of how Roman laws were made. Few of the many forms taken by Roman 'law' had been originally conceived as 'perpetual'. The exception under the Republic was statute-laws (*leges*) passed by the popular assemblies and binding on the whole state. Even after emperors had assimilated the powers of the sovereign *populus* into their own prerogatives, imperial constitutions still, strictly, had only the 'force' (*vigor*) of statute and were not statutes, *leges*, themselves. All other forms of imperial legal enactment, which were authorised by their holding of the combination of magistracies devised originally by Augustus, were, in a formal sense, ephemeral. Edicts were issued by a magistrate and were

[20] *CT* 12.1.59 and 16.2.12, (12 Sept. 364).   [21] *CT* 12.1.64.   [22] *CT* 12.1.96.

valid only for his term of office, rescripts and subscripts were relevant, technically, only to the person and problem addressed, and formal letters, *epistulae*, to designated recipients, Senate, People, Provincials, or officials, were personal statements which often (but not invariably) contained legal rulings.

All forms of law, bar statutes, lacked permanence. However, had every edict, *epistula*, rescript or subscript died with its imperial author, much of the functioning body of Roman law would have required renewal with every change of emperor. In practice, both the impermanence of the edict and the *ad hominem/feminam* nature of rescripts were subverted by the Roman flair for improvisation. Firstly, the most comprehensive of all edicts, that of the Roman Praetor, became perpetual. Under the Republic, the praetorian edict had passed from one set of praetors to their successors with often only minor modifications. A parallel habit can be observed in provincial government in the same period, when uncritical acceptance of a predecessor's provincial edict was a convenient short-cut for lazy governors, like Cicero.[23] Finally, under Hadrian, the praetorian edict received its final, codified form, to be known from the third century on as the Edictum Perpetuum.[24] Secondly, the broadening of the scope of the rescript to act as precedent with the status of a general ruling is reflected both in the writings of the jurists, who regularly cited rescripts, with their addressees, in support of their analyses of legal problems, and, most spectacularly, in the authoritative codification of rescript-law from Hadrian to Diocletian by Gregorius, supplemented by Hermogenianus, in the 290s. Thirdly, language is never static, and the meaning of *lex* itself evolved. Retaining its connotations of authority and permanence, and its link with sovereignty, *lex* came to be applied to imperial constitutions, often, especially later, with the reinforcing adjectives of '*generalis*' or '*edictalis*', both explicitly denoting general (but not necessarily universal) application.[25]

None of this sufficed, however, to clarify the status of past imperial rulings beyond question. In the absence of a comprehensive law-code, how old could an imperial constitution be, yet still retain validity? Had an 'ancient' law been superseded by a more recent ruling? Who decided? Although by the fourth century, the answer to the last question was usually that the emperor was required to rule, in the third century, provincial judges still had some discretion. In 250, a dispute came to a

---

[23] Cic. *Fam.* 3.8.4 (to his predecessor, Appius Claudius), 'Romae composui edictum; nihil addidi nisi quod publicani me rogarunt, cum Samum ad me venissent, ut de tuo edicto totidem verbis transferrem in meum.'

[24] For the evolution of the term 'edictum perpetuum' see Pringsheim (1931/61).

[25] For this distinction, see Sirks (1985); a law could be 'generally' applicable in, say, Illyricum or Rome, but not universally valid throughout the Empire.

hearing before the Prefect of Egypt, Appius Sabinus.[26] It concerned the liability of villagers in the Arsinoite nome for liturgies in the metropolis, to which they had been summoned by the *boule* of the metropolis. After skirmishes on various points, the villagers' advocate, Seleukos, produced and read a 50-year-old law of Septimius Severus, ruling that villagers were not liable. The Prefect then turned to the spokesmen for the Arsinoite boule and asked them to read him a law too. Although they were unable to produce a more recent counter-measure, the *bouleutae* still maintained that they had a case, as they could argue that Severus' law was no longer valid. Severus' ruling (they said) could be ignored on two grounds. One was that Prefects since had supported the needs of the cities, 'which define the force of the law'. Secondly, the situation had changed over the fifty years, since Severus had made his ruling 'while the cities were still prosperous' and this was no longer the case. This last argument was rejected by Sabinus, not because it contravened Severus' law, but because the decline in prosperity applied to the villages as much as to the cities. The Prefect's final decision supported the villagers, and enunciated the principle with regard to the enforcement of old laws that 'the force of the laws will increase with time'.

Although this outcome accords with the principle that imperial law prevailed, unless contradicted by a later ruling, it was by no means predictable. Egyptian litigants customarily accepted the decisions of their Prefects, as well as of emperors, as precedents. Both sides in the Arsinoite dispute alleged that prefects' rulings since Severus favoured their case, although none appear to have been produced for citation in the record. Other documents from the province reveal that, under the early Empire, precedents derived from prefects' and imperial rulings, spread sometimes over more than a century, were collected and manipulated by litigants.[27] Prefect-law was, therefore, a reality in Roman Egypt. However, it was unlikely that any Prefect would go as far as directly to contradict an explicit imperial ruling (although the proceedings of 250 suggest that Prefects since Severus could at least be plausibly represented as having contradicted his ruling in favour of the liability of villagers, because of changed circumstances). Nor does the tone of the proceedings of 250 imply any disrespect to the laws of emperors as such, described by the advocate of the boule as 'to be held in awe and reverence'. The issue before the court was simply whether *this* law, given its age, had been

---

[26] Skeat and Wegener (1935) has text and commentary of *P. Lond.* Inv. 2565, containing the bulk of the court record.

[27] E.g. *P. Oxy.* II, 273, petition of 186 refers to precedent of 87; *SB* VI 9016, material from trial of 48 cited in court minutes of 160; *P. Stras.* material combined from 90 and 207. On this in general see Katzoff (1982).

superseded by more recent decisions. And, of course, production by one side or the other of a recent imperial decision would have clinched the matter.

Repetition of laws, therefore, added strength to the law. Citizens of the Empire required to know what the most recent thinking on the law was and it was a form of reassurance to learn that there was a recent enactment relevant to their case, and that emperors had more than once reached the same decision. This had also been true in the second century: the Prefect of Egypt, M. Sempronius Liberalis, ruled at Memphis in 155 that 'not only to the divus Hadrianus but also to his son, our Lord (Antoninus Pius) did this seem good'.[28] Rescripts from the third century, from Caracalla onwards drew attention to the frequency of their repetition by the use of such formulae as 'saepe rescriptum est',[29] 'iam pridem rescriptum/decretum est',[30] or 'saepe constitutum est'.[31]

While reiteration was built into the rescript system, which provided responses to multiple individual queries, it also extended to the more generalised formats of the edict and the official letter. Here, too, the existence of numerous previous laws lent authority to new enactments; in 399, for example, courts were ordered to punish the abettors of runaway decurions and guildsmen without referring their cases, 'since there exist so many laws which provide for the infliction of certain punishment on the harbourers of fugitives'.[32] Repetition, in other words, when made explicit by the legislator, was a way of advertising and sanctioning predecents, of confirming the validity of past laws while also affirming their continued validity in the present. In 349, Constantius II responded to an appeal from the *vicarius* of Mesopotamia for a reiteration of the law restricting the career aspirations of members of the governor's office staff; Constantius obliged, accepting that 'the authority of a repetition of the law is desired'.[33] When, in 384, Theodosius I was called upon to legislate about the duties of the children of decurions at Edessa, his advisers produced an earlier law of his 'divine ancestors', issued by Valens at Antioch a mere nine years before.[34] Theodosius scrupulously summarises the earlier law, then confirms it; 'Since this is true, we order, by both the present law, and by the previous one, which is still in force' – that the

---

[28] *P. Mich.* Inv. 2964, discussed by Pearl (1971).
[29] E.g. *CJ* 1.54.2 (228); 2.43.3 (244); 2.55 (213); 4.2.3 (239); 4.10.2 (260); 4.19.6 (245); 4.65.11 (244); 5.54.2 (213); 6.30.4 (250); 7.57.3 (227); 9.34.4 (244); 10.60.1 (Severus Alexander); *FV* 275 (Diocletian). Note also Caracalla's reinforcing of his authority at *CJ* 4.31.1, 'et senatus censuit et saepe rescriptum est...'
[30] E.g. *CJ* 5.51.5 (Gordian); 7.64.7 (285).
[31] Formula favoured by Diocletian and his colleagues, e.g. at *CJ* 4.44.3; 7.45.1; 7.56.4; 7.60.1; 10.53.5.   [32] *CT* 12.1.162.   [33] *CT* 8.4.4.
[34] *CT* 12.1.105 (Theodosius); 12.1.79 (Valens).

children of chiefs of the bureaux should be recalled to their municipal duties at Edessa. In 397, Honorius issued a letter which, apparently, did no more than confirm the existing benefits due to the Church; 'We decree nothing new by the present sanction but rather confirm those privileges which were evidently granted formerly.'[35] Laws could be repeated so that new regulations could be appended; privileges of the clergy, for example, over tax-exemptions were reaffirmed by Constantius II in 343, 'in accordance with the previous sanction' and exemptions from billetting and the trade-tax were added.[36] Usurpation, clearly, might interrupt the smooth flow of valid legislation. Acts of usurpers were routinely annulled, but it sometimes became necessary also to reinstate the acts of previous legitimate emperors; the Church in Rome, Africa and Gaul was assured in 425, after the fall of the usurper John that 'the privileges granted by previous laws' should be preserved.[37] Even without the intervention of a usurper, ideological conflicts between successive emperors created uncertainty; Valentinian I, for example, a Christian, but honoured by Ammianus for his neutrality in religious matters, had to reassure the pronconsul of Africa that the *sententia* of Constantius II on some religious matter was still in force, despite challenges from some pagans under Julian.[38]

Repetition of laws, then, was not, as a rule, occasioned by disobedience or the ignoring of previous legislation, but by a combination of factors which prove the opposite. Given that many laws were issued to people, or groups, who had asked for them (and often may have had a shrewd idea of the expected response), reiteration signals both that citizens wished to be sure of what the law was, and that the law was observed and, where applicable, enforced, at least by some, even in areas, like the flight of decurions from the cities, where legislation is now deemed to have been ineffective. Emperors repeated laws because they understood the public need for reassurance that old laws were still valid, and that the new laws had behind them the authority of precedent. A dead law, therefore, was not one that was repeated but one that was never evoked. As Ammianus, a contemporary, well versed in the ways of emperors, perceived, the worst fate that could befall a law was that wished by him on Julian's legislation

---

[35] *CT* 16.2.30. The clause is cited 'post alia', and the innovative aspect of the law may lie in the sections excluded, for whatever reason, by the compilers of the Code. Supporters of the notion that repetition = ineffectiveness might note that many 'repeated' laws in the Codes are isolated from their context and may have been originally no more than reassuring additions to a main clause, introducing a new regulation on some other matter.   [36] *CT* 16.2.8.

[37] *CT* 16.2.46 (Africa). Copies of the same law, with local modifications, from which different extracts are preserved, were sent to Rome (16.5.62), the *comes rei privatae* (16.5.64), and Gaul *(CS* 6).   [38] *CT* 16.2.18 (370).

forbidding Christians to teach the pagan classics, that 'it should be buried in perpetual silence'.[39]

Context: law and place

Most government by an emperor was carried out long-distance. Those who travelled – a rare breed in the fifth century – could receive petitions in person. Stay-at-homes relied on the efficiency of the operation of official channels. From the late fourth century, *suggestiones* and *relationes* passed through the offices of the urban and praetorian prefectures, but, as we shall see, there was still room for others to make approaches, through friends at court. Self-interested embassies with their own axes to grind wended their slow (and expensive) way across the empire. Wherever there was a dispute over obligations and rights, whether of *coloni* or others burdened or privileged by hereditary status, or of taxation, groups whose self-interest was affected appealed for a ruling in their favour. Christians, once assured of imperial support, were not slow to use the emperor's goodwill to further their struggles for dominance against local pagans or heretics. And, of course, any form of violent breach of the law was liable to provoke cries of outrage from injured parties. Many laws, therefore, would have been responses to grievances voiced by parties in a position to have access to the emperor's ear, or to attempts by political or religious factions to take advantage of the errors of opponents by enlisting the emperor on their side. And where laws were evoked to serve the interests of a faction, we may expect that faction to ensure that the law was effectively enforced.

From the perspective of the small-town politician, religious or secular, the emperor's will was a tool to be manipulated. How this worked can be seen from specific cases. Here, for example, is Augustine's representation of violence against Christians in a small African town – and its consequences.

On 1 June 408, a procession of pagan residents of the Numidian town of Calama wended its way through the streets in the customary annual celebration of the Kalends. Provocatively, its route took the cortege past the local Christian church. There, the clergy, well knowing that they had recent imperial laws on their side, tried to put a stop to the pagans' celebrations. Enraged at this interference, the pagans threw stones at the church. Over the next week, the situation rapidly deteriorated. After the Christians approached the local council with their complaint, citing the laws, but to no avail, more serious disturbances broke out. More

[39] Amm. Marc. 22.10.7 'obruendum perenni silentio'.

stones were thrown and, in a second night of violence, the church was stoned again, then set on fire and one unfortunate was killed. As the flames from the church rose into the night sky, the clergy fled in terror of their lives. The mob ran riot, unchecked by any citizen of Calama; only a traveller (*peregrinus*) passing through intervened to protect the lives and property of the Christians from the looters.

As the stricken clergy struggled to come to terms with their anger and grief – ably assisted by the counselling of a neighbouring bishop, Augustine[40] – they might have reasoned, as many have done since, that the laws were ignored and the Roman empire ungovernable. Similar actions elsewhere had gone unpunished. Pagan processions were to continue even in Italy, close to the heart of government, well into the fifth century, benignly tolerated or ignored by the local authorities. Riots were, as they had been for centuries, a recognised method of popular self-assertion. Nor could the Christians hope for justice from the local authorities. Twice they had tried and failed to exploit the town's procedures for redress and protection; the council had ignored their citing of 'very recent laws'[41] and had refused permission for the outrages committed by the pagans to be entered in the official records. The central power at Ravenna could have seemed a long way off to the persecuted Christians of this small town on the periphery of empire.

Their despair was premature and, in the event, the response of the Christians of Calama was to be devastating. Within a few weeks, Possidius, bishop of Calama, was on his way to Italy, to make a direct appeal to the central power, carrying in his baggage, among other documents, a letter from Augustine dealing with appeals for restraint from a worried citizen of the town.[42] By other bearers, Augustine also sent letters of his own to the new court favourite of Honorius, Olympius, who had overthrown Stilicho in August. In these he used every argument known to him to goad the emperor into action. Olympius must move fast to establish that 'the enemies of the Church will understand that the laws sent to Africa while Stilicho was still alive about the destruction of idols and the reform of heretics were indeed promulgated at the will of an emperor most God-fearing and faithful', a point reiterated a few sentences later, when Augustine demands an assurance that even fools should understand 'that the son of Theodosius, not Stilicho, authorised the sending of the laws issued in support of the Church of Christ'.[43] Olympius could

---

[40] Aug. *Ep.* 91.10, 'ut nostri in tam gravi dolore vel consolarentur afflicti vel sedarentur accensi'.   [41] Aug. *Ep.* 91.8, 'contra recentissimas leges'.

[42] Aug. *Ep.* 91, recounting events at Calama in reply to *Ep.* 90 (the writer was called Nectarius), which conceded that the town deserved punishment, if judged by the standards of the public laws.   [43] Aug. *Ep.* 97. 2 and 3.

have been left in no doubt of what would happen if Possidius' appeal was ignored; the sincerity of the emperor's intentions, if not his very control over his own policies would be called into question and his credibility as a ruler undermined.

Honorius' response was to mobilise the full forces of the governor and, if necessary, the *comes Africae* to punish the guilty.[44] The judges throughout Africa had, according to Honorius, failed in their duty to enforce the law, or to report cases of disobedience to the emperor himself. Now, these same 'conniving' judges were ordered to seek out the culprits, bring them to trial and, if they were convicted, have them sentenced to the mines or deportation, whatever their rank. After the response to the specific outrages complained about, a general law was added, threatening capital punishment in the future to anyone attacking churches or clergy. These were to be reported by the municipia and rural police (*stationarii*), and the culprits named. Where the attack was perpetrated by a mob, recognised individuals were to be arrested and made to inform on their confederates. If the mob proved impossible to control by the forces at the disposal of the civilian authorities, armed apparitors were to be drafted in. Finally, for good measure, Donatists and other heretics, Jews and pagans were admonished that the laws against them were still in force and governors were ordered to enforce them on pain of losing their rank, while the conniving or negligent office staff-members would be fined twenty pounds of gold and the three heads of staff (*primates*) would receive further punishment.

From Honorius' standpoint, it was his plain duty to enforce the laws, both the ones already passed about pagan rites, and those which safeguarded persons and property. The apparent failure of the provincial authorities to deal with law-breaking could have come about, in his view, only through the connivance of the judges,[45] who concealed what was going on, allowing dreadful crimes to go unpunished and unreported. What the legislator failed to observe is that Possidius' embassy, which was ready to leave by August 408, must have been planned almost immediate-

---

[44] *CS.* 14 (15 January 409 at Ravenna), is almost certainly the reply to Possidius' embassy, although Calama is not indicated by name. The text of the law refers to other indignities inflicted on Catholic bishops, such as having their hair torn out, indicating that Possidius, or the African bishops, made the most of their envoy, by adding other complaints requiring to be brought to the emperor's attention.

[45] Buck-passing to corrupt or venal judges was an imperial habit, for which cf. Gratian's complaint about the authorities at Rome who had tolerated the bad behaviour of a contumacious priest, *Coll. Avell.* 13.1.7, 'nostrorum videlict iudicum socordia fretus, qui privatae gratiae imperialia praecepta condonant et religionem quam nos iure veneramur, quia fortasse ipsi neglegunt, inquietari patienter accipiant'. Also see Jones (1964) 409, echoing emperors' rhetoric on their own governors who 'were often incompetent, generally too compliant to the interests of local magnates, and almost invariably venal'.

ly after the Calama incident and that the bishops may well therefore have taken a deliberate decision to by-pass the governor, believing, with good reason, that the propaganda effect of imperial intervention would more than repay the inconvenience to Possidius of a journey to Italy 'in the depths of winter'.[46] But imperial power could not lightly be invoked. By looking outside Africa, the bishops risked undermining their position in their own communities, by being made to appear unable to deal with a situation for themselves. Indeed, what Honorius perceived as long-term connivance by the governors and their staffs may have been rather a constructive inactivity by provincial authorities better informed about conditions 'on the ground' than was the distant emperor, combined with a general, prudent reluctance to involve the central power on the part of local leaders who understood the subtle mechanisms of small-town power games; the Africans had to sort out their problems for themselves. Nor was the insensitivity and harshness of the imperial response likely to endear the emperor's suppliants to their fellow citizens, hence the touchiness of Augustine's final communication to Nectarius, claiming that he was unaware that any request from Possidius' embassy for excessive punishment for Calama had been granted, especially considering that Possidius loved his town much more than Nectarius did.[47] As every bishop knew, in the exertion of ecclesiastical influence, based on the teachings of Christ, 'love' and power were indissoluble.

Laws, then, were activated, obeyed or enforced in complex local contexts, of which the lawgiver could have had little detailed knowledge. Embassies with a grievance would have been in no hurry to enlighten his ignorance, particularly as it was clearly in their interest to inflame his anger as much as possible against the disobedient and those who had flouted his authority by ignoring his laws – hence Augustine's warning to Honorius that he must show himself to be his own man and not Stilicho's creature. Obedience to the law, once activated, was encouraged, if not guaranteed, by the fact that most laws were asked for, by someone, to serve their own ends, and the group requesting the law was therefore bound either to enforce it themselves, or to see it enforced.

It would be mistaken to picture local observance of laws purely in factional terms. The laws guaranteed rights and could be invoked against the criminal. This could be done in generalised, rhetorical terms, as when Augustine censured the leaders of the *colonia* of Sufetana over the massacre there of sixty monks, lamenting that 'among us the laws of Rome are

---

[46] Aug. *Ep.* 97.2, 'etiam media hieme'.
[47] Aug. *Ep.* 104.1.1, 'an aliquid audisti, quod nos adhuc latet, fratrem meum Possidium adversus cives tuos, quos – pace tua dixerim – multo salubrius diligit ipse quam tu, quo plectantur severius, impetrasse?'

buried, the terror of the governors' courts is trampled underfoot, and emperors are accorded neither respect nor fear'.[48] But another negotiation involving Augustine shows how laws could be exploited by local leaders to curtail criminal behaviour, or its consequences. Writing to Alypius, Augustine lamented the depredations of the so-called *mangones*, raiders and slave-traders, who took children away and sold them overseas.[49] He then considered the text of a law of Honorius sent to the prefect Hadrianus, ordering that crooked 'traders' be beaten with lead thongs, proscribed and sent into perpetual exile. Although, as he observed with scrupulous accuracy, the law did not actually specify the situation of the child-slaves, but only spoke 'generally' (*generaliter*) of families sold overseas, this law was clearly applicable and a copy was attached for Alypius' benefit.

Augustine, however, was not a law-enforcement agency. His priorities as bishop differed from those of the imperial governors. While consistent in his expression of respect for the law, it was also his job as bishop to mitigate the consequences of harsh legislation. In the case of the *mangones*, Augustine's main objective was to free the prisoners and he would therefore exploit the law only as far as he needed to in order to achieve his humane purpose. For him, 'using' the law was all-important; enforcing it, to the letter, was not.[50] Similarly, Augustine 'used' a recent law on legal procedures, of which he had a text to help a client confronted with a law-suit brought by a more powerful adversary. When one Faventius, a conductor of a local estate, under the protection of the church at Hippo, was kidnapped by an official of the proconsul, Augustine invoked a recent law, pointing out that Faventius had first to be questioned by the local authorities and his replies entered on the public records as to whether he should have an interval of thirty days in custody to organise his affairs. The language of the letter follows closely the text to be exploited by the bishop.[51] This text he sent directly to the official respon-

---

[48] Aug. *Ep.* 50.   [49] Aug. *Ep.* 10* (new Divjak letter).

[50] Id. 4. 1, in tantum ea (lege) nos uti coepimus, in quantum sufficit ad homines liberandos, non ad illos mercatores ... tali poena cohercendos.

[51] Aug. *Ep.* 113, ut faciat quod imperatoris lege praecipitur, ut eum apud acta municipalia interrogari faciet, utrum sibi velit dies triginta concedi, quibus agat sub moderata custodia in ea civitate in qua detentus est, ut sua ordinet sumptusque provideat, and *Ep.* 114, ut ad gesta municipalia perducantur atque illic interrogentur utrum velint triginta dies in ea civitate ubi tenentur agere sub moderata custodia ad parandos sibi fructus vel rem suam, sicut necesse fuerit, ordinandam..., cf. *CT* 9.2.6 (21 January 409), an velint iuxta praeceptum triumphalis patris nostri xxx diebus sibi concessis sub moderata et diligenti custodia propter ordinationem domus propriae et parandos sibi sumptus in civitate residere. The date, six days after the issue of *Const. Sirm.* 14, suggests that Augustine's copy of this law could have been part of a package brought back to Africa by Possidius. The Theodosian law referred to is *CT* 9.2.3, not *CT* 9.3.6 as suggested by Mandouze (1982) s.v. Generosus 3, p. 533; he also argues that the affair may predate 409, but the linguistic parallels suggest specific reference to the 409 law.

sible, Florentius, and, to be sure that he received it, a second copy was sent by a messenger. Florentius was reminded that all powerful men were also subject to imperial power and thus to the laws,[52] and should obey them, a reminder delivered, the bishop wrote, 'as a request, not a threat'.[53] Unfortunately for Augustine, his client had already been removed. Undeterred the bishop appealed to his colleague at Cirta to pursue the matter with the proconsul. A postponement of the hearing was to be requested. The grounds were, as before, technical: Faventius had been snatched against his will, there had been no hearing before the town authorities and no chance of a postponement for thirty days. In fact, Augustine hoped to use the law's delays for his own ends; the real motive, as he admitted, was to buy time for the conclusion of a mediated settlement between Faventius and his more powerful adversary.[54] The outcome of the case is unknown.

This incident also illustrates the difficulty noted earlier of making simple generalisations about the relationship of rules and power. The emperor's official, charged with upholding the law, was prepared to subvert the rules, exerting what was in fact arbitrary power by making an illegal arrest. Faventius happened to have a patron able to invoke recent law to protect his rights, albeit with limited effect. Had there been no Augustine, Faventius' legal rights would have been ignored by the emperor's own law-enforcement officer, either through ignorance or negligence. Such incidents of arbitrary behaviour by officials are common enough in the annals of Late Antiquity. What is less often observed is that the presence of patrons such as Christian bishops, alert to abuses of power and aware of such legislation as suited their purposes, would have acted as an unobtrusive but omnipresent check on the arbitrariness of officials. Patrons like Augustine 'used' the law to help their clients, and patronage did indeed affect the observance of legislation, but not always to its detriment.

Enforcement

The workings of law-enforcement, as is clear from the above, were, in some areas, largely a matter of chance. The state accepted some, limited obligations. Governors had their armed retinues and soldiers could be called upon to deal with civil disturbances, or arrest such offenders whose crimes required them to be hunted down. One fourth-century martyr-act describes how a whole band of soldiers arrived at a suburban villa to arrest

[52] Aug. *Ep.* 114.1, Augustine plays on words denoting power and command; Hoc autem scio, quod omnis potestas sub imperio constituta imperatoris sui legibus servit.
[53] Aug. *Ep.* 114.3, eam (legem) cum his litteris identidem misi non terrens sed rogans.
[54] Aug. *Ep.* 115.

two martyrs; normally, commented the author, just a couple of soldiers would do. There are few signs of organised police forces in the sources, although various groups, called *stationarii*, or by some other label, can be identified as responsible for enforcing writs on litigants, and bringing defenders to court. These officials took action only when litigation had been properly initiated in the governor's office in writing by a plaintiff, who would take responsibility for establishing proofs: they had no role as a detective force, in ferreting out evidence, nor would they act as a state prosecuting service, by laying charges for themselves. The onus therefore lay on the person who brought suit, who had to do all the work himself, and who faced a corresponding penalty, if he failed to prove his case. This must frequently have deterred private enforcers of the state's law.

However, in some areas, the state took a more active role. Some regulations, such as those concerning tax-collection, were in a state of constant activation, whether they were observed in detail or not, simply because the imperial administration required to receive its revenues. Tax-collectors went about their business and could call on armed assistance, if necessary. And the 'advocates of the fiscus' were actively responsible for litigation about taxes, and investigations about the status of allegedly caducous or ownerless property. Their work could receive assistance from informers, whose presence was required at any investigation, where ownership was challenged to the benefit of the fiscus or a petitioner for a grant, but whose status remained suspect and disreputable. So much were the activities of informers frowned on that, despite their potential usefulness, Constantine refused to allow informers to act at all.[55] Later emperors limited the number of times they could act, even justifiably, without penalty to two, while a third attempt would incur capital punishment.[56] Words for informers' activity, such as 'calumny' and 'betrayal' signal public repudiation for a class of people loathed by emperor and upper classes alike. Only, it seemed, when information was to be laid against heretics, as in an investigation of the Manichees, launched by Theodosius I in 382, was the 'odium' attached to informers laid aside.[57]

Nor could the emperor's men turn a blind eye to serious public disorders. The Roman plebs retained a form of restricted right to riot, over the absence of grain to be supplied by the state,[58] for example, or alleged tactless remarks from a Prefect of the City over the price of wine,[59] and

---

[55] *CT* 10. 10. 1–3.   [56] *CT* 10. 10. 12. 2 (380); 28 (418, west).   [57] *CT* 16. 5. 9 (382).

[58] Amm. Marc. 19. 10. 2–3, Tertullus, the Prefect of the City of Rome, already persecuted by riots, shows his sons to the crowd to arouse their pity.

[59] Amm. Marc. 27. 3. 4, the Elder Symmachus' house was set on fire after a 'certain low plebeian fabricated, without proof or witness', that Symmachus preferred to quench his limekilns with his wine, rather than sell it at the price demanded by the plebs.

some disturbances, such as the lynching of the controversial bishop George of Alexandria in 361, could be overlooked or lightly censured. As a general rule, however, the state could not ignore blatant challenges to its own authority. Ammianus had high praise for the Roman Prefect, Leontius, who personally took on mutinous mobs and arrested and publicly punished their leaders[60] and had little time for the Christian factions who rioted against each other in 367 over the disputed papal election of Damasus, a series of disturbances ended only by the decisive action of the Prefect, Praetextatus, who banished Damasus' rival, Ursinus.[61] However, the forces of law and order had often to be supplemented by private initiative. When the house of another unpopular Roman Prefect, Lampadius, was attacked by an assemblage of 'the lowest of the low', the owner himself fled, leaving his friends and neighbours to defend his property by showering stones and roof-tiles down on the would-be arsonists. Ammianus did concede that the mob had a real grievance; Lampadius had seized building materials for his prestige projects without paying for them.[62]

The enforcement of religious prohibitions was an area new to government, which, with the exception of persecutions of Christians and, occasionally, others, had tolerated religious diversity. What happened to temples or those engaging in forbidden sacrifices seems still to have depended on local attitudes, rather than active enforcement of the closure of temples by the central authority, which in many respects was responding to, rather than initiating Christian oppression of opponents.[63] There were active persecutors of pagans among officials, such as Maternus Cynegius, who, as Prefect of the East (383–8), closed temples in the East and actively persecuted pagans at Alexandria. More often, it was local leaders, especially bishops, who took advantage of the imperial fiat. Marcellus of Ancyra was described as the 'first to use the law'[64] issued to Cynegius in 385, which banned sacrifices, to sanction his destruction of pagan shrines. Although such initiatives doubtless enhanced the power of the faith, they were also divisive. Marcellus' own fate illustrates what could happen when episcopal extremism violated local solidarity. While supervising the destruction of a temple by 'soldiers and gladiators' hired for the purpose, he was lynched, the murderers were later identified – but the provincial council took no action against them, on the grounds that Marcellus' relatives should be grateful that he was privileged to die in so noble a cause.[65]

---

[60] Amm. Marc. 15. 7. 2–3; Matthews (1987).   [61] Amm. Marc. 27. 3. 12–13.
[62] Amm. Marc. 27. 3. 8.
[63] For analysis of the law as 'leading from behind,' see Hunt (1993).
[64] *CT* 16. 10 9, with Theodoret, *HE* 5. 21.   [65] Sozom. *HE* 7. 15.

Viewed from the pagan perspective, Christian local 'initiative' in enforcing the law could be taken to excess. In his oration in defence of the temples, Libanius complained of looting of the peasantry by those engaged in destruction of temples, on the grounds that they had been involved in sacrifice. The proper procedure, he maintained, was to invoke the law on sacrifice in a court of law. Insisting that these poor rustics would of course have obeyed the law anyway, Libanius demanded to know why no-one had come forward to launch a prosecution; 'ill-will and jealousy would have given cause to the neighbours to institute proceedings', but no-one did, 'or will, given his fear of perjury, not to mention flogging'.[66] Libanius' case was in fact that the Christians had failed to use the legal remedies available to them. Indeed, they avoided the courts of law, precisely because they had no case, but continued with their depredations, as if they had, and therefore acted in violation of imperial law. This line of argument is significant, because it illustrates not only the conventional, and less conventional, systems of religious law-enforcement at work, but also the terms of the discourse of those who wished to put the other side in the wrong. Repeatedly, orators 'used' the law to wrong-foot opponents, not only in real life, as Augustine did, but also in pleading a case, as if it were a case at law. In this quasi-courtroom, 'they', the enemy, were the law-breakers, while the speaker, invariably, was the champion of right, justice and the lawful authority of emperors.

Efficacy and accountability

Not all laws, then, existed in order to be enforced or 'obeyed', and the activation of many depended on private initiative. Even in such delicate areas as the abolition of sacrifices or the (illegal) destruction of temples, enforcement depended on the policy adopted by officials and the local authorities – hence the survival of many local traditional and non-Christian religious observances. Emperors themselves could prove dilatory in enforcing the edicts of colleagues: a notable example was Constantius I's open tolerance of Christians during the Great Persecutions. All knew, though few admitted, that laws were rendered effective by those whose interest it was to 'use' them in defence of their own or their clients' interests, or to further their local aims. The efficacy of law therefore relied on an unstable and unpredictable alliance of imperial and local self-interest, the long-term viability of which was guaranteed only by the community of interest between emperor and local elites. On this interpretation, physical distance from imperial centres would have little effect on

[66] Lib. *Or.* 30. 15–16.

the efficacy of law in general, although demonstrations of imperial power or anger with law-breakers were naturally more likely to happen in the vicinity of the emperor and his entourage. Knowledge of law, and access to texts, would be a surer guide to the extent of its use than the presence of the imperial lawgiver.

This does not explain why so much emphasis was laid in the texts of laws on the disobedience of law-breakers and the idleness or corruption of officials, which the law was designed to remedy. The creation of an image of the imperial legislator as the guardian of the law was one motive. A second was that blanket condemnation of criminal types and the hammering of 'venal' judges and suchlike miscreants was part of the language of power, an assertion of the supremacy of the emperor, backed, as he so often insisted, by the *consensus universorum*, and a statement that this power would be used to punish offenders and ensure the accountability of his officials to both himself and the governed. Consequently, the language of accountability became a part of the continual dialogue between the emperors and the once-sovereign *populus*. Those who are accountable are also subject to criticism from those to whom they answer. Imperial tirades against officials therefore should be analysed as a part of a wider phenomenon, which might be termed a 'culture of criticism', which also found expression in the speeches of orators, the strictures of historians like Ammianus and the representations of bishops and others who criticised the misconduct of officials. Of course, disobedience, corruption, extortion or incompetence were not new. What was new was the willingness of those with access to the late antique media of communication to complain about such behaviour, and to encourage others to do so. Far from being coralled into habits of subservient acclamation, citizens were encouraged to hold their government to account.[67] The result of all this was that complaints increased in volume, and more may have been done to remedy them; what the evidence does not show is that there was actually more to complain about.

All this is not to maintain that laws were always effective. Evidence independent of law shows that imperial attempts to regulate inconvenient entrepreneurial activities or counteract abuses of patronage and many other matters were a failure. However, the ineffectiveness of some laws is not evidence for disrespect for all law. The increased publicity accorded breaches of the law does not, in itself, indicate any statistical increase in illegal behaviour; if anything, the highlighting of abuses could have assisted in their control. It may therefore be suggested that the system, despite many malfunctions, operated with surprising effectiveness. The sophisti-

[67] *CT* 1.16.6.1 (331).

cated and centralised nature of imperial rule, backed by clear, but flexible, lines of communication from the emperor to the farthest corners of empire; the inbuilt responsiveness of the legislative procedure to expressed public needs; the self-interest of the groups who evoked legislation in ensuring its enforcement; the voicing of criticism of imperial officials, even in imperial laws; and the existence of articulate and influential interest-groups, notably bishops, able and willing to criticise – all these may have combined to ensure that Roman law in Late Antiquity was more frequently invoked and effectively enforced than at any previous period in Roman imperial history.

5   In court

Much of law was concerned with how the state regulated disputes be-
tween its citizens and punished those who offended against social norms.
Readers of Late Antique law-codes would have come early to regulations
on civil litigation, much of it based on the codified Praetorian Edictum
Perpetuum; they would have had to wait rather longer before reaching the
criminal provisions set out in Books 9 of the Theodosian and Justinianic
Codes, and Books 47–8, the so-called 'Libri Terribiles'[1] of the *Digest*.
How litigants went about conducting lawsuits in civil, and in criminal
cases is not easily envisaged, as ancient authors were, on the whole, not
given to literary descriptions of trials from the inception of the suit to its
final outcome. Even the apparent exceptions, such as martyr-acts, are
selective in their presentation, and take what was common procedure at
the time for granted. Most revealing of what happened in the hearing
itself are a small selection of verbatim court records, from Africa (on the
Donatists) and Egypt, which show judge, advocates, witnesses and litigants boisterously engaged in verbal disputes, requiring, on the part of the
advocates, a knowledge of the law and prompt reactions to the devices of
opponents.[2]

Late Roman justice was, and is, commonly assumed to have been
weighted in favour of the rich, who could afford better legal representation and perhaps also the services of more influential friends. While this
was doubtless true on many occasions, the poor also had their protectors,
not least bishops, and being made to appear the weaker party may even
have been an advantage in some cases; as we shall see, patrons found it an
effective device to present their clients as being the victims of oppression
by their opponents.[3] Moreover, a distinction must be drawn between the
socially accepted exercise of patronage on behalf of clients, which entailed

---

[1] Described as such by Justinian, *Const. Tanta* 8a, et post hoc duo terribiles libri positi sunt
pro delictis privatis et extraordinariis nec non publicis criminibus, qui omnem continent
severitatem poenarumque atrocitatem.
[2] The so-called *Acta Purgationis Felicis* and the *Gesta apud Zenophilum*, preserved in Optatus, App. 2, *CSEL* 26, on which see above, ch. 3, pp. 74–5.   [3] Below, ch. 8, pp. 165–6.

writing letters to a judge, and bribery or other forms of corruption designed to pervert the course of justice. As will be suggested below (chapter 8), there are a number of reasons for the rhetorical portrayal of late Roman judges as 'venal' and corrupt.

However, one question relevant to the weighting of justice in favour of the better-off should be disposed of at the outset. Did court charges exist and did they prevent access to litigation by the poor? The balance of the scanty evidence available for the fourth century is that, in the time of Constantine, charges for court services did exist but were not imperial policy. A vehement edict issued in 331 by Constantine,[4] not only attacked the 'venality' of the judge's 'curtain', which screened the room where he heard cases, but also forbade the levy of charges by the chiefs of the office staffs, their assistants, the other apparitors assisting with the running of the court and those who wrote up the records, the *exceptores*. There was therefore a perhaps surprisingly generous attitude towards access to the legal process, which was in theory available to all, more so than was to be the case with many later systems, including our own. However, there were practical problems with restricting a steady increase in the levying of charges (*commoda*) or 'tipping' (*sportulae*), especially as the courts did incur expenses, which had to be met. Under Julian, the *consularis* of Numidia posted in the forum at Timgad a schedule of the charges (*commoda*) to be made by his court officials.[5] The *officialis* in charge of issuing summonses could levy charges on a sliding scale, depending on how far he had to travel within or beyond the city limits; the minimum was 5 modii of wheat or the monetary equivalent. The *scholastici*, who drafted the summons and response received 5 modii for the summons and double that for the defendant's rebuttal, and the final document, containing both arguments and outcome was assessed at 15 modii. The *exceptores*, who wrote out the documents, received 5 modii for the summons, 12 for the defence, and 20 for the final document. Limits, however, were placed on the amount of parchment that could be used; one large roll for the summons, four for the defence, and six for the summing up. On a reckoning of 30 modii to the solidus, these are moderate charges.[6] However, it cannot be ascertained how far these charges were enforced, or how typical they were of charges elsewhere, although Valentinian and Valens clearly thought exactions made by advocates, staff-chiefs, *exceptores* and enforcement officers were excessive, and should be controlled by the *defensores civitatis*, whose job was to look after harmless rustics.[7] By the time of Justinian, who attempted to

---

[4] *CT* 1.16.7.   [5] *FIRA* 2nd edn. 1. 64 = *CIL* 8. suppl. 17896.
[6] Jones (1964) 497 points out that 30 modii is a man's ration for a year. Evidence is lacking for the scale of fees in the higher courts.   [7] *CT* 1.29.5 (370/3).

regulate[8] and reduce charges, litigation was substantially more expensive and emperors had accepted the existence of so-called *sportulae*, or tips, as inevitable. Even in the fourth century, the combination of fees exacted, the perhaps substantial extra costs of hiring an advocate, travel and accommodation, and the unpredictability of the process if it went to appeal, resulting in yet further expense, would have given pause to less well-off litigants, encouraging them to resort to informal arbitration, episcopal hearings or other forms of alternative dispute resolution.[9]

In Late Antiquity, all hearings, civil and criminal alike, were conducted before a judge (*iudex*), empowered by the state.[10] This had not been normal procedure in Rome under the Republic and Early Empire, particularly for criminal cases conducted under the *quaestiones*, established over a period from the second century BC, when juries had delivered verdicts. However, hearings before a single *iudex*, had been the normal system of jurisdiction in the provinces and gradually become no longer 'extraordinary' but normal procedure,[11] for all types of case. Jury-courts largely ceased to function as such, although the Senate occasionally resurrected its traditional prerogative of sitting as a special court.[12] The fact that the same *iudex* heard both civil and criminal cases led to a merging of the two procedures, and similarly the procedure for appeals, although the initial stages of bringing suit retained an important difference; the accuser in a criminal trail had to bind himself by a written undertaking to undergo the same penalty as threatened the defendant (*inscriptio*). Civil cases fell under the *ius civile*, the law governing citizens, which went back to the Twelve Tables of c. 450 BC and the *ius honorarium*, the law of the praetorian edict.

For most provincials involved in civil litigation, the judge most likely to deal with their cases in the first instance was the governor, the bulk of whose job, from Diocletian onwards, was jurisdictional, or a deputy appointed by him. In Late Antiquity, the parties had no choice of judge, and, once involved in litigation, were obliged to submit to its rules and the judge's decisions. This differed from earlier practice in civil suits. Under

[8] The law is lost but see Just. *Inst.* 4.6.25. On tips and charges, see *CJ* 3.2, de sportulis et sumptibus in diversis iudiciis faciendis et de exsecutoribus litium. There is no separate section for this topic extant in the Theodosian Code. For fees/tips in other contexts, see *CT* 1.31.2 (voluntary); 8.4.6; 9; 27; 12.6.3; cf. 10.1.11 (1 per cent fee exacted by susceptores, later (12.6.2) doubled; 14.4.4; 6.31.1.
[9] See below, ch. 9, 'Arbitration' and 10 'Episcopalis audientia'.
[10] See above, ch. 2, pp. 53–5.
[11] For evolution of *cognitio* see Buti (1982). Jurists did not use the term extensively, see *Dig.* 48.19.1.3; 48.19.13; 48.16.15.1, all on criminal hearings.
[12] As in the case of Arvandus, tried for treason in 469, on which see Harries (1994a) 159–66. For the quinqueviral court responsible for the trials of senators on criminal charges, see *CT* 9.1.13 (376, west); 2.1.12 (423, west).

the Republic, the praetor could authorise the appointment of a *iudex datus*, agreed by the parties; although the emphasis was on the parties' consent, the authority of the magistrate to appoint a deputy derived from the jurisdictional authority vested in him as a representative of the state and holder of *imperium*.[13] The parties also accepted that their case would be defined by a written formula handed down by the praetor. The agreement of the parties both to the appointing of the *iudex* and the formula had two effects. One was that the parties, having consented to the nomination of the judge in the first place, were under greater pressure to abide by the outcome than they may have felt, when hauled before a state judge in Late Antiquity. This in turn may have led to a more critical attitude on the part of Late Roman litigants towards judges and a greater readiness to resort to appeal, if a decision went against them. Secondly, consultation over the appointment of the judge allowed for a large element of arbitration in the resultant hearing. In Egypt under Antoninus Pius, the governor is found agreeing to the nomination of a *mesites* (arbiter) by the parties and empowering the arbiter to go between the parties and 'pass judgement' (*krinei*),[14] and in 338 at Oxyrhynchus, two litigants requested a named individual as judge (*dikastes*) and the governor agreed.[15] But, the judge, however chosen, still derived his authority from the state, not the litigants, and their 'choice' was advisory only. Other elements of continuity from the past still present, at least in the early fourth century, should also not be entirely discounted. Constantine legislated that *iudices* should conduct lengthy investigations, so that decisions could be reached, not by the judge's unilateral verdict, but by the agreement of the parties themselves,[16] showing that the judge's arbitral role was still notionally important. Other relics of ancient procedures continued till well into the fourth century: the written formula, handed down to the judge by a superior authority, traditionally the praetor, and determining the nature of the case, was only formally abolished in 342.[17]

Judges had no formal training and relied heavily on the legal expertise of their *consilium*. In a digression on the Persians, Ammianus commented on the fact that Persian judges were experienced lawyers, who had little

[13] *Dig.* 2.1.5 (Julianus, *Digest* 1). More maiorum ita comparatum est, ut is demum iurisdictionem mandare possit, qui eam suo iure, non alieno beneficio habet. See also id. 13, 16–18.

[14] *P. Chrest.* 87, 'Choose the arbiter (*mesites*) you want.' (X) having chosen Domitius and Agrippinus having agreed, Julianus said 'Domitius will arbitrate between you and pass judgement.'   [15] *P. Chrest.* 56 = Meyer, *Jur. Pap.* 87.

[16] *CT* 1.18.1, 'Compromise' solutions could well have favoured the richer or more powerful party, who could impose a less generous settlement on his weaker opponent than he was perhaps entitled to by law.

[17] *CJ* 1.57.1, Iuris formulae aucupatione syllabarum insidiantes cunctorum actibus radicitus amputentur.

need of advisers and looked down on the Roman habit of stationing legal experts behind the unlearned (*indoctus*) judge, to keep him on the right lines.[18] While some advice was on offer from emperors, judges had to use their own discretion as to how they behaved. Many, especially from among the *indocti*, must have found themselves sharing the perplexities of Aulus Gellius, who, in the early second century, found himself serving as a judge in private suits. In a literary conversation, his friend, the philosopher Favorinus, poses four questions relating to the proper conduct of judges (which go unanswered).[19] These were, first, should a judge use knowledge acquired prior to the hearing but not adduced in the trial itself, when reaching a decision? In Late Antiquity, the answer would have been clear: a decision not based on what was set down in the court record was highly vulnerable on appeal. Secondly, should a judge, having heard a case and perceived the chance for a negotiated settlement, postpone giving a decision, in order to take on the role of mutual friend of the parties and mediator? This shifting between the role of adjudicator and mediator might have been harder for a busy Late Roman judge, but was precisely the kind of flexibility in dispute settlement envisaged for the bishop, who was expected to act as judge and conciliator. Thirdly, should the judge raise questions, which are in the interest of a party to have aired, even though the party concerned had not raised them for themselves, the danger being that such conduct would be perceived as advocacy, not adjudication?[20] Finally, should a judge say things and ask questions in the course of a trial, which could help understanding, but might also create the appearance of inconsistency? In both the latter cases, the judge had to rely on his own good sense. The late antique records show that judges followed the instructions of Constantine, in that they were indeed active in cross-examination, although, on the whole, they followed lines of enquiry already indicated by the parties, or their advocates, and did not embark on initiatives of their own.

Gellius, a young and worried judge, whose main interests lay elsewhere, with grammatical studies, reveals the amateurish nature of the early imperial judicial system. This was still the case in Late Antiquity. Although advocates were to become increasingly professionalised, the *iudex* himself remained dependent on what he had picked up, the expertise of his advisers, and his own sensitivity to what Papinian had described as the 'religio' of those who judge.[21]

[18] Amm. Marc. 23. 6. 82.   [19] Aul. Gell. *Noctes Atticae* 14.2.12–19.
[20] Id. 16, 'Patrocinari enim prorsus hoc esse aiunt, non iudicare.' Tampering with what was discussed in the hearing in this way would have been one of the very few opportunities available to a corrupt judge improperly to influence the outcome.
[21] *Dig.* 22. 5. 13, quod legibus omissum est, non omittetur religione iudicantium...

Denuntiatio or *editio*

The first stage in civil proceedings was the summoning of the defendant by the plaintiff. Constantine insisted on official involvement in the process right from the start; the notification of suit (*denuntiatio*) had to be issued either through the court of the governor or the legal secretariats.[22] This ensured that the written instrument, also known as the *postulatio simplex*, was correctly drawn up, and the next stage was the issuing of an edict by the relevant magistrate ordering the defendant to appear. In response to the summons, the defendant would also draft a written *contradictio*, declaring an intention to rebut the charge and perhaps including grounds for the defence.[23] The alternative was to petition the emperor directly;[24] the response to this was a rescript, detailing the legal question at issue (in some respects the equivalent of the ancient formula) and referring the case to a competent judge. Once either the edict or the rescript was in place, *litis contestatio*, joinder of issue, could take place, and the case could be inaugurated, provided, of course, that the rescript was legally impetrated and the litigants legally qualified to act.[25] However, even the summons could be problematic for other reasons. The defendant could be in one of a number of prohibited categories, listed by jurists in Justinian's *Digest*. These included magistrates, priests or other sacred officials, judges hearing a case, litigants involved in another case, lunatics, children, a bride or bridegroom, or the principal relatives and guests at a funeral.[26] A summons could also not be issued in violation of *pietas*, duty towards the gods, close relations and patrons.[27] Defendants could not be dragged from their homes, but could be summoned from the doors of their houses, baths or the theatre.[28]

At some point early in the fifth century, the *libellus*-procedure came into use, as a means of launching litigation. The petitioner addressed the office of the governor through a *libellus*, which described the defendant and the nature of the accusation. The first known incidence of this is in a papyrus of 427,[29] in which one Cyrus, a trader of Alexandria, lodged a suit for a debt against a fellow trader; the record in fact consists of the *dialysis*, a record of settlement, in which Cyrus agreed that the defendant had come forward and given satisfaction, so that the case was now closed. A document of the same year shows Cyrus engaged in another suit; his opponents addressed their refutation of his *libellus* to the Prefect's office, omitting arguments – in effect reserving their defence – but undertaking

---

[22] *CT* 2.4.2 (322).
[23] This procedure is envisaged in *FIRA* 1.64, the schedule of court charges drawn up by the consularis of Numidia, on which see above.   [24] See above, ch. 2, p. 27.
[25] *CT* 2.4.4 (385).   [26] *Dig.* 2.4.2–4.   [27] *Dig.* 2.4.4–8.   [28] *Dig.* 2.4.18.
[29] *P.Oxy.* 1880.

to defend themselves in court and not pull out until the case had been concluded, 'so that we may be free of any blame'.[30] The counterplea had been validated and, in answer to the 'formal question', a standard element in legal procedure, the defendants had placed on record their consent to co-operate with the court. Although technically new, the *libellus*-procedure was a natural development of methods of litigation already current in the fourth century. Petitions to the governing power were a standard way of gaining access to a judge and a legal hearing and, once the *denuntiatio litis* was also channelled through the governor's office, the two processes could conveniently be fused. How long different procedures survived, or whether indeed the *libellus* ever became the standard mode of litigation in the West, is uncertain; in Rome in the 440s the *denuntiatio litis* procedure in property suits was still assumed to be the norm, with no hint that it was about to be replaced with something else.[31]

From the time of the issuing of the summons, the clock began to tick towards the statutory time-limit for concluding the case. This was usually four months, and certain devices aimed at subverting the limit by obfuscation or other forms of delaying tactics were outlawed. While the aim of the time-limit was clearly to concentrate minds and ensure a conclusion to the case, this was not always realised in practice. For some litigants, it was not advantageous to have any outcome at all, and their energies could therefore be ingeniously and unconstructively bent on ensuring that time ran out before a decision could be reached.[32] This could be done in the first place by failing to appear, although if the defendant was persistently absent, the hearing could take place without him. Sureties could be extracted against non-appearance from people subject to the jurisdiction of the judge, although proceedings for non-compliance over the sureties then had to be conducted independently of the main suit.[33] There were also provisions about what should happen if litigants were prevented by others from making an appearance.[34] Once the litigants were present, challenges could be lodged as to the legal capacity of the parties present, and whether they were competent to act either for themselves or as representatives of others.[35] The unfortunate Symmachus, as Prefect in 384, was driven to distraction by three spurious objections lodged by one Gaudentius, the representative of one party to a dispute, against the

---

[30] *P. Oxy.* 1881.   [31] *NVal* 8.1.

[32] Amm. Marc. 30.4.13 attacks lawyers for time-wasting.

[33] *Dig.* 2.8.2.5: In fideiussorem, qui aliquem iudicio sisti promiserit, tanti quanti ea res erit actionem dat praetor. If a defendant failed to appear on a first summons, then a further interval was allowed of thirteen days (Ulpian at *Dig.* 5.1.68–70).

[34] *Dig.* 2.10: 'De eo per quem factum erit quominus quis in iudicio sistat.'

[35] For these delaying tactics, see Symm. *Rel.* 19, and for the right of challenge, *CT* 2.12.3 = *CJ* 2.12.24.

standing of the other, Liberius. These were, first, that a previous agent had been employed, secondly, there had been no deed of agency read out in an earlier court confirming Liberius' status, and, third, the person represented by Liberius was herself now dead. Symmachus managed to refute all three objections by a sophisticated use of corroborative evidence and a constitution of Julian,[36] but his patience and concentration had already been tried and were to be yet more sorely tested by what was to come.[37]

There might also be debate at some early stage over the competence of the court; soldiers, senators and others had privileges over where, and before whom, their cases should be conducted, which were set out in the various rules applying to *praescriptio fori*. Trials were expected as a rule to 'follow the forum' of the defendant. This applied even to senators, who were expected to sue before the governor of the province of the defendant, but could defend themselves before the Prefect of the City.[38] In criminal cases, however, senators outside Italy were made liable to preliminary hearings before the governors of the province where the alleged crime took place; this was not to affect the status of the accused, whose ultimate punishment was to be referred upwards to the emperor or his deputies.[39] Cases of complaints involving taxation were to be heard before the representative of the fiscus,[40] but governors did not have to await the consent of the fiscal representative before hunting out accused people to produce them in court.[41] Lawsuits involving women were heard in the place of residence of their husbands and in accordance with their status.[42] Military courts were a separate operation, and civil cases were not expected to end up in front of military judges, although this could be hard to enforce.[43] 'Dilatory' objections might be lodged, requesting that the start of the case be delayed; these had to be entered at the start, and serious failure to comply with this rule was punishable, under Julian, with a fine.[44] A second form of objection, the peremptory objection, arguing that the suit could not proceed at all on some technical ground, could be lodged at any stage prior to the verdict.[45]

---

[36] *CT* 2.12.1, a procurator could continue a case after the decease of his client, provided he had been mandated to do so.

[37] For regulations limiting durations of suits to thirty years see esp. *CT* 4.13. This is not evidence for the incidence of such delays, which were expensive for all parties.

[38] *CT* 2.1.4 (364).   [39] *CT* 9.1.13 (Gratian, 376).   [40] *CT* 2.1.5 (365).

[41] *CT* 2.1.11 (398, west).   [42] *CT* 2.1.7 (392).

[43] *CT* 2.1.7 (397, east). For the complexities of the *praescriptio fori* for soldiers, see *NTh.* 7.1–4.

[44] *CJ* 4.19.9 (294), objections to be entered at the start of a suit; *CJ* 8.35.12 ordering an advocate who omits lodging an appeal for a delay at the start, does so later, ignores a warning against it and persists, to be fined one pound of gold.

[45] *CJ* 7.50.2 and 8.35.8, both of 294.

The hearing

How the formal arguing of the case proceeded is a subject of debate. On one interpretation, advocates on both sides put forward, first, the *narratio* of the case, during which the basic points and arguments were laid out, and then the rebuttal. This allowed advocates to offer explanations of their clients' cases, adorned with appropriate rhetorical flourishes. A group of papyrus records exist, containing summary outlines of cases, with notes in the margins and preceded by the problematic symbol of the crossed 'N' (Ꞥ).[46] This has been interpreted as standing for *narratio*, the preliminary statement of the case, made before the judge, and followed by a rebuttal from the defendant. However, it was then argued that real court records show such a high degree of intervention by both the opposing advocate and the judge that it would be impossible to deliver a *narratio* in court as a coherent statement at all, therefore the 'N' documents must in fact be the initial plea to the governor, the *denuntiatio*, and not part of the trial proceedings.[47] Yet more recently, papyrologists have concluded that the 'N' stands, not for *narratio* but for *nomikos*, advocate or jurisprudent, and that these documents were notes or instructions for the advocates, to use when drawing up their statements.[48] All this leaves the existence of set speeches at the start of the formal hearing in a state of uncertainty, although it must presumably have suited the judge to have at least some preliminary notion of what the litigants were talking about.

In court proceedings, the advocate was a central figure, and the outcome of the case could depend on his juristic and forensic skills.[49] Augustine commented on the universal need of everybody for a lawyer, when in any kind of material difficulty, although he also warned that the power of the profession could be overrated by the ambitious Christian; 'To be an advocate, he says, is a great thing. Eloquence is very powerful indeed, to have in every matter those implicated in the case hanging from the tongue of their learned counsel, and expecting from his lips loss or gain, death or life, destruction or survival.'[50] But such beliefs were a form of exile (from the truth), Augustine opined, – another 'river of Babylon'. This did not deter numerous ambitious men from seeking advancement through ad-

[46] *P.Lips.* 41 (Hermopolis, late 4th C.), *P. Thead.*16 (after 307), *P. Princ.* 119, re-edited by Hanson (1971) (*c.*325), *P. Col. Panop.* 31 (Panopolis, *c.* 329), *P. Col.* Inv. no. 181 (27) (Karanis, 4th C.).   [47] Lewis and Schiller (1974).   [48] *P. Col.* VII, no. 174: 165–72.

[49] Crook (1995) does not survey the Later Empire. For the extensive evidence on late imperial advocates, see, briefly, Jones (1964) and, for Early Empire, see Crook (1995).

[50] Aug. *Enn. in Ps. 136.3.* Advocatum esse, inquit, magna res est. Potentissima eloquentia: in omnibus habere susceptos pendentes ex lingua diserti patroni sui, et ex eius ore sperantes vel damna vel lucra, vel mortem vel vitam, vel perniciem vel salutem... Nescio quo te miseris: alius et iste fluvius Babylonis est.

vocacy and the law in general. Rules were brought in by emperors to regulate the numbers and qualifications of advocates at the bar of the great prefectures, a popular avenue for advancement, and the fifth century saw a debate about whether they should be pensioned off after twenty years, to allow in 'new blood'.[51] But not all advocates should be viewed as the ancient equivalent of the modern British QC. In the provinces, the less linguistically gifted may have resorted to representation by a friend in court in a manner similar to those illiterate groups of villagers in Egypt who dealt with the written formalities of their lives by exploiting the skills of one of their number, or legal petitioners who used the expertise of their friends to couch their complaints in the accepted moralistic jargon of the time. Some litigants, indeed, chose not to be represented by an advocate at all.

Advocates, or legal representatives, were required to be on the alert, even in relatively simple cases. Late in the third century, the advocate Isidorus spoke before the *strategos* about the wrongs inflicted by one Syrion on defenceless children, whose sheep he had stolen.[52] Syrion was charged with 'greed' and 'violence', the latter 'often' entered on the official records, by formal complaints (the children's agents had been alert to infringements of their rights). Worse, Syrion had 'defied' the orders of the governor to restore the sheep he had stolen (also on record). When an excuse was offered that Syrion was absent on necessary treasury business (one of the valid excuses for not responding to a summons), Isidorus was quick to challenge that he was shirking his trial and the judge responded by granting a formal interval, so that the case could be heard on Syrion's return. Even in this simple case, much was required of the small-town lawyer, who had not only to be fully briefed on the day but also cognisant of the past history of the dispute and alert to dodges by the opposition.[53]

Various forms of evidence could be adduced, accompanied by extensive cross-questioning by the *iudex*, supported by his team of advisers, or assessors. As Roman imperial culture became in general more reliant on the written word, so documentary proofs acquired equal or greater weight than oral testimony.[54] Written documentation was all-important. These documents could be private, but endorsed by three or more witnesses, who subscribed their names in their own hands, or through the agency of

---

[51] *NTh.* 10. 1–2 (April 439); *NVal.* 2. 2 (August 442); 3 (August 443); 4 (October 454).
[52] *P. Thead.* 15.
[53] Cf. *P. Princ.* 3.119, (early 4th C.), once thought to be a petition but argued by Hanson (1971) to be the speech of an advocate arguing a complex case over land, which lack of cited documentary evidence suggests may be a weak one. Political overtones are present in the involvement of Dionysius, an ex-protector, who, although initially the accused, has lodged a counter-petition against his accusers, alleging *calumnia*, false accusation.
[54] *CJ* 4.20.1 (undated, Greek).

others, or documents drawn up by notaries. Records could also be produced from the public archives. As it was possible – and a useful delaying tactic – to interpose an accusation of forgery, handwriting experts could also be brought forward and required to testify under oath.[55]

Despite the growth in importance of the written word, oral testimony remained important. A general rule that more than one witness was required to establish a point continued to be observed in Late Antiquity,[56] although emperors had a tendency to reduce the number of witnesses required to avoid time-wasting,[57] and Constantine made a short-lived attempt to privilege the witness of a single bishop, even if isolated from other proofs.[58] While attempts were made to ensure fairness by excluding certain categories of witness, such as close relations by blood or marriage, altogether,[59] the social status of the witness was regarded as one indication of the reliability of his (or her) testimony.[60] Constantine's privileging of the witness of *honestiores* in a law of 334 was a simplistic expression of priorities set out by the jurists, who included status as just one of the aspects of a witness to be considered by the judge.[61] Callistratus, who was exceptionally interested in trial procedure, advised that character was also relevant, as was financial position (the poor could more easily be bribed) but that Hadrian was right to advise judges to be flexible over whether to pay most attention to the number of witnesses, their status and authority, or general opinion about the case.[62] That assumptions about reliability were based on status at all is one of the peculiarities of Roman justice, and one which could easily be abused to the detriment of the poorer and less well-connected litigant.

In determining the law that was to apply, the production of a genuine

[55] *CJ* 4.21.20.3.
[56] *Dig.* 22.5.12 (Ulpian), that when the number of witnesses required was not specified, two would suffice. See also *CJ* 4.20.4 (284); 4.20.9 (334), which also privileges the witness of *honestiores*.
[57] *Dig.* 22.5.1.2. Arcadius Charisius, under Diocletian and Constantine, observed that a larger number was mentioned by statutes, but imperial constitutions reduced the requirement to a 'sufficient number' to avoid the 'annoyance' of superfluous witnesses.
[58] *Const. Sirm.* 1 (333).
[59] For excluded categories, including freedmen of the litigants, the under-age, beast-fighters, prostitutes and advocates involved in the case, see *Dig.* 22.5.3.5; 5.9; 5.10; 5.19; 5.25. For those not compelled to appear, id. 5.4; 5.8.
[60] For the importance of character to the outcome, cf. Aulus Gellius, *Noctes Atticae* 14.2.1–21 for a case in which a plaintiff of good character lacks proofs or witnesses in a case against a defendant of known bad character, who sought not only acquittal but conviction of the plaintiff for false accusation. Gellius' advisers support the defendant, on evidential grounds, his hero, Favorinus, (21) cites Cato as precedent for finding for the plaintiff. Gellius' decision was to opt out – 'non liquet'. On this, see Holford-Strevens (1988): 219–20. [61] *CJ* 4.20.9.
[62] *Dig.* 22.5.3.1 and 2 (Callistratus). See also 22.5.21, Arcadius Charisius advised that if all witnesses were of 'the same high status and good reputation' and the judge agreed, a decision could be reached but, if not, the case was to be decided by whether the evidence fitted with the circumstances, not by the number of witnesses.

and preferably recent imperial rescript or general law could prove decisive.[63] Much therefore depended on the diligence of advocates in tracking
down, or assembling private collections of, useful laws.[64] In an Egyptian
hearing before the *defensor civitatis* on the ownership, and tax liabilities, of
some disputed land, the advocate of the villagers, who were seeking to nail
down the defendants as owners of the land, scored an early advantage
with his production of a law of Constantine on the *praescriptio longi
temporis*, establishing that, if land had been in the possession of an
individual for forty years or more, he became its legal owner.[65] The
response of the *iudex* was first to establish the gist of the law (and therefore
its relevance) and then to insist that its actual wording was read out,
before establishing that the forty-year tenure could also be proved. In this
case, after further interrogation of the parties, the judge ascertained the
facts and, in accordance with standard procedure, delivered his ruling
from a written tablet.[66]

The verbatim transcription of the interrogation had several purposes.
One was to establish that the judge had carried out the proceedings fairly.
If he had not done so, he could be called to account. Secondly, the
transcript would include all the arguments advanced by the parties, and
the legal (or debating) points scored by each side. The Egyptian hearing
before the *defensor* was dominated by the sharp lawyer employed by the
victorious villagers, who interrupted the opposition's leisurely and tendentious preamble by producing his law, and scored a second hit when he
helped the judge to establish that the ultimate losers did indeed know
about a town house, of which they had at first denied all knowledge. The
third purpose of transcripts was to provide a full record for a higher court.
However conclusive the transcript might be, delay in implementing the
decision was easily achieved. Justified or not, the defeated party in a civil
suit had the right of appeal.

Appellatio

All Roman citizens had the right of appeal and the lengthy sections devoted
to it in the Theodosian Code, Book 11, show that its complexities were of
importance to lawyers. By the fourth century, this meant appeal from the

---

[63] But cf. Symm. *Rel.* 34. 13 which challenges the issue of a rescript based on *litterae* of
Constantius II; quaeso, igitur, ut gesta, quae fidem relationis adseruint, audire dig-
nemini, legesque percensentes, quarum plerumque duritiam pro clementia vestra de-
cretis moderatioribus temperastis.

[64] For survival of laws through private collections, see above, p. 21.

[65] *P. Col.* VII, no. 175.

[66] *CT* 11.30.40 (383), Omnem, quae de libello scripta recitatur, dici volumus atque esse
sententiam.

court of first resort, usually that of the governor-*iudex* or his deputy, to that
of the emperor, by which was meant the jurisdiction of the praetorian
prefects, or prefects of the cities of Rome and Constantinople, who judged
'vice sacra', in place of the emperor and are often denominated in inscriptions as 'v.s.i', *vice sacra iudicans*. For an appeal to reach the stage of even
being heard, both parties to the case and the judge had to comply with
documentary formalities, on which strict time limits were imposed.

Appeals could normally be made only from final decisions, delivered in
writing and read out by the *iudex*. Although a *iudex* might, in cases of
doubt, refer a point of law to the emperor, in the form of a *consultatio*, this
could be frowned upon by the central authority, if the judge was in effect
avoiding his own responsibility for reaching a decision for himself.[67]
Litigants were forbidden to appeal from a preliminary or 'interlocutory'
decision (*praeiudicium*), which, unlike the final *sententia*, was not written
down or read out, although Valentinian II, perhaps in response to a query
from Symmachus, allowed for the forwarding of such appeals on the
grounds that, if the rule had been broken, the fine could still be exacted
from the offender.[68] Appeals could also be lodged before the final verdict,
if 'peremptory prescriptions' or objections were at issue, as these could
determine the final outcome.[69] In general, imperial policy was to discour-
age appeals that were procedurally incorrect[70] and those lodged to delay a
capital sentence. Appellants against *praeiudicia* were penalised by fines of
up to thirty pounds of silver by Constans in 341.[71] Appeals against capital
sentences were more problematic. Constantine took a hard line in ruling
that people convicted of homicide, adultery, magic and poisoning by their
own free confession or clear proofs were not allowed to appeal,[72] but his
sons, by 347, allowed appeals in criminal cases in general. This principle
seems to have been accepted in law thereafter, although the accounts of
trials and condemnations in Ammianus, for one, suggest that, in extreme
cases, where the emperor's minions were directly involved, the right of
appeal against the death sentence was in practice non-existent.

Once an appeal was lodged, all parties to a first hearing incurred
obligations. The appellant had the right to withdraw the appeal for three
days after it was officially lodged.[73] The judge, in the meantime, was

---

[67] *CT* 11.29.1 (313/4) limits, but does not prohibit, *consultationes*.
[68] *CT* 11.30.40 defines *praeiudicium* as 'quidquid . . . libelli absque documento et recitatione
decernitur'; 11.30.44(384) refers appeals over *praeiudicia* to the emperor. For Symmachus' referral of an incorrect appeal, see *Rel.* 16 and p. 115.
[69] *CT* 11.30.37; 11.36.23.   [70] *CT* 11.36.2; 3; 5; 11; 15; 16; 18.
[71] *CT* 11.36.5. Lesser infractions incurred fines of 15lb silver.
[72] *CT* 11.36.1 (314/5) reiterated by Constantius II, *CT* 11.36.7.
[73] *CT* 11.30.56 (396) clears up confusion on the point from which the three days' grace was
reckoned.

obliged to furnish to the parties a copy of his decisions (*opinio*) and the grounds for them within ten days; the litigants then had a further five days to lodge objections.[74] The judge or his staff were then obliged to forward the whole dossier to the appeals court within twenty, later thirty, days of the original verdict.[75] Documentation had to be complete to avoid referral back, or an incorrect but nonetheless irreversible, rescript.[76] While the appeal was pending, appellants were not to be victimised by imprisonment, or harrassed by officials.[77] Dodges indulged in by appellants looking to play the system by exploiting loopholes were also prevented by legislation. Nothing could be included in the *libelli*, the submissions by the parties, which had not already been considered at the trial (and therefore included in the court *acta*), still less brought up for discussion at the appeal hearing.[78] Attempts to influence the appeal court by a personal supplication were penalised under Valentinian and Valens by a fine of half the amount in dispute.[79] However, later modifications suggest a more sympathetic understanding of the plight of litigants kept in suspense by delays in the system, along with a less welcome shift of the onus for keeping the appeal alive from the officials to the litigants; personal supplications were allowed, if the appeal had not been heard within a year, and the appellants were also expected to furnish their own dossier of the records and the referral by the judge.[80]

Litigation on appeals aimed to ensure that only those qualified to appeal did so, that procedures were correctly implemented, and that delays were kept to a minimum. All parties were kept in line by a system of fines. Constantine imposed a fine of thirty folles on appeals from *praeiudicia*, increased, as we have seen, in 341, to thirty or fifteen pounds of silver depending on the amount involved in the litigation. Judges were not permitted discretion in setting the level of fines.[81] More indicative of the emerging culture of official and judicial accountability asserted in legislation was the imposition of fines on the *iudex* and his office-staff for delays in forwarding appeals or refusal to accept them in the first place. The latter was the more serious offence. In 343, the judge was liable to a fine of ten pounds of gold, his office-staff for fifteen;[82] by 356, both governor and his staff faced penalties of thirty pounds of gold, but this was modified by Valentinian I, who restricted the liability of the governor to twenty pounds. By the 390s, the governor's penalty was between twenty and thirty pounds, but that of the office-staff had increased to fifty, for

[74] *CT* 11.30.1 (317/15); 11.30.24 (348).
[75] *CT* 11.30.4; 8; 22; 25; 29; 31; 33; 34; 48; 51; 58–9; 64; *CJ* 7.32.64.
[76] *CT* 11.30.9; 35.   [77] *CT* 11.30.2; 4.   [78] *CT* 11.30.11 (321); 52 (393).
[79] *CT* 11.30.34 (364).
[80] *CT* 11.30.47 (386); 54 (395); 66 (419). See id. 47 for supply of trial dossier by appellants.
[81] *CT* 11.30.43 (384).   [82] *CT* 11.30.22.

failing to advise 'their' governor properly.[83] Imperial concern that officials should assert themselves, if required, was not confined to the late fourth century; Constantine had employed characteristically vigorous language to attack the 'damnable connivance' of officials, who were to remind the *iudex* of imperial decrees, oppose him if he persisted in getting things wrong and, if necessary, lay hands on him ('manibus iniectis'), drag him from the court and hand him over to the tax office to be fined.[84] By 399, little had apparently changed; Honorius reminded imperial administrators to stand up to the governor stubbornly, prove him wrong by citation of *acta* and show him what had been established by law.[85] As usual, all this was given a moral dimension. Imposition of sanctions for wrongdoing over appeals was justified by strictures on the motivation of *iudices*, who supposedly felt sensitive about appeals as reflecting on their competence, and therefore suppressed or delayed references to the appeal courts because of their 'guilty consciences'.[86]

What the laws could not control was the politics of apportioning blame. Permanent officials in service to temporary governors might have been either culprits, genuinely responsible for maladministration, or scapegoats, their legal liability for their own and their masters' wrongdoing a weapon in the hands of *iudices* seeking to justify their own actions. It was always open to 'victimised' governors to get in first with their own complaints about officials. Symmachus, for example, as Prefect in 384, had bitter things to say in a *Relatio* to Valentinian II, about the *censuales*, of whom he was conducting an audit, and various members of his office-staff and that of the *vicarius Romae*. These had colluded with others to deport a key trial witness to Africa, despite a lodging of an appeal by the witness before Symmachus and his predecessor.[87] The situation was further complicated by the meddling of a senator, Fulgentius, who used two *agentes in rebus* and a Palatine official to kidnap a second witness and detain him by force. Such manoeuvres were perhaps especially intricate in Rome, where local power-struggles were enlivened by the competing jurisdictions of Prefect and Vicarius, and the various agendas of individual senators and imperial administrators, but they were not unrepresentative. Although *officia* were anonymous in the laws, the individual bureaucrats who composed them were far from 'faceless'.[88]

[83] *CT* 11.30.51, 'obsecundantem officii gratiam'; 58; 59.   [84] *CT* 11.30.8.1.
[85] *CT* 11.30.58, nisi huic pertinaciter restiterit, atque actis ita contradixerit et, quid iure sit constitutum, ostenderit.
[86] *CT* 11.30. 13 (326); 25 (356); 31 (363), 'prava id conscientia faciente', and stipulating that, to avoid excuses or delays in future, the date on which the dossier was entrusted to the apparitor charged with its delivery would be recorded.   [87] Symm. *Rel.* 23.4.
[88] For further whistle-blowing on corrupt officials, cf. *Rel.* 44, drawing attention to one Macedonius, who depleted the salt-workers guild by granting illegal exemptions.

Vice sacra iudicans: **Symmachus as Prefect, 384 CE**

As evidence for the workings of late Roman justice, Symmachus' *Relationes* to the emperor Valentinian II have their drawbacks. The cases which came before Symmachus, or other Praetorian and City Prefects, acting as the supposedly final court of appeal, would have been the most intricate and difficult, and should not therefore be interpreted as symptomatic of the (mal)functioning of late Roman justice as a whole. Moreover, the form of the reportage leaves some details unclear, as, along with the covering letter, which survives, Symmachus would have included a full dossier of the case. However, both the details of the cases themselves and the overall political context in which this senatorial pagan *iudex* conducted his work reveal something of the pressures exerted even on powerful and eminent judges by non-legal considerations, while his responses to these pressures will supply a different perspective on ancient and modern assumptions about the 'corruption' of judges.[89]

The legal grounds for a referral were usually that a new ruling was required. In the case referred to above,[90] involving the curator Gaudentius and the procurator Liberius, the grounds seem to have been the impossible complexity of the case, which resulted in the breach of the statutory time-limits for completion, after running, already, for many years. As so often, the case involved several generations of a single family. The property in dispute belonged to Prisca, deceased. She had two children, Marciana the Elder, now deceased but still represented by Liberius, and Placidianus, who had married and produced at least two children of his own, Marciana the Younger, represented by Gaudentius, and Placida; Placidianus and Placida were also now dead. Liberius, on behalf of Marciana Senior's estate, was suing the younger Marciana, then in possession, for a share of Prisca's estate. His method was to employ two forms of action under a single procedure,[91] the 'complaint of unduteous will' (*querela inofficiosi testamenti*) and a claim that Prisca had made unreasonable gifts to Placidianus, which had then been inherited by his two children (*querela inmodicarum donationum*)[92]. The aim of Liberius was to push forward, the aim of Gaudentius, the representative of the party in possession, was to be as obstructive as possible. The ingenuity of both confirms that disputes in Late Antiquity could drag on for years, not because of bribery, corruption or incompetence, but simply thanks to the chicaneries of lawyers.

At the hearing before Symmachus, the lawyers at last turned to the

[89] On which see ch. 8.   [90] *Rel.* 19; Vera (1981).   [91] *CT* 2.20.1.
[92] *Dig.* 31.87.3 envisaged a grandmother who gave away her whole estate to her grandchildren; this counted as 'excessive presents' and, in the event of a challenge, half the gifts could be revoked.

subject of the 'immoderate gifts' which 'derived from' Placidianus' estate and had gone to his children. Now a further complication was introduced, the estate of Marciana Junior's sister, Placida, also deceased, as Liberius claimed for his client (the elder Marciana), the amount left to the younger Marciana in the will of her dead sister. Symmachus' letter is unclear as to how this worked, perhaps reflecting confusion in the mind of its author, and Gaudentius exploited this uncertainty: whose estate were they discussing and why had Liberius not mentioned Placida in his petition? Deadlock on this point was, predictably, the result. Then a second front was opened by Liberius, who proposed that the property in dispute should be placed with him in trust, while a valuation was made. This would have robbed Gaudentius of his strongest card, the fact that his client was in possession, and he naturally objected, arguing that the petition should be discussed before the question of the trust. It then transpired that the time agreed at an earlier hearing with the praetor for valuing the overseas property was too short (perhaps thanks to the calculated inefficiency of Gaudentius). Consequently, time was running out, and, in despair, Symmachus forwarded the whole to the emperors' lawyers. It would have been little consolation to him to have reflected that the deadlock illustrates how, even in the so-called post-classical period of Roman law, there were still legal brains at work, for whom the niceties of law held real practical interest, even if these were matters of technicalities, rather than of legal philosophy.

Most attested referrals by Symmachus were not, strictly, for legal reasons. When he referred to Valentinian a technically illegal appeal against a *praeiudicium*, on the grounds that the appellant had received bad advice, his concern was clearly that the law should not be applied with inconsiderate harshness.[93] Compassion was also, at first sight, a motive, when, in a criminal case, a young prosecutor, Africanus, committed himself to face the same penalty as threatened the accused,[94] then found himself unable to prove his case. The legal consequences were clear and Symmachus would have been entitled to enforce the penalty. However, he referred the case to the emperor's *clementia*, stating that Africanus, though a rash young man, had done good service. What he did not say in his letter was that there was an oddity at the trial – witnesses expected to testify for Africanus stated the opposite – which indicated sharp practice by one side or the other, and that Africanus was an imperial *agens in rebus*, a secret agent with, perhaps, some influential backers.[95] Where politics

---

[93] *Rel.* 16.
[94] By the process of *inscriptio*, on which see ch. 6. For the case, see Symm. *Rel.* 49.
[95] Cf. also *Rel.* 32, involving a protector disputing over land. Again the referral is technically unnecessary.

and imperial interests might be at issue, the prudent prefect preferred to keep his diplomatic distance.

Justice could also be contaminated by politics on a higher level. When Symmachus judged the complaint of one Scirtius,[96] that he had been dispossessed of his land, he was capable of sorting it out for himself, but chose to tell Valentinian all about it, because (he wrote) the offence was so outrageous and his own conduct so scrupulously correct. A further motive emerges in the course of his account, the blackening of the character of a political opponent, the Christian senator, Olybrius, whose agent is shown behaving in a violent and illegal manner, with, it is implied, the connivance of Olybrius himself. Olybrius' agent frustrates the implementation of Symmachus' decree awarding possession to Scirtius, various witnesses of the act of obstruction are kidnapped 'in violation of the laws', most of the people on the estate go into hiding after 'hints' from Olybrius' agents, and Scirtius' household slaves are carried off to a suburban villa, which belonged to Olybrius. Despite this attempt to remove witnesses wholesale, the council of Praeneste agrees to testify in Scirtius' favour against his ostensible opponents, the heirs of one Theseus. This flushes out the procurator, Tarpeius, who, it turns out, represents Olybrius, in alliance with the Theseus group, thus effectively implicating the 'clarissima et illustris domus' of Olybrius in all the preceding wrongdoing. The Christian senator is exposed as an unscrupulous land-grabber, working through others from behind the scenes to oppress the weak (Scirtius) and pervert the course of justice, to his own aggrandisement.

This moral wrong-footing is consistent with the language of both emperors and petitioners of the period. The wrongdoer is accused of abuse of power and violation of the laws, the speaker is either weak and oppressed himself, or acting for others against the powerful. Much of this may be true and reveals Olybrius as a not untypical member of the land-hungry (and Christian) Anicii, whose most prominent representative, Sex. Petronius Probus, held vast estates all over the Empire, although his title to some of them was, in the view of Ammianus, questionable.[97] Olybrius himself was City Prefect in 369–70, Praetorian Prefect of Illyricum in 378 and consul, with Ausonius, in 379.[98] But Ammianus' portrait of Olybrius as prefect, fifteen years before Symmachus' attack, provides a corrective to the stereotype of the unscrupulous man of power. As Prefect, Olybrius had been mild and fair, severely punishing false accusations, remitting taxes and consistently just and humane; his only faults were that, in private life, he was over-fond of luxury, the theatre and

---

[96] *Rel.* 28.   [97] Amm. Marc. 27.11.1.
[98] *PLRE* I, Q. Clodius Hermogenianus Olybrius 3, *PLRE* I, pp. 640–2.

love-affairs.[99] But although land-grabbing was not, for Ammianus, one of Olybrius' principal faults, Symmachus' version of his character may also stand; Olybrius acted, according to Symmachus, through agents, thus retaining deniability. The agents' activities could have proceeded unchecked, without damaging the public moral purity of their main beneficiary.

Symmachus' *Relationes* cover a number of his duties as Prefect, many of which had no connection with the law. His legal papers document exceptional cases, the ones he could not resolve for himself. They were not, therefore, representative of Symmachus' activities within or beyond his court, as a whole. However, a total of forty-nine *Relationes* in six months, an average of just under two per week, is far from negligible.[100] For political as well as administrative and juridical reasons, Symmachus felt the need to keep in constant touch with the distant, and potentially hostile court. Herein lay his difficulty, and one not confined to him. He could not interpret, still less make, law for himself,[101] therefore any case of doubt had to be referred; the vulnerable *iudex* could not risk even appearing to exceed his powers. There was no independent judiciary. Secondly, as *iudex*, Symmachus effectively encouraged the emperor to exert his discretionary powers of *clementia* on behalf of clients recommended by the Prefect. Thus the emperor's function as guarantor of strict law was undermined by his own *iudex*. Neither, however, would have seen Symmachus' interventions in this light; patronage was a traditional and honourable activity – and only subversive of the legal process when indulged in by someone else. How honourable its effects were, depended, as Symmachus knew, on the standpoint of the beholder and the identity of the patron; the *clementia* laudable in an emperor became, when indulged in by his deputies, corrupt and venal *gratia*.[102]

---

[99] Amm. Marc. 28.4.1–2.
[100] Cf. the average rate of production of laws surviving in the *CT*, of 21 per annum. Most *Relationes* of Symmachus did not, however, require a legislative response.
[101] Symm. *Rel.* 30, nos venerari potius quam interpretari oracula divina consuevimus.
[102] Symm. *Rel.* 49.4.

Crime and the problem of pain

The dark reputation of Late Antiquity as a period of cruelty and terror is based to a great extent on the operation, or abuse, of its criminal law. The severed heads of some usurpers and rebels went the rounds of the Empire as a warning to others and an ever more ghastly proof that the challenge was no more.[1] Traitors, murderers, magicians and other criminals were routinely burned alive, the public floggings of slave and free inflicted both pain and social humiliation, judicial torture was extended up the social scale, innocents on remand rotted in prison, their cases unheard. All this provokes horror in the modern student of the time and general condemnation of the 'judicial savagery' of the age.[2]

The harshness of the judicial climate in general, reinforced as it was by the menacing rhetoric of imperial laws, which routinely threatened the wicked with harsh penalties cannot be denied. In the language of the laws, emperors stand self-convicted of imposing terror on the citizens of the Empire, while their content reiterates the desirability of harsh punishments, and reveals the slow but sure erosion of the immunities of the better-off.[3] From the pagans Libanius and Ammianus, as well as from the Christians Lactantius and Eusebius come harrowing accounts of oppression by ruthless judges, the 'rack', the 'claws' and the sadism of torturers. By contrast, although the Early Empire had its share of judicial cruelty, as evidenced in the torture of slaves or the public entertainments provided by the inventive executions of criminals in the arena, writers, although waxing indignant about many abuses, never combine in the chorus of protest that is heard from the historians and bishops of Late Antiquity.

---

[1] Zos. 4. 58. 5 (Eugenius' head shown to followers after execution in 394); 5. 22. 3 (Uldin of the Huns sends head of Gainas to Arcadius); Amm. Marc. 26. 10. 6 (head of Procopius exhibited in Philippopolis on its way to Gaul).

[2] E.g. MacMullen (1986); Angliviel de la Beaumelle (1992) 92 on the 'banalisation de la torture'.

[3] Foucault (1975/1977) interprets public torture and punishment as assertion of the state's control of the body of the criminal. For Late Antiquity, this interpretation reinforces the function of imperial law as imposition of the emperor's will, through the language of power.

Such weight of evidence cannot be discounted, but the significance of these eloquent late antique protests against a cruel and oppressive system is perhaps due for re-evaluation.[4] Most obviously, the fact that these highly partial, rhetorical, sources saw fit to protest at all is a reflection of a culture prepared to question and criticise the abuse of power; orators and writers spoke or wrote as they did because they could expect a sympathetic response from their audience. We know so much about the sufferings of Christians in the Great Persecution, or of the friends and associates of Libanius, Ammianus and others, because writers made the sufferings of their friends or co-religionists the subject of highly-wrought accounts, designed to create sympathy for the victims and odium for their persecutors. The 'savagery' of the torturer is played up, perhaps artificially,[5] in the interests not of dispassionate truth but of the polemical purpose of the writer. For that purpose to be achieved, some sympathetic response had to be created in the audience; readers and listeners had also to believe that the infliction of excessive pain, at least in some contexts, and on the innocent, was wrong. In other words, criticism of judicial cruelty is not evidence in itself for the extent of that cruelty, but for public willingness to criticise the operations of justice as cruel and inhumane.[6]

In what follows, an attempt will be made to ascertain both what happened in criminal prosecutions and what was thought, by legislators and others, of the various processes involved. Discussion will focus in particular on the not always effective legal safeguards afforded to defendants, the interrogation of witnesses and suspects, often under torture, known as the *quaestio*, the function of punishment, and the impact of Christianity (and associated moral values), which fostered what may be called a 'culture of criticism', and which, in almost every city of the Empire, employed a combination of public strictures and private arm-twisting to mitigate the full rigours of the criminal law.

Accusation

The function of terror, which, in Late Antiquity, was often regarded as beneficial,[7] was to deter the wicked and ensure justice. Therefore, when a

---

[4] There is some evidence for the invention of atrocities; Ammianus' information that Procopius was beheaded (26. 9. 9) is ignored by Sozom. *HE*. 6. 8, alleging that Procopius (like the legendary Procrustes) was torn apart by bent trees.

[5] E.g. Ammianus, the arch-critic of torture when employed by Constantius II, Valentinian and Valens, makes no reference to the probable use of torture by the interrogators employed by his hero, Julian, at Chalcedon in 362, on which see Angliviel de la Beaumelle (1992) 93. 100–1.

[6] Cf. Honoré (1978): 37 (imperial constitutions denouncing abuses) 'are testimony more to the acuity of a sense of injustice than to the prevalence of injustice itself'.

[7] See Scott (1985).

criminal accusation was lodged, the accuser was compelled to bind himself, in writing, 'with shaking pen' to undergo the penalty threatening the accused, if he failed to prove his charges.[8] In the reign of Constantine, however, there was some debate over whether a verbal accusation alone might suffice, and that emperor and his successors insisted that the bond of accusation could be incurred only after time and reflection, 'when anger has been calmed and peace of mind restored', and therefore had to be in written form.[9] The seriousness of criminal charges suspended privileges available in civil suits, in particular the *praescriptio fori*, the right of some privileged groups to choose trial outside the province where the dispute originated; under criminal procedures, the accused stood trial in the province where the alleged offence took place,[10] although Gratian in 376 compromised over the trials of senators by permitting referral of the punishment of senators to an Italian court, after an initial hearing in the province where the suit originated.[11] Other safeguards were put in place. Accusations had to be made by the prosecutor in person, not through a deputy, and could not be lodged by those already indicted themselves for criminal offences,[12] as these could clearly be malicious.[13] Julian ruled that defendants had the right of access to records, 'nor should their release be postponed by the cunning of the accuser'.[14] Prosecutions were not allowed to drag on for more than a year, and if a defendant was detained in prison, the case was to be heard within one month.[15] In cases of alleged adultery, the right of accusation, hitherto available, after an interval, to third parties outside the injured family, was limited to the husband, in the first instance, and after him to the father, brothers and cousins of the culprit; the motive, Constantine declared, was to prevent malicious accusations, which ruined the marriage relationship.[16]

Although prison sentences were not part of the Late Roman penal system, they were extensively used for purposes of detention before trial. Excessive pressures on the courts due to the numbers of the accused could result in overcrowding, hence Eusebius' sardonic observation on the Diocletianic persecutions, that the prisons became so full of bishops and clergy that there was no room for real criminals.[17] The problem for lawyers and others concerned for fairness was that the innocent could suffer a long term in gaol, and perhaps not survive at all. Again, therefore, some safeguards were necessary. No one was to be arrested and im-

---

[8] *CT* 9.1.5 (320); 8 (366); 9 (366); 11 (373); 14 (383); 19 (423, west).   [9] *CT* 9.1.5.
[10] *CT* 9.1.1 (317); 10 (373); 16 (386). Theodosius I (*CT* 9.7.9, 383) insisted that soldiers too, if accused of adultery by the husband, had to 'follow the forum' of the accuser.
[11] *CT* 9.1.13.   [12] *CT* 9.1.12 (374).   [13] *CT* 9.1.15 (385).
[14] *CT* 9.1.6 (prefecture of Salutius Secundus).   [15] *CT* 9.1.7 (338).
[16] *CT* 9.7.2 (326). Constantine clearly regarded the protection of *inscriptio* as inadequate against slander.   [17] Eus. *HE* 8. 6. 9.

prisoned before the formalities of entering the *inscriptio* in the public records had been completed.[18] Defendants were not to be put in bonds in prison, until convicted,[19] and, when produced in court, were to be only loosely chained.[20] Male and female prisoners were to be segregated.[21] By the late fourth century, prisoners' rights, which had been acknowledged from Constantine onwards, were more systematically upheld. Theodosius I, followed by Honorius, allowed to accused people an interval of thirty days for the arrangement of their affairs.[22] Moreover, named officials were made liable for the proper treatment of prisoners, while in custody. Constantine insisted that prisoners were kept in daylight and issued dreadful (but vague) threats against prison guards, who caused the deaths of prisoners, and provincial governors who failed to inflict capital punishment on the guilty.[23] Theodosius I further tightened the rules by insisting that prison registrars made full reports about the prisoners in their charge, and made the governor's staff liable to fines (twenty pounds of gold) and the governor to a fine (ten pounds of gold) and exile.[24] By the early fifth century, the formal involvement of bishops in the supervision of prison conditions provided a further guarantee of humane treatment: food (*alimoniae*) was to be provided to poor prisoners and they were to be allowed baths and the right to be questioned about their treatment every Sunday.[25]

Whether these regulations were always remembered or observed in practice is debateable. However, as has been argued above, the existence of the laws themselves, the declared responsibility of the state for prison conditions, the naming and potential penalising of those liable if the rules were broken, and the formal supervisory role granted to bishops gave support to those wishing to make an issue of prison conditions. Thus when Libanius, not best known as a social reformer, took up the issue of prison conditions, he may well have expected a sympathetic hearing from the emperor, whose law of 380 he knew and cited.[26] In an eloquent attack on abuses by the powerful,[27] he 'informed' Theodosius I that innocent people were being accused by the strong and wealthy elite and packed off to gaol by the governor's officials, 'despite denials, assertions of wrongful accusation, and appeals to written law (*graphe*) and customary usage

---

[18] *CT* 9.3.4 (365).   [19] *CT* 9.2.3 (380).   [20] *CT* 9.3.1 (320).   [21] *CT* 9.3.3 (340).
[22] *CT* 9.2.3 (380); 6 (409). For Augustine's exploitation of this rule see above, pp. 92–3.
[23] *CT* 9.3.1 (320).   [24] *CT* 9.3.6 (380) = *CJ* 9.4.5.
[25] *CT* 9.3.7 (409) = *CJ* 1.4.9 (in a section on ecclesiastical powers and duties. Justinian's compilers removed this from the criminal sections of the Code, showing the importance they attached to the clause empowering bishops to supervise the judge).
[26] Lib. *Or.* 45. 32.
[27] For restrictions on *potentiores*, see *CT* 9. 1. 17 (390) insisting they be produced in court when bound by *inscriptio*, and 9.11 (388) to the Augustal Prefect (of Egypt) outlawing the use of private prisons.

(*nomoi*)'. The rich accusers, who had presumably flouted the requirement concerning *inscriptio*, then, according to Libanius, went off on holiday and forgot about the matter completely. This neglect resulted in long confinement for their victims, who starved, could not sleep because of the crowded conditions and suffered the extortions of their gaolers, who cynically recommended appeals to visiting deaconesses for assistance.[28] In such conditions, many died, while negligent governors indulged in pleasurable distractions (dancers, mimes, chariot-racing) or heard taxation suits, or frivolous cases, in preference to serious business.[29] In blaming the governor, at length, Libanius echoed the attitudes of imperial legislation in general, as did his insistence that laws were no more than waste paper if magistrates failed to enforce them. But, as has been argued above,[30] complaints about the ineffectiveness of laws were not necessarily indicative of the failure of legislation in general. Libanius expressed views that carried more weight because publicly endorsed by imperial law; his position of influence in Antioch ensured that he would be heard; and the oppressed in prison, socially and economically weak as they were, were not left to suffer in silence.

Quaestio

To get at the facts was the job of every *iudex*. In criminal trials, he was entitled to submit to 'the Question', under torture, slaves and, increasingly, free men. However, it was only when members of the elite began to run the risk of interrogation by torture that the literary sources became vociferous in their protests. Ammianus, *protector domesticus* and member of, probably, the Antiochene elite, is a prime example. In 371, he witnessed the public interrogations and mass executions of a number of prominent citizens of Antioch implicated in the so-called 'philosophers' conspiracy' against the emperor Valens. In treason trials, all immunities were void, but, whatever the legal situation, that of the sufferers was given the full dramatic and theatrical treatment beloved of Late Roman writers. In the presence of the Praetorian Prefect, Domitius Modestus, and the leading investigators, 'the racks were tightened, the lead weights brought out, along with the cords and lashes, everywhere echoed with the ghastly sound of the brutal cries of the torturers as they went about their work, amidst the creaking of the chains – "hold him steady, shut him in, tighten, release"'.[31] But this purple passage is only one of many devices employed by the historian to maximise pity and terror. From the low-key beginning of the affair, when two minor palatine officials in debt to the treasury are

---

[28] Lib. *Or.* 45. 8 (sleep); 9 (food); 10 (lamp-oil and 'women do-gooders').
[29] Lib. *Or.* 45. 16–31.   [30] See above, ch. 4.   [31] Amm. Marc. 29. 1. 23.

accused of plotting to murder the *comes rei privatae*, he systematically builds up a picture of accumulated terror, as ever more people are drawn, almost at random, into the web of conspiracy and, after fearful sufferings, dispatched to a humiliating death by strangulation or by fire. Looming in the background of the inquisition is the menacing figure of the emperor Valens, who is the more terrifying, because his uncontrollable rages and propensity to believe rumour, rather than truth, render him the more unpredictable and therefore dangerous. Because of his character, and that of his following, normal processes of law were set aside: 'The judges called his attention to what was provided in the laws but went on to conduct the cases in accordance with the ruler's will.'[32]

Ammianus' indignation, it should be noted, was directed against abuse of the law, not, primarily, the law itself, and was fuelled by the fact that the victims were known to him. Whatever his motive, his horror at Valens' treatment, while it evokes sympathy in the modern reader, should not be glossed into a reinvention of Ammianus as a twentieth-century western liberal. He, like most contemporaries would have been, to a great extent, inured to the physical (and mental) pain caused by, among other things, disease, poverty, childbirth and war. Pain is an area in which societies may differ profoundly from each other and Roman society was very different from our own. Our task, in this difficult area, must be to try to understand the 'otherness' of Late Antiquity.

It is indicative of the problem that modern observers have with the infliction of pain in judicial contexts that the recent translators of Justinian's *Digest* rendered the heading of the section in Book 48, *De Quaestionibus* as 'Torture'. True, the entire contents of the section concern the liability to torture of witnesses and accused persons (usually, in the time of the jurists, of servile status). But torture was not applied only in the course of judicial interrogation. It could be used to exacerbate the death penalty in particularly heinous cases: such was the fate of the popular leader, Petrus Valvomeres (to deter similar disturbances in the future),[33] and of the corrupt official associates of the *comes* Romanus in Africa in the 370s.[34] When torture was used in the course of the *quaestio* (which was not inevitable), the infliction of pain was not intended to be gratuitous, but was designed to get at the truth, in accordance with the long-standing (but not universally held) belief that only torture guaranteed truth, even when the testimony was apparently offered voluntarily.[35]

[32] Id. 27. The right of people accused of wrongdoing to accuse others – a practice which expanded Valens' hit-list in 371 – was outlawed by Valentinian and Valens in 374 (*CT* 9.1.12), renewed, with modifications, by Honorius in 423 (*CT* 9.1.19).
[33] Amm. Marc. 15.7.4.   [34] Id. 29.5.50.
[35] Hence Ulpian's definition of *quaestio* (*Dig.* 47.10.15.41), 'Quaestionem' intellegere debemus tormenta et corporis dolorem ad eruendam veritatem.

In Late Antiquity, more is heard of the horrors of torture in the context of the *quaestio* than in earlier periods, not surprisingly, as its scope extended further up the social hierarchy and direct experience of it would fuel the indignation of the elite literary classes as the pain inflicted on slaves could not have done. But was Late Antiquity therefore a harsher age? Even under the Republic, nobles did not escape torture altogether, when autocrats elected to abuse their power. The young Octavianus Caesar tortured a praetor suspected of criminal designs[36] and 'bad' Julio-Claudians inflicted 'serviles cruciatus', torments appropriate for slaves, on fellow aristocrats suspected of *maiestas*[37] and indeed on free men and citizens in general.[38] What is not clear is whether, under the early Empire, the rights of the upper classes, or of free citizens in general, were protected by formal statute or assumed as a matter of right and custom. Even in the Antonine and Severan periods, when jurists were most actively seeking to define every aspect of law that occurred to them, little attention is given to the exemption of *honestiores* and other privileged categories, as such, from judicial torture. Instead, as we might expect of the generally responsive character of Roman imperial law, exemptions were taken for granted unless, or until, they were challenged and an imperial ruling sought. Thus rescripts on the subject dealt with the cases and categories of people, whose rights were challenged in a particular instance. The assumption that decurions in general were not liable underlay – and was formally reconfirmed by – a rescript of Antoninus Pius that even a condemned decurion (who might have forfeited his status) was exempt.[39] In a similar marginal category were descendants of *equites* or decurions, whose status depended on non-hereditary criteria; the reaction of Diocletian and Maximian was to cite the authority of Marcus Aurelius for the right of exemption from 'plebeian penalties' for descendants of *eminentissimi* and *perfectissimi*, and of Ulpian for the sons of decurions.[40] In all these cases, which involved men who were not only free but of the curial class, what stands out is that, already, by the second century, challenges were emerging to the immunities, not just of the free, but of marginal groups among the elite. Moreover, the number of situations in which torture could be invoked increased; Antoninus Pius, for example, allowed the torture of slaves in civil suits involving money, if no other means of getting at the facts was available.[41] As many of these questions, which elicited imperial responses, may have originated with the courts, perhaps in the belief that the torture of a suspect or witness would elicit the truth, they

---

[36] Suet. *Aug.* 27.4.   [37] Tac. *Ann.* 3.50, of Tiberius.
[38] Garnsey (1970) 143–5; Jones (1972) 114–16.   [39] Discussed by Garnsey (1970) 146.
[40] *CJ* 9.41.11.
[41] *Dig.* 48.18.9 pr., posse de servis habere quaestionem in pecuniaria causa, si aliter veritas inveniri non possit.

suggest a hardening in judicial attitudes towards immunity from torture, which was already far advanced by the mid-second century. By the reign of Severus, the liability to torture of the free was taken for granted – although interrogation by torture could not be used on a free man whose testimony was consistent.[42]

Soldiers – or, more accurately, the military in general – did well out of the chaos in parts of the Empire in the third century. Given their status, it is indicative of the erosion of the protection granted the privileged by custom, if not by law, that the exemption of soldiers was queried with the emperors, probably in the late 280s. As what had been customary before, had now to be stated in writing, Diocletian's response sought to cover most eventualities. Soldiers as a class, including those who had been honourably discharged without serving their full term, were exempted from torture and 'plebeian punishments'; this protection applied also to the sons of soldiers and veterans, but did not extend to soldiers cashiered for dishonourable reasons.[43] However, while the liablity of the freeborn is now taken for granted, another part of the same rescript sought to mitigate the apparent harshness of the rules on the *quaestio*, by issuing a reminder about how trials were expected to be conducted. Not even in trials for public crimes, said the emperors, should enquiries begin with the use of torture; rather, plausible and likely proofs of other kinds should be adduced and, if torture was deemed necessary, its use must depend on the *condicio*, social status, of the prospective victim. Thus, they concluded, the provincials would appreciate the innate *benivolentia* of their rulers.[44] At about the same time, the author of the *Sententiae* ascribed to Paulus opined that a defendant should be subjected to the *quaestio*, if the other evidence against him seemed convincing, but, if such evidence were lacking, torture should not lightly be used but instead further pressure should be exerted on the accuser.[45]

The 'benevolent' Tetrarchs may also have provided a precedent allow-

---

[42] *Dig.* 48.18.15 pr. (Callistratus), ex libero homine pro testimonio non vacillante quaestionem haberi non potest.

[43] *CJ* 9.41.10: Milites neque tormentis neque plebeiorum poenis in causis criminum subiungi concedimus, etiamsi non emeritis stipendiis videantur esse dismissis, exceptis scilicet his qui ignominiose sunt soluti. Quod et in filiis militum et veteranorum servabitur.

[44] Id. Oportet autem iudices nec in his criminibus, quae publicorum iudiciorum sunt, in investigatione veritatis a tormentis initium sumere, sed argumentis primum verisimilibus probabilibusque uti. (2) Et si his veluti certis inducti investigandae veritatis gratia ad tormenta putaverint esse veniendum, tunc id demum facere debebunt, si personarum condicio pateretur. Hac enim ratione etiam universi provinciales nostri fructum inenitae nobis benivolentiae consequerentur.

[45] *Dig.* 48.18.18.1 (Paulus, *Sent.* 5), Reus evidentioribus argumentis obpressus repeti inquaestionem potest, maxime si in tormenta animum corpusque duraverit. (2) In ea causa, in qua nullis reus argumentis urguebatur, tormenta non facile adhibenda sunt, sed instandum accusatori, ut id quod intendat comprobat atque convincat.

ing for the further expansion of torture in the *quaestio*, through the judicial
licence exercised in the persecution of the Christians. Christians were not
subjected to the *quaestio* for the normal reason, to force a confession, but
the reverse; the problem for *iudices* was that Christians were all too ready
to confess that 'Christianus sum'. Thus in the trials of Christians, 'the
question' was used for the opposite of its normal purpose, to force the
'criminal', who had voluntarily confessed, to recant by performing an act
of sacrifice.[46] It might therefore perhaps be more correct not to refer to the
tortures of Christians as being exactly equivalent to the *quaestio* process,
which was to establish facts, although the terminology of Eusebius suggests that the torture of Christians to compel sacrifice may have evolved
as a perversion of the *quaestio* procedure.[47] Whatever the technicalities,
the effect of the suspension of some legal rights could have had an
unanticipated effect. Where imperial policy enjoined universal sacrifice
regardless of rank, what must have counted in the eyes of the judge was, of
necessity, the Christians' religion, not their social status.[48] Thus, paradoxically, the precedent set by the persecution of Christians may have
further undermined the protections afforded by social status under the
Christian Empire.

From the reign of Constantine onwards, the erosion of legal privilege
continued. Slaves, of course, continued to be liable to torture, as they had
been under the Republic. In cases of adultery, the slaves of both husband
and wife were liable – provided they had been in the house at the time of
the alleged crime.[49] In 326, the year of the executions of Crispus and
Fausta, Constantine ruled that slaves could be tortured to reveal the value
of confiscated property to agents of the fisc.[50] Torture could also be
applied to slaves who broke rules about status and occupation; they were
not to be allowed by their masters to serve as *tabelarii*, a job open only to
men of free birth.[51] Men and women of free, but 'humble' or 'ignoble'
status were now routinely at risk. Senators and *equites* were forbidden to

---

[46] Note the latitude given to interrogators at Eus. *HE* 8.2.5, recording Diocletian's edict
that the leaders of the Church are to be chained and 'forced to sacrifice by every possible
means'.

[47] Eus. *HE* 8.10.2–10 cites verbatim a letter from Phileas, bishop of Thmuis, on the
martyrdoms at Alexandria during the Great Persecution. The bishop comments (6) that
martyrs suffered torment without respite, not only during the period of 'interrogation' by
the judge, but also, at the hands of his assistants, throughout the day; the underlings were
left in charge to exploit signs of weakening and to add to the tortures at will.

[48] There were earlier precedents for the ignoring of the exemptions of special categories, e.g.
at Eus. *HE* 5. 1. 44, and 50–2, where the governor allows a Roman citizen martyr of Lyon
in 177 to go to the arena, in violation of his right to relatively painless decapitation.

[49] *CT* 9.7.4 (385); the restriction, showing residual concern that even slaves should not be
tortured unnecessarily, should be noted. Cf. *CT* 9.1.14 (383) that slaves were not to be
tortured in criminal trials, if the *inscriptio* had not been lodged.

[50] *CT* 10.1.5. For the background to 326, see Barnes (1981).   [51] *CT* 8.2.5 (401).

hand over property or gifts to the lowly mothers of their illegitimate children; the mothers could be tortured to recover the property, which might also be confiscated to the fisc.[52] The convention accepted by Pius, that torture could be used in cases involving money, also surfaces again in legislation on the conduct of cases where a sum is claimed from a deceased debtor. This may be due to possible problems in such cases with forged documents, as not only was written evidence, *chirographa*, required but also their authenticity had to be established by the interrogation of the letter-carriers, who, if not of high rank, was subject to 'the terror of torture'.[53] Cases of forgery were clearly criminal, and fell under the ancient Sullan Lex Cornelia de falso, but the chance that documents cited in a civil suit might be challenged as forgeries introduced a dangerous complication into civil litigation. Innocent disputants over property could face an interposed criminal prosecution for forgery, along with the possibility of torture, and the situation was made worse by Gratian (and his quaestor, the poet Ausonius), who, in 376, allowed the interposition of a forgery charge, without the protection of *inscriptio*.[54] The law made worrying reading, even for decurions, who from as early as the reign of Constantine lost the protection of their status, if accused of forgery.[55]

Part of the emperors' drive for accountability among their officials consisted of threats of torture for those of ignoble status suspected of misbehaviour. Lowly officials were reminded of their duties. The *cancellarii* of governors were not to be hand-picked in the first place and were to remain in the province for three years after the departure of their boss, so that they could be produced for interrogation about his behaviour, if required.[56] Accountants were to remain in their job for no longer than a fixed period of years, so that they could be prosecuted after a reasonable interval, for their wrong-doing.[57] Emperors also pointed the finger at their procurators, including those of the imperial factories, mints and tax offices,[58] the overseers of imperial estates,[59] and the keepers of public records.[60] The aim was to ensure accountability, by making these minor officials available for prosecution, and, by the threat of trial and torture, to deter misconduct in the first place. Thus, while Valentinian expressed

---

[52] *CT* 4.6.3 (336). Whether the legislator, Constantine, considered the relevance of this to his own family background may be doubted; Helena, his low-born mother, concubine of Constantius I, had died a few years before.   [53] *CT* 2.27.1 (421).

[54] *CT* 9.19.4; Honoré (1986); Harries (1988).

[55] *CT*. 9.19.1 (316). As also did decurions who elected to become tax assessors. The immunities of chief decurions, *decemprimi*, remained protected.

[56] *CT* 1.34.3 (423, east).

[57] *CT* 8.1.4 (334), 'greedy and fraudulent' accountants liable to torture and restricted to two years; 8.1.6 (362), five years' restriction, plus a year on retired list to allow prosecution. The incentive for 'good' officials was retirement after this with rank of *perfectissimus*.

[58] *CT* 1.32.3 (377).   [59] *CT* 2.1.1 (349).   [60] *CT* 8.1.7 (362); 11.1.11 (365); 8.2.5 (401).

the principle of deterrence in a mild form, hoping that his *tabellarii* would be deterred from their usual fraudulent ways by fear of torture, Constantius II resorted to more colourful rhetoric; 'prison shall confine the villains when convicted, tortures shall tear them, the avenging sword shall destroy them'.[61]

Infringement of the immunities of the powerful predictably made a greater impact on the record. The main preoccupation of the sections in the Theodosian and Justinianic codes, *De Quaestionibus*,[62] is with defining the charges, which could provoke investigation by torture of the hitherto exempt. By assimilating lesser offences to more serious crimes, emperors could entangle even the great in the more painful snares of the law. *Maiestas* (*laesa*), treason, was long held as the worst of crimes and could be defined as anything which damaged the 'majesty', or interests, not only of the emperor, but also of the Roman state in general.[63] Gradually, other crimes had come to be regarded as equivalent to treason. These included the forgery of the imperial subscription,[64] 'unspeakable practices' ('nefanda dictu'), namely magic and sorcery,[65] and divination by members of the imperial *comitatus*.[66]

Because of the chronic insecurity of fourth-century emperors and the elasticity of the definition of *maiestas* in Roman law from Augustus onwards, the actual content of law and the theoretical immunities enjoyed by senators and others mattered less in practice than the necessity of safeguarding imperial security. In his account of Valens' harsh treatment of the 'philosophers' conspiracy', Ammianus conceded that the emperor's life was indeed in danger, but that his excessive rages and credulity of rumours caused the innocent to suffer along with the guilty.[67] Guilty or not, the eminent implicated in the affair endured the full rigours of the *quaestio* ; victims of torture included the former *praeses*, Fidustius, the former *vicarius*, Euserius, the philosopher Pasiphilus (*condicio* uncertain).[68] Torture of high-ranking imperial officials was employed in the notorious case of the forgery of letters from the Frankish general, Silvanus, in 355[69] and even debtors to the fiscus were subjected to torture by Valens' ferocious father-in-law, Petronius.[70] Irrespective of the emperor's

---

[61] *CT* 11.1.11 (Valentinian); 2.2.1 (Constantius II).   [62] *CT* 9.35; *CJ* 9.41.
[63] Cf. Ulpian at *Dig.* 48. 4. 1, including under the definition of *maiestas* illegal assembly of armed men, occupation of public buildings, riotous assemblies, murder of magistrates, bearing of arms against the state, privately negotiating with enemies of the Roman people. See also Jones (1972): 106–7; Harries (1994): 163–6 (case of Arvandus in 469); Bauman (1967): 266–92 discusses the development of the *lex Iulia de maiestate* in the *Digest*.   [64] *CT* 9.35.1 (369).   [65] *CT* 9.35.2 (376).   [66] *CT* 9.16.6 (357).
[67] Amm. Marc. 29.1.15–22.
[68] Amm. Marc. 29.1.9, Fidustius 'excarnifactus ad interitum'; 35, Euserius 'sub cruenta quaestione confesso'; 36, Pasiphilus 'crudeliter tortus'.   [69] Amm. Marc. 15.5.13.
[70] Amm. Marc. 26.6.7.

needs, the judge's control of his own court and his need to get at the facts, by whatever means, meant that the use of torture in practice went beyond what was legally authorised. In the notorious trials of senators at Rome under Valentinian, his evil agent, Maximinus, took it upon himself to assimilate adultery to treason and subject senators suspected of both adultery and treason, as well as slaves, to 'the Question'.[71] That torture of those accused of adultery was at times accepted court practice is assumed in Jerome's account of the women of Vercellae, accused of adultery, who steadfastly protested her innocence, even after her alleged lover, who was also tortured, had 'confessed'.[72] Such local initiatives may also suggest that the questions raised with emperors over immunities, the extension of torture in practice and the erosion of judicial privilege was driven, not by the emperor, but by the needs of the courts.

The imperial response, then, to questions of immunity, perhaps generated by pressure from the courts, could often show more concern for legal rights than did his petitioners. The aim of the *quaestio* was always to elicit the facts, but only within the context of defined judicial proceedings. Thus Gratian legislated that no one, not even a slave, could be subjected to the *quaestio* before the proper preliminaries had been completed and the prosecutor had bound himself by *inscriptio*.[73] Regulations on the annulment (*abolitio*) of proceedings also ruled out the use of torture for no purpose. Valentinian and Valens in 369 ruled that annulments were not allowed once the defendant had been put to the question – unless he himself agreed; this was not to apply to cases of treason, peculation or abandonment of the imperial service.[74] By the early fifth century, this ruling had been modified to allow a unilateral abandoning of the trial by the accuser, within thirty days of its commencement, and also thereafter, subject to the agreement of the defendant – but still only if no free man, even a plebeian, had been tortured.[75] This allowed for the wasteful torture of slaves, but not free men; thus there survived into the fifth century some residual distinction between the rights in court of slave and free.

The infliction of pain, then as now, aroused mixed emotions. Christians were constantly aware of the workings of the *quaestio*, not only from their experience of what they saw in the forum, but because the interrogation process allowed their martyrs to bear effective witness to their faith. But although, as we shall see, the literary representations of persecution gave full coverage to the tortures inflicted on their heroes, the Christian attitude to the *quaestio* was not always negative. Interrogations read into

[71] Amm. Marc. 28.1 passim.
[72] Jer. *Ep.* 1. His interest focussed on her courageous endurance of pain, not the technical illegality of the proceedings.   [73] *CT* 9.1.14 (383).   [74] *CT* 9.37.2.
[75] *CT* 9.37.4 (409).

the public court record could serve to bolster the case of the orthodox against the heretic, notably in the case of Felix of Apthungi in Africa, whose clearing on the charge of *traditio*, the handing over of sacred books to the persecutors, was preserved and referred to a century later.[76] In the course of interrogation of the scribe who had written a letter incriminating Felix, and allegedly at his dictation, the proconsul Aelianus, with some prompting from the advocates, established that the scribe, Ingentius, had lied. After a stern warning on the consequences of not telling the truth, the proconsul persisted with further questions – causing Ingentius to be caught out again. Only at this point did the proconsul pose the all-important question that was the preliminary to the use of torture, 'of what condition are you?' It then emerged that Ingentius was a decurion and therefore exempt, although this did not deter the proconsul from taking him into custody, pending further investigations. This, of course, was a *quaestio* in which torture was not ultimately used, and illustrates what may have been a common restraint in practice among provincial judges, reflecting the exhortations of Diocletian to use other forms of proof first. From the point of view of orthodox Christians, the lucky escape of Ingentius was immaterial; the calumniator of the orthodox bishop had been convicted, provisionally, of forgery and Felix himself freed of all blame.

The same acceptance of interrogation by legitimate authority is present in the most famous dream-*quaestio* to survive from Antiquity, Jerome's interrogation by God the Judge on the criminal (?) charge of being a Ciceronian, rather than a Christian.[77] 'In spirit', he is dragged before the tribunal of the *iudex*, which is surrounded by bystanders bathed in shining light. He is 'thrown to the ground' before the judge and asked his *condicio*. When he claims to be a Christian, the judge accuses him of lying; he is in fact a Ciceronian and is ordered to be whipped. Though suffering from the blows, Jerome is in still greater agony from the 'fire' of his guilty conscience, and starts to cry out and beg for pity. At last the bystanders intervene by interceding for the poor young man, and Jerome promises to reform. Nor was it just a dream: 'witness the tribunal, before which I was cast, witness the judgement, which I feared so much – may it never be my fate to experience such an interrogation (*quaestionem*) – that I had bruised shoulders and after my sleep still felt the blows...'. Although flogged unmercifully by his divine tormentors, Jerome never criticises the ministers of God, the lawful authority, for inflicting pain on him; he was guilty, and deserved what he got.

Many *quaestiones* were conducted in public, somewhere on, or in the

---

[76] *Acta purgationis Felicis* preserved in Optatus of Milevis, App. 2.   [77] Jer. *Ep.* 22.30.

vicinity of, the tribunal of the *iudex*. A fourth-century school book refers to interrogations in the forum and the fixed order of torments to which the accused man (who is presumed guilty) was subjected.[78] Eusebius refers to the bringing of the gridiron 'to the centre' to assist in the torture of Peter of Nicomedia, and often draws attention to the reactions of those who looked on, and to what 'we ourselves' saw.[79] On these occasions, the *iudex* himself conducted the questioning,[80] allowing for the display of various emotions; in the case of the governor of Palestine, Urbanus, these were characteristic of the bad ruler – anger, intemperate threats and cruelty. Eusebius also accepted as a fact of life the right of governors to vary both tortures and penalties, which gave Urbanus the latitude to invent unheard-of tortures for Christians, including the compulsion to fight gladiators.[81] As Ammianus was to do for victims of Valens' persecution at Antioch, so Eusebius did not spare the details required to achieve his emotional and dramatic effects; 'Men endured fire, iron, crucifixion, wild beasts, drowning in the sea, amputations of limbs, burning, the piercing and gouging out of eyes, the mutilation of the whole body, hunger, the mines and imprisonment.'[82]

In Eusebius' view of torture there was, however, an ambivalence, which arose out of the wider purpose of his history. Torture was evil, because Christians were innocent of wrongdoing (no position is taken on the torture of criminals), yet it was also the means through which the martyr was able to testify to the strength of his or her faith and earn the promised heavenly crown. A further dimension is present at the outset of his account of the reign of Diocletian, when Eusebius represents the Great Persecution as the divine punishment visited on Christians for wickedness in times of prosperity and divisions among themselves (although this, admittedly, also gave scope for the martyrs to win glory). On this argument, not only the persecutions, but also the tortures employed by the persecutors were consistent with the will of God. Pain, therefore, was not in itself an evil. Endurance by Christians manifested and strengthened faith, while its infliction by God on sinners hereafter in the burning fires of Hell was a fit reward for the wicked. That principle also applied in this world to persecutors such as Galerius, the painful details of

---

[78] Dionisotti (1982).
[79] *HE* 8.6.2 (Peter); 8.9.4 (eyewitness); 8.10.8 (bodies of the tortured on the ground a pitiful sight to onlookers).
[80] Eus. *HE* 8.10.6 (interrogations at Alexandria); *Mart. Pal.* 7.5–6 (Urbanus interrogates Pamphilus on philosophy and literature, then orders him, in vain, to sacrifice). For the judge as interrogator, see also *Dig.* 22.5.3.1 (a judge's assessment of witnesses, 'an ad ea quae interrogaveras ex tempore verisimilia responderint') and 3, Hadrian's repudiation of written *testimonia*, ('nam ipsos interrogare soleo').   [81] Eus. *Mart. Pal.* 7.4.
[82] Eus. *HE* 8.14.13.

whose last illness are luridly recounted by both Lactantius and Eusebius as proofs of the efficacy of divine retribution.[83]

What concerned writers on torture was not only pain itself, but the context in which it was inflicted and the character of the victims. When the ruling power used torture on the innocent, or allowed anger and arbitrariness to prevail over law, the legitimacy of its acts could be questioned. But these doubts fall far short of a systematic challenge to the use of torture on principle. Even that most subtle of thinkers, Augustine of Hippo, was not averse to the infliction of pain, if good could come of it; a *quaestio* conducted 'acrius', resulting in a quicker confession, allowed greater scope for mercy later on,[84] when the discretion of the *iudex* could be exercised, as the law allowed, in the direction of leniency.[85] Like Eusebius, he argued that what mattered was the moral character of the victim, not the infliction of pain itself. A robber (*latro*) who endures punishment for his crimes is tortured but will not admit what he knows is true. 'Do we say "what great endurance ('magna patientia')"? No, we would say, "what detestable stubborness ('detestanda duritia')".'[86] Even those who did affirm a faith under torture could win no glory if they were wrong. Augustine pictures a Donatist. He proudly confesses his faith under torture, he does not blush but boasts of his iniquity. Better if he had concealed it: 'for this is not sanity, based on good understanding, but senseless obstinacy'.[87] From this combination of letters to imperial officials on the *quaestio*, and addresses to his congregation, it would appear that *duritia*, pig-headedness, worried the bishop more than the pain inflicted 'acrius', as he would put it, in the course of 'inquisitio'.

However, it was Augustine, in more reflective mood, who produced, in the *City of God*, one of the most comprehensive critiques of judicial torture to survive from Antiquity.[88] In his analysis of the role of the *iudex* in human associations (*humana societas*) he argued that the judge is compelled by the necessity of his ignorance of the inner awareness (*conscientiae*) of those whom he judges to resort to torture to find out the truth. Proofs may therefore be extracted from innocent witnesses, who are made to suffer in a case affecting another, a principle reiterated by Augustine elsewhere, when he denies that the precedent of Adam, 'in whom all

---

[83] Eus. *HE* 8.16.4–5; Lact. *De mort. pers.* 33.
[84] Aug. *Ep.* 133.2 (to the tribune Marcellinus), Inquirendi quam puniendi necessitas maior est; unde plerumque necesse est, exercetur acrius inquisitio, ut manifestato scelere sit ut appareat mansuetudo.
[85] Aug. *Ep.* 134.4, cur non flectas in partem providentiorem, lenioremque sententiam, quod licet iudicibus facere etiam non in causis Ecclesiae?   [86] Dolbeau (1992b) 287.
[87] Id. 288. Non est haec sanitas cum sensu sed duritia sine sensu.
[88] Aug. *De civ. D.* 19.6.

sinned' should be visited on his descendants.[89] Secondly, an innocent man may be accused and be forced to suffer undoubted pain for an uncertain crime, not because his guilt has been discovered but because it is not known that he is not guilty. Thus, the bishop concluded, the ignorance of the judge (*ignorantia iudicis*) spells disaster for the innocent (*calamitas innocentis*).

As part of his general purpose to advocate the claims of the heavenly city over those of earthly or 'human' associations, Augustine's argument placed the responsibility for the inequities of the *quaestio* firmly with the flawed nature of *humana societas* as a whole. Thus, although in theory a judge might be conscious of the unfairness (not the cruelty) of torture and therefore could refuse to act, nevertheless in fact he will act, because he is compelled to his duty by the values of the society of which he is part. He will not think it wrong that innocent witnesses should be tortured in cases involving others than themselves, or that innocent people make false confessions under torture and are therefore punished, despite being innocent. There is also a third type of person caught out by the functioning of the system, the accuser who brings a prosecution to benefit the *humana societas*, of which he is part, but whose prosecution fails, because the witnesses lie, or the defendant holds out under torture; the prosecutor, (who was of course bound by the *inscriptio* to suffer the penalty threatening the defendant) is now condemned, having failed to prove his case, even though the *iudex* is in fact still ignorant of the truth. None of this is deliberate wrong-doing; the judge is not morally responsible for what he does, because he is expected by society to pass a judgement.

Nowhere, in this extended reflection on the injustice of the *quaestio*, does Augustine object to the infliction of pain as a matter of principle. His argument seems to leave open the option that, if it could be guaranteed that torture would be inflicted only on the guilty, this could be acceptable. Thus the Augustine of the *City of God* is still recognisable as the bishop who publicly differentiated the torture of Donatists and villains from that of martyrs on grounds of the moral rightness of the victims, while taking for granted the presence of pain as a fact of contemporary life.

It is this, almost casual, acceptance of the inevitability of pain and its use in judicial contexts which seems most alien to modern western perceptions. In this respect, however, it may be twentieth-century western society which, albeit enlightened in its assertion of the rights of the imprisoned and oppressed, is nevertheless out of step with much of recorded history. Before the invention of anaesthetics, pain from a variety

[89] Aug. *Ep.* 250. 2, where A. questions whether his opponent can give any reason 'si animas innocentes pro scelere alieno, ex quo non trahunt sicut ex Adam, in quo omnes peccaverunt, originale peccatum, spiritali supplicio puniamus'.

of natural causes was something to be anticipated and endured. Public executions, of varying barbarity, were regular crowd-pullers in England, down to their abolition in 1867. When Libanius commented on the pleasure shown by an Antiochene crowd, as it gloated over the 'bleeding backs' of a group of bakers, being publicly flogged at a cross-roads for fixing the price of bread,[90] he may have more accurately pictured the typical Late Roman response to judicial infliction of pain than we might care to admit.

[90] Lib. *Or.* 1.208. One obvious reason for the crowd reaction was the grievance of the high price of bread and resultant starvation of the poor. But Libanius, on another occasion, pleaded that suspect shopkeepers should not be flogged, and the reaction of spectators, an essential part of a public punishment, was never predictable; cf. Foucault (1975/77), 57–69 on contrasting crowd reactions, while Roman imperial Martyr Acts show that a crowd could also react with compassion or disgust at what were perceived as excessive tortures.

7   Punishment

At no period in their history were the Romans known for leniency towards the condemned. Despite the wide availability of the right of appeal, access to it on the part of condemned criminals merely seeking to delay their inevitable punishment was severely restricted.[1] Given the reputation of Late Antiquity for cruel and inhumane treatment of those on the wrong side of the law, we would expect evidence of increased ingenuity in the use of public punishment, especially of those condemned on a capital charge. However, as we have seen, the barbarous treatment of people imprisoned on remand and the subjection of the innocent to torture were both publicly questioned, and the high profile given, for various reasons, to judicial torture may signal, not necessarily a greater intensity of use but a profounder questioning, at least in some quarters, of the implications of the *quaestio* procedure. In the area of punishment, changes occurred in Late Antiquity which suggest that more humane values had a real impact, and the variety of public penalties, to which the guilty were liable decreased. At the same time, more is heard of arguments against the death penalty on theological grounds. The Christian insistence on greater humanity in punishment, within limits, is, as we shall see, representative of a society still conditioned to accept state cruelty and individual suffering, but also increasingly prone to exploit the rhetoric of pain to question and, where possible modify, the assumptions inherited from the Early Empire, on which Roman penal practice was based.

Pain was caused by design in both interrogation and the infliction of the final penalty. Although clearly distinct components of the judicial process, *quaestio* and *supplicium* (punishment) could in practice merge together. A defendant or witness could die under torture. This was often the fate of Christians in the Great Persecution, who showed their faith by enduring the *quaestio* unto death, while some victims of 'the Question' in the fourth century were so badly mauled by the torturers that there was

---

[1] See above, p. 111.

little left of them to be subjected to the final penalty.[2] Moreover, as we have seen, torture itself could be a part of the final punishment, in cases of aggravated wrong-doing. As the early imperial jurist, Claudius Saturninus, observed, punishments of some wrongdoers could be made harsher to set an example to the rest.[3]

The prime motives for inflicting punishment in Late Antiquity were those inherited from the Early Empire, retribution and deterrence. Christians, however, were profoundly to influence the penal debate; their distaste for the death penalty was justified on the grounds that, once a criminal was executed, the chance to reform (and do better in the afterlife) was denied him. The combination of the first two, traditional, motives explains the highly public nature of executions, again a continuation of early imperial practice.[4] For first- and second-century writers, this was self-evident. The so-called Pseudo-Quintilian concludes a formulaic practice declamation with the observation that criminals were hung on crosses on roads where they would be visible to frighten as many people as possible, 'for all punishment is aimed not so much at the crime as at deterrence'.[5] Over a century later, the Severan jurist, Callistratus, whose *De Cognitionibus* is an important source for trial procedure, observed that many supported the practice of hanging notorious bandits on gallows in the places where they had committed their crimes, so that others also would be deterred from doing the same.[6]

In Late Antiquity, little changed. Emperors exacted legitimate retribution through 'the avenging sword'[7] and a variety of other punishments. A particular death penalty was not always specified; a criminal convicted under Constantine's laws on forgery could be 'done to death or delivered to the flames',[8] and a freedman who denounced his master or a parricide could be killed 'by the sword/iron or by fire'.[9] The deterrent effect could be enhanced if the punishment fitted the crime. Constantine's edict of 320 against abduction stipulated that nurses who inveigled their charges

---

[2] Amm. Marc. 29.1.44. Alypius, former vicar of Britain was accused by one Diogenes, a degraded character, whose body did not suffice for punitive tortures and was burned alive.

[3] *Dig.* 48.19.10. Nonnumquam evenit, ut aliquorum maleficiorum supplicia exacerbentur quotiens, nimium multis personis grassantibus exemplo opus sit.

[4] See Coleman (1990) passim.

[5] Ps.-Quintilian, *Declamationes minores* (ed. M. Winterbottom) 274. Omnis enim poena non tam ad delictum pertinet quam ad exemplum.

[6] *Dig.* 48.19.28.15. Famosos latrones in his locis ubi grassati sunt furca figendos compluribus placuit, ut et consectu deterrentur alii ab iisdem facinoribus. It is possible that 'furca', the gallows, where death was quick, has been substituted by the Justinianic compilers for 'patibulo', or some other word for 'cross.' Callistratus' original text probably referred to crucifixion, not hanging. See Parente (1979).

[7] 'Gladio ultore', mentioned in the *CT* at 9.6.1; 6.3; 7.3; 9.1; 14.3; 22.1; 24.2; 34.10; 40.21.

[8] *CT* 9.22.1, aut capite puniri debet aut flammis tradi.

[9] *CT* 9.6.1 (326, freedman accuser); 15.1. (parricide).

into co-operating with their abductors should be punished by having their mouths and throats (responsible for the 'wicked persuasion') closed by the pouring in of molten lead.[10] This inventive attitude to penal policy had precedent in the Early Empire, and was not confined to 'bad emperors'; the virtuous Galba ordered a soldier who illegally sold part of his food allowance to be starved to death, and a money-changer who cheated on the weights had his hands cut off and nailed to the table where he had conducted his fraudulent deals.[11] Alleged precedents to be found in the less reliable biographies of the *Historia Augusta* are more likely to reflect fourth-century notions of how an emperor might punish the guilty; Macrinus tied adulterers together before burning them alive, even though adultery did not carry the death penalty in the third century,[12] and Severus Alexander had a courtier suffocated by smoke in the Forum Transitorium at Rome for selling favours illegally, a practice colloquially known as 'selling smoke'.[13]

In all these displays of imperial rigour, the connection between crime and punishment was most effectively made if it was dramatic, explicit and widely publicised – hence the language of Constantine's edict on abduction and Severus Alexander's alleged use of a herald to proclaim that 'he who sold smoke is punished by smoke'. The theatricality of punishment is also illustrated in Theodosius I's rhetoric against homosexuals, who were to suffer the well-merited punishment of fire, 'while the people look on', so that 'all' will understand the consequences of 'shamefully' betraying one's own sex.[14] Whether the use of fire itself as the preferred form of execution had other social overtones is debateable. Christians may have perceived its use as foreshadowing or, in the case of martyrs, exempting from the fires of hell, in which the damned would suffer for all eternity[15] but the use of burning as a form of execution by non-Christian emperors would appear to rule out any notion that fire was a favoured method of execution, because perceived by the authorities as the instrument of the vengeance of God, administered through his agents, the emperors, on earth.[16]

The smoke of the fires of Late Antiquity, stoked up with criminals and the unfortunate, may obscure important changes in attitude, which con-

---

[10] *CT* 9.24.1.
[11] Suet. *Galba* 7.4. and 9.1. The biographer did, however, comment that Galba as a judge was excessively harsh.   [12] *SHA Macrinus* 12.10.   [13] *SHA Severus Alexander* 36.6.
[14] *Coll. Mos. Rom.* 5.3.1.2 (full text, posted in the Atrium of Minerva), with a shorter version, from the copy posted in Trajan's Forum, at *CT* 9.7.6, spectante populo flammae vindicibus expiabit, ut universi intellegant sacrosanctum cunctis esse debere hospitium virilis animae nec sine supplicio alienum expetisse sexum, qui suum turpiter perdidisset.
[15] E.g. at *Mart. Pionii* 4.5. Pionius warns of the 'judgement by fire' to come; at id. 7, he states it is better to burn now, as a Christian, than 'to burn after death'. For further discussion of the fires of Hell, see below, pp. 146–7.   [16] Contra Callu (1984) 348.

trast with the penal policies and practices of the Early Empire. Although life for the elite in Late Antiquity was less comfortable, in that more crimes and more categories of people were subject to the death penalty, the range of penalities to which criminals in general were subject had decreased. In the second and third centuries CE, jurists' analyses of 'ultimate penalties' (*summa supplicia*) gave pride of place to exposure to wild beasts in the arena, a fate to which were subject brigands, deserters, murderers, arsonists, abductors, forgers and those guilty of sacrilege.[17] Arsonists were also, appropriately, liable to be burned alive, as were the sacrilegious and deserters, while robbers and other kinds of criminal were also threatened with crucifixion. Condemnation of parricides to be sewn in a sack, *culleus*, with appropriate animal company and flung into water was still operative in the reign of Constantine, who gave the reason for this exceptional penalty; parricides were to be deprived of the two essential elements, the air when still alive, and the earth, when dead.[18]

Both execution *ad bestias* and crucifixion are last heard of in the legislation of Constantine, who, in law issued in the years following his victory over Maxentius, condemned to crucifixion slaves who informed on their masters,[19] and slaves or freedmen who were found guilty of kidnapping were condemned *ad bestias*.[20] How long afterwards these punishments continued in use is uncertain. Firmicus Maternus wrote a work on astrology in the 330s, which gave information on the bizarre deaths awaiting those born under a particular star sign. Although its accuracy as a reflection of conditions in the last years of Constantine has been challenged, Maternus' use of terms in current fourth-century use supports the reliability of his picture of the contemporary penal system, as reflected in the fates awaiting those born under unfavourable signs.[21] Some born under the sign of Pisces could expect death by the beasts, the cross, or, 'after judgement by the public (i.e. criminal) court, they will be burned to ashes by the avenging flames'.[22] Others, born under Libra, would be subjected, by imperial order, to crucifixion, torture or hang-

---

[17] Grodzynski (1984) 340–1.

[18] *CT* 9.15.1 (319). As parricides were exceptionally wicked too, and their penalty unlikely to be a matter of controversy, virtual silence on the *culleus* after Constantine cannot be taken as significant. However, at *CT* 11.36.4 (339) adultery is assimilated to parricide, perhaps for effect – the adulterer is to be put in a sack and burned alive.   [19] *CT* 9.1.5 (314).

[20] *CT* 9.18.1 (315). Hitherto the penalty had been the mines. Constantine also decreed that free men were to be executed by gladiators in the arena, and that those already sentenced to the mines should not be recalled.

[21] Grodzynski (1984) 397–403, arguing against Cumont's dismissal of Firmicus as a mere translator of ancient writings into Latin and citing such examples of contemporary terminology as *publica animadversio, publica sententia, publica custodia, ultrices flammae*.

[22] Firm. Mat. *Mathesis* 8.7. Ad bestias obici, in crucem tolli, publica sententia flammis ultricibus concremabuntur.

ing.[23] Soon after writing the *Mathesis*, Firmicus converted to Christianity, leaving unexplored the implications of the thesis that punishments (and therefore crimes as well) were foreordained by the stars; had it been pursued, the effect of Firmicus' work on ideas of human responsibility, predestination and free will could hardly have been ignored.[24]

The decline and probable disappearance of the *ad bestias* penalty in the fourth century can be partly ascribed to Christians' distaste for the perpetuation of spectacles, in which their own martyrs had suffered and the doubts felt among some of the elite, pagan and Christian, about the desirability of such public entertainments in general (although this did not inhibit imperial or senatorial generosity in this respect overall). Too much should not be made of Christian influence in isolation from the broader moral context of the fourth century.[25] The failure of the Christian establishment, as represented by the bishops, to counter the popularity of theatrical shows and chariot-races, which could leave churches embarrassingly empty, reveals the limits of the Church's ability to impose its will on a recalcitrant plebs. It is more likely, therefore, that the beasts lost their diet of criminals due to a combination of Christian pressure, imperial policy and a shift in fashion, which may also have favoured the gradual disappearance of gladiators.[26] The demise of crucifixion, the second of the 'summa supplica', has more obvious links with the growing power of Christianity. Constantine admitted probable Christian influence in his penal policy when he abolished branding on the face, because the face was created in the image of heavenly beauty, although he allowed branding on the hands or legs.[27] Whether or not it was also Constantine who formally abolished crucifixion in favour of hanging,[28] the change over time to the more humane penalty is certain; the *furca*, gallows, on which death was instantaneous, replaced the protracted agonies of the cross.

The apparent abandonment of two painful and humiliating forms of the death penalty, when taken with other developments in penal policy, affected the operation of the 'dual penalty' system inherited from the

---

[23] Id. 8.25, in crucem iussu imperatoris tolletur aut praesente imperatore torquebitur aut iussu principali suspenditur.

[24] Cf. Augustine's problems with punishment, grace and predestination, discussed by Rist (1994) 273–6.

[25] As argued for Constantine's moral legislation by Evans Grubbs, J. (1995: 317–42).

[26] The defining enactment abolishing gladiatorial combat for the later codifiers was *CT* 15.12.1 (325), which also decreed sentencing to the mines for those hitherto sent to the arena. But for further constitutions, still restricting condemnation to 'the arena' see *CT* 9.18.1 (315); 9.40.2 (316), both predating abolition; 8 (365); 11 (367).

[27] *CT* 9.40.2 = *CJ* 9.47.17 (316).

[28] Attested by Aurelius Victor *Caes.* 41.4, eo pius ut etiam vetus teterrimumque supplicium patibulorum et cruris suffregendis primus removerit; Ambrosiaster, *Quaest. Vet. Test.* 115, et antea cruci homines figebantur, quod postea edicto prohibitum manet. See also Parente (1979) for meanings of *patibulum, crux, furca*.

second century CE, under which *honestiores* could expect to be spared the more humiliating punishments dealt out to their social inferiors. The erosion of the immunities of the elite to torture by the expansion of its use up the social scale, and the assimilation of other crimes to the rules and penalties of *maiestas* undermined, but did not destroy, the class distinctions between the 'better' and 'worse' elements in society. For those convicted of counterfeiting money, Constantine decreed that decurions, or sons of decurions, should be banished and their property confiscated, 'plebeians' should receive 'perpetual punishment' and slaves should suffer the 'supreme penalty'.[29] Slaves could still expect worse treatment than anyone else: slaves and freedmen who accused their masters were to be burned alive (except in cases of treason),[30] as were male slaves who had affairs with their mistresses.[31] At the end of the century a further chance reference shows that old hierarchical distinctions were still in force; harbourers of robbers were warned by Gratian and Theodosius I that they faced corporal punishment or forfeiture of property, 'in accordance with the rank of the person and at the discretion of the judge'.[32] On many other occasions, however, emperors appear to impose a capital penalty for criminal wrong-doing regardless of rank; capital punishment or the death penalty was imposed for, among other crimes, criminal violence (*vis*),[33] conspiracy to cause the deaths of *illustres*, senators or imperial servants,[34] *haruspices* (soothsayers) who visited private houses (their hosts were liable to exile and loss of property),[35] those who consulted soothsayers,[36] murderers of suspected magicians,[37] forgery and counterfeiting money, or deliberately abetting the same,[38] assaults on holy virgins and widows,[39] or failing to destroy defamatory writings.[40] Adulterers could also face the

---

[29] *CT* 9.21.1 (323/5).

[30] *CT* 9.6.1 and 2 (376); 3 (397) specifies the 'avenging sword' for the same offence.

[31] *CT* 9.9.1 (329).

[32] *CT* 9.29.2 (383/391), dated to the second consulship of Merobaudes (383) and headed by the names of Gratian, Valentinian II and Theodosius I, but addressed to the praetorian prefect (Nicomachus) Flavianus, who held office in 391. See also *Breviarium* 9.22, where the *Interpretatio* explicitly limits the judge's discretion to the fine.   [33] *CT* 9.10.1 (317).

[34] *CT* 9.14.3 (397, east). This was generated by troubles in Constantinople in that year.

[35] *CT* 9.16.1 (320).   [36] *CT* 9.16.4 (357).

[37] *CT* 9.16.11 (389). This is directed against those 'charioteers, or any other class of man', who take the law into their own hands, by justifying murder after the event with the claim that the victim was a magician, either in order to cover up a connection with the dead man's illegal activity or using it as a pretext to kill a private enemy.

[38] *CT* 9.19.2 (320); 9.21.2.4 abettors of counterfeiting, authors and accessories to the fact; 9.21.5 + 22.1 (343) makes penalty for counterfeiters burning by fire and for tampering with weights of coins, fire or some other death; 9.21.9 counterfeiting held equivalent to *maiestas*.

[39] *CT* 9.25.2 (364) capital punishment for those attempting *attemptare* holy women. 9.25.3 (420) lets off those who try to 'get round' (*ambire*) holy women with deportation and confiscation.   [40] *CT* 9.34.7 (Valens); 10 (406).

death penalty, not, as in earlier centuries, through private family vengeance, but through the agency of the state, although the extent of its use is uncertain.[41] Allowing for the incomplete nature of the texts, it may still be concluded that, for serious crimes of violence, treason, magic, or forgery, along with the *de facto* death penalty for adultery already noted, members of the elite, if convicted, could now be liable to the same, or similar, penalties as their social inferiors.

Those convicted of lesser offences could still find that their fates were determined by their social status. Those members of the lower social orders sentenced to the mines were often subjected first to flogging, as a further physical humiliation; although their forced labour would be economically productive, deportation to the mines, public works or imperial factories was not for primarily economic reasons, but as a means by which the state could control and degrade the bodies of its criminals.[42] A sentence to the mines could be inflicted for apparently minor offences. 'Rustic or poor' people who took their cases to appeal unsuccessfully before the Praetorian Prefects were sent to the mines, as were those who wasted courts' time with the wrongful use of powerful names in lawsuits over property and unjustified claims over free status.[43] Those who shirked their duty under the law could also expect graded penalties: under Valentinian and Valens, abettors of deserters of lowly status went to the mines, and those of higher 'locus' or 'dignitas', station or rank, lost half their property, but Theodosius ruled that those harbourers of deserters 'whose status made them liable to corporal punishment' should be first beaten with cudgels, then sent to hard labour in the mines, while their richer counterparts should supply ten recruits per deserter or monetary compensation.[44] Slaves and lower class criminals who violated tombs, or were guilty of kidnap or violence, and slave women who married decurions to help them avoid their obligations along with estate overseers who abetted the offence, also went to the mines.[45] New in Late Antiquity was hard labour in the mines for conniving at heretical assemblies; this was inflic-

[41] Senatorial women executed for adultery at Rome, Amm. Marc. 28.1.44–5. Jer. *Ep.* 1, attempted execution of innocent for adultery at Vercellae. Both instances come from Italy in the 370s. See further Beaucamp (1990) 139–70; Clark (1993) 35–6.
[42] Millar (1984) 147, 'labour was seen, and used, as a form of violence to the body, which was closely comparable to flogging, the cross or exposure to beasts'. Economic functions were significant 'not least in their very distinct direction and limits; but they should nevertheless be seen as secondary'.
[43] *CT* 1.5.3 (331), where a rich failed appellant suffered exile for two years and the loss of half his property; 2.14.1 (400), misuser of powerful name also flogged first; 4.8.8 (372) on free status.   [44] *CT* 7.18.1 (365); 8 (383/91).
[45] *CT* 9.10.4 (390, violence); 17.1 (340, tombs); 18.1 (315, slave or freedman kidnappers to beasts, free convict to be killed by gladiators, but previous convicts not to be recalled); 12.1.6 (318, union of decurions with slaves).

ted on overseers, who were also flogged first, and procurators of estates where the meetings took place. The one hope for these unfortunates was the exercise of imperial *clementia* through amnesty, such as that proclaimed by Honorius for all exiled by deportation or relegation, sentenced to the mines or engaged in various kinds of obligatory occupation 'on islands or desolate places'.[46]

One form of penalty which bore most heavily on the propertied classes was *infamia*, or loss of status. This deprived the offender of the legal rights of Roman citizenship, which included bequeathing or receiving property in a will, or making a legally binding contract. In Late Antiquity, *infamia* still threatened those convicted of traditional offences, such as conniving at the insertion of the name of a powerful person into the titles of a contested property,[47] breaking the conditions of an arbitration agreement by seeking a referral to a judge,[48] or lodging petitions for estates owned by the emperor;[49] senators, *perfectissimi* and civic magistrates were also liable if they gave recognition to children of theirs born to female slaves or freedwomen, their daughters, and other types of disreputable woman.[50] However, two categories of person featured especially prominently in the imperial codes. One consisted of public servants, who were made accountable for their misdemeanours in office: *spectabilis* judges were threatened with *infamia*, and a fine of twenty pounds of gold, if they delayed execution of a sentence for a serious crime, or allowed the criminal to be spirited away by clerics or to lodge an illegal appeal, while lesser *iudices* and their staffs, if liable, had to pay half that amount;[51] judges who failed to provide full documentation for appeal cases, or to forward the dossier within thirty days, also lost their civil rights, as did those judges who violated the immunities of decurions by subjecting them to flogging with a leather-weighted lash.[52] The other newly penalised group was the religiously incorrect: Manichaeans and Donatists were given notice that their testamentary rights were withdrawn, as also were apostates.[53]

Penal policy was further complicated by considerations of responsibil-

---

[46] *CT* 9.38.10 (405), perhaps also applying to those forced into imperial factories. For tied labour in *gynaecea* and other imperial enterprises, see *CT* 10.20 and Millar (1984) 143–5.
[47] *CT* 2.14.1 (400).   [48] *CT* 2.9.3 (395).   [49] *CT* 5.15.21 (367–70).
[50] *CT* 4.6.3 (336).   [51] *CT* 9.40.15 (392).
[52] *CT* 11.30.9 (318/9); 24 (348); 34 (364), all on appeal. 11.30.16 (331) imposes *infamia* on frivolous appellants, who waste the prefects' time. For decurions, see 12.1.85 (381), where the judge is also fined 30lb gold.
[53] *CT* 16.5.3 (372) and 7 (381) on Manichaeans; 16.5.54 (414) and 6.4.3 (405) on Donatists; 16.7.5 (apostates). *Coll.* 15. 3. 2 removes protection of status from Manichees; even *honorati* or those with *dignitas* were liable to confiscation of property and sentence to the mines. For a suggested connection between the right to make a will and right religion, see Watson (1995b).

ity, which were often related to the social status of the convict and its consequences for his freedom of action. Slaves, for example, might act either by their own volition or on the orders of their masters, and the penalty for some offences varied accordingly; thus slaves convicted of *vis* on their own account were executed, but if acting on their master's instructions, were merely sent to the mines, while the master suffered *infamia*[54]. Similarly, when slaves or *coloni* desecrated a tomb (probably by removing parts of it to be used for building purposes elsewhere), if acting without their master's or landlord's knowledge, their fate was the mines, otherwise the master faced exile and any house of his containing material from the tomb was confiscated.[55] The liability of women was limited in some circumstances, while wards could also not be held responsible for criminal activities they saw but could not be expected to understand.[56] Nor could the insane be held responsible for their actions.

Conversely, a penalty could be increased or lessened, if there was proof of the exertion of *force majeure*. *Potentia* and its derivatives were not, as a rule, regarded favourably by Roman writers, and criticism of abuses of power was a constant theme of late antique law and rhetoric. Whether it follows from this that *potentes* were in fact behaving worse in Late Antiquity than at any previous time in Roman history is less clear,[57] and depends on how the legal sources in particular are interpreted. It is clear that, from the second century onwards, Roman law took account of the potential of powerful individuals (whose exact social status is left vague) to fix the system to suit themselves. Both Gaius in his commentary on the Provincial Edict and Ulpian in his influential manual on the duties of a provincial governor (*De Officio Proconsulis*) emphasised that it was the governor's duty to protect the weak against the strong.[58] The same points were made, in more dogmatic and simpler form by the Constantinian author of the *Opiniones* ascribed to Ulpian; among numerous duties prescribed for the governor was prevention of *iniuriae*, wrongs, inflicted on *humiliores* by *potentiores viri*.[59] Dodges engaged in by litigants, abetted by powerful allies, were dealt with. How complex these could be, even in the second century, is illustrated by the example anticipated by Gaius; if a man transferred his property to a *potens*, making him therefore a party to a

[54] *CT* 9.10.4 (390).   [55] *CT* 9.17.1 (340).
[56] *CT* 9. 21. 4 (321), see above, ch. 2, p. 52. See also *CT* 12. 1. 6, where the penalty is affected by the location, urban or rural, of the offence.
[57] Contra Schlumberger (1989) 'There is no doubt that from the third century onward, they (the *potentes*) attained a power and range of activity that were without precedent in ancient history. The phenomenon must be considered ... a special characteristic of Late Antiquity.'
[58] *Dig.* 4.7.1.1 and 3pr. (Gaius, *Ad Ed. Prov.* 4); id. 1.16.9.5 (Ulpian, *Off. Proc.* 2).
[59] *Dig.* 1.18.6.2. Ne potentiores viri humiliores iniuriis adficiant ... See also *Dig.* 4.2.23.1. For *potentiores* in Roman legal sources, Wacke (1980).

lawsuit, he was liable to be faced with prosecution, because in the process he had made his adversary's legal condition worse.[60] In certain circumstances, the law could provide limited assistance to the weak. Thus interference by a *potens* could mitigate a penalty: if a tenant lost the use of his farm because of coercion by a powerful person, the landlord, who had responsibility for supplying what was stipulated in the rental contract, was liable only for return of the rent, not for the value of the produce lost.[61]

The consequence of a system which allowed the penalty for an offence to be influenced by the social status of the offender was that inevitably account was taken of the criminal as well as the crime. This did not – yet – lead to a focus on the reform of the criminal. However, it did allow for the proposition that status might also determine motive. In a statement about the removal of boundary stones preserved in the *Digest* but also used by the author of the *Collatio* of Roman and Mosaic Law,[62] rich men who removed boundary stones were punished by exile for a period of years, more for younger men, less for older ones, because their motive was clearly to increase their landholdings; by contrast, poorer people who did the same were sentenced to two years in the mines if the offence was deliberate, but less if the disturbance was accidental. This explicit connection of status, motive and penalty is seldom found in the written sources but is consistent with the general view of legal writers that power always contained within itself the potential for abuse. It should also be noted as symptomatic of the complexities of attitudes over power, that this suspicion of *potentes* coexisted with the apparently incompatible assumption that 'the better class of people' should not only be better treated under the law, but also could be more relied upon, for example as witnesses, than their social inferiors.[63]

The justifications of punishment

The state's justification for punishing its citizens publicly and painfully was that they deserved it and that the display of terror would act as a salutary deterrent for others. Terror was not entirely a negative concept, if

---

[60] *CT* 2.14.1 (400) makes no reference to legal condition, but prescribes *infamia* for powerful men, who connive at the abuse, while culprits acting on their own initiative were to be flogged and sent to the mines.   [61] *Dig.* 19.2.33.   [62] *Dig.* 47.21.2 = *Coll.* 13.3.
[63] For an eccentric attempt to allocate moral points by status, see Ambrosiaster, *Quaest. Vet. Test.* 124. A poor man gains more than the rich man, if he can show *misericordia* and *iustitia* and it is also less wrong for him to steal, as he does it from want; he loses points for *superbia* and *libido*, which are vices appropriate for the rich. A rich man does better if he shows *humilitas*, (poverty should make the poor man humble anyway), *doctrina, studium* and *pudicitia*.

fear ensured obedience.[64] While the Prefect Symmachus fulminated against a hardened criminal, who failed to be influenced by 'respect for rescripts, the sternness (*severitas*) of the laws, the bond of agreements or reverence for the courts',[65] Augustine bemoaned a more serious infraction in similar vein, lamenting the destruction of law, and the 'trampling underfoot of the *terror* of the courts and the judges', as evidenced in a massacre at Sufetana.[66] Fear was not only beneficial to the operations of the state. It could be represented as a positive emotion within families,[67] if combined with love, and could also be a motive for Christians to observe the laws of God; Ambrosiaster, an enthusiast for power and terror, argued in a brief history of law that, because the destruction of Sodom and Gomorrah was buried 'by the forgetfulness of antiquity', Moses had to receive the Ten Commandments 'to inspire terror, in order to correct and restore order, and renew faith in God'.[68] Although representations of the Last Judgement and the torments of the damned in Christian writings might also have been designed to frighten the faithful into virtue, terror in this regard was of only limited use and could be detrimental; Augustine, for one, insisted that fear of hell was not the same as fear of sin and that, while a man might be terrified into love of God, he could not manage both emotions at once.[69]

For *terror* to be justified, it had to be wielded by a lawful authority, be it state, father, husband, or God. The 'avenging sword' or the 'avenging flames' of the imperial codes represented legitimate punishment inflicted by a lawful authority on wrongdoers. The same meaning for the word *ultio* and its cognates is found in Ammianus, who described the goddess Nemesis, or Adrastia, as the one who brings retribution on the wicked, the 'avenger of godless crimes',[70] and recollected the justified retaliation of past rulers on their enemies.[71] In his own day, Constantius is pictured

---

[64] For fear as positive in early Byzantium, see Scott (1985) 103–4. For *terror* as negative, *CT* 3. 6. 1; 11. 11. 1; *CJ* 12. 60(61). 1. On *terror* and violence in government, see Matthews (1989) 256–62.

[65] Symm. *Rel.* 31.1, neque rescriptorum veneratione neque legum severitate vel pactionum fide aut iudiciorum reverentia permovetur... (2) vim rescripti, statutum praecelsae potestatis elusit; dehinc proconsularibus evocatus edictis leges pari arte frustratus est.

[66] Aug. *Ep.* 50, apud nos Romanae sepultae sunt leges, iudiciorum rectorum calcatus est terror, imperatorum certe nulla veneratio nec timor.

[67] Aug. *Enarr. in Ps.* 118, 31.3, sic patres a filiis piis et timentur et amantur; sic pudica coniunx virum et timet, ne ab illo deseratur, et amat, ut fruatur...

[68] Ambrosiaster, *Quaest. in Vet. Test.* 4.1, terroris causa ad disciplinam corrigendam et fidem in deum reformandum. Cf. id. 83. 3 on Mosaic Law, 'quae neque obsolesceret et magis metum incuteret. maior enim timor est, ubi auctoritas manifesta est'.

[69] Aug. *Ep.* 145.4; Rist (1994) 274; 'He may be compelled before he wants to do good, but he cannot be under compulsion when *actually* wanting to do good.'

[70] Amm. Marc. 14.11.5, ultrix facinorum impiorum.

[71] Amm. Marc. 23.6.7 (Tomyris, on Cyrus); 31.5.7 (Aurelian drives out the Goths).

exacting limited retribution from the Limigantes in 358, and, in 361, promises his troops at Nicopolis that Julian will pay the due price for trampling justice underfoot.[72] How legitimate the exacting of retribution was might also depend on the opinions of those involved. Ammianus recounted a past case at Smyrna, when a woman justified her murder of her husband and son by alleging they had killed her son by a previous marriage; the Council, uncertain whether this was justified retribution (*ultio*) or a criminal act (*scelus*) postponed the hearing for a hundred years.[73] Under Valentinian and Valens, the Austriani rose up to 'avenge' the execution of their kinsman, burned to death for treachery; although Ammianus himself believed the execution to be just, he dutifully reports the self-justification of the rebels for seeking revenge, namely that they were kindred of the victim and that his death was unjust.[74] Punishment, whatever the method, was justified in Ammianus' eyes, if the object of the penalty deserved it – as did, for example, Paul 'the Chain' and his fellow-informers, who met their just deserts, when condemned to be burned to death at the hearings at Chalcedon in 362.[75]

Legitimate retribution was also approved of by Christian writers, who believed in its efficacy, both in this world and the next. The painful or humiliating deaths of the persecuting emperors; the speedy fall of Urbanus, the sadistic inventor of tortures in Palestine; the sordid demise of the arch-heretic Arius; the death of the emperor Julian in campaign against the Persians, all could be cited and dwelled upon as warnings of the retribution inflicted by the anger of God. And beyond death was the judgement of God in the hereafter and the torments that would ensue for the wicked. The so-called *Apocalypse of Paul*, which probably dates from the third century, advertised itself as a text 'discovered' in Tarsus in the reign of Theodosius I.[76] The text purported to be the account by the apostle Paul of his visit to Hell, escorted by an angel. The torments of the damned were intense and appropriate to their crimes on earth, in which breaches of church discipline were prominent. In a river of fire, men and women were immersed up to their knees, navels, necks or hair; their crimes were, respectively, idle disputing after church, fornication after

---

[72] Amm. Marc. 17.13.1–2 (Limigantes); 21.13.13 (Julian). At 22.12.1 Julian presents his Persian campaign as 'retaliation for past injuries'.   [73] Amm. Marc. 29.2.19.

[74] Amm. Marc. 28.6.2–4, *huius necem ulcisci, ut propinqui damnatique iniuste causantes.* There may, however, be irony in Ammianus' reference shortly after to the claim of the *comes* Romanus to 'avenge' the murder of Zammac by his brother Firmus (29.5.2).

[75] Amm. Marc. 22.3.11. *Apodemium enim ... Paulumque notarium cognomento Catenam, cum multorum gemitu nominandum, vivos exustos, qui sperari debuit oppressit eventus.*

[76] For recent edition of text and translation, see Elliot (1993) 616–44. It was known to Origen (*Hom. in Ps.* 36), Prudentius (*Cathemerinon* 5.125), Augustine (*Tract. Ioh.* 9.8.8) and Sozomen (*HE* 7.19).

communion, slander in church and plotting spite against their neighbours. Paul is obliged to watch a priest who administered communion
after eating, drinking and fornication being torn by iron hooks;[77] a bishop,
who did not give just judgements or show compassion to widows and
orphans is stoned, receiving 'retribution according to his works';[78] a
deacon who ate church offerings and committed fornication is seen in the
fiery river with worms coming out of his mouth, while a bad lector is
slashed across the lips with a 'great fiery razor'.[79] Further ingenious
tortures are devised for usurers, disparagers of the Word of God, illicit
breakers of fasts before the proper time, fornicators with prostitutes and
failed ascetics, distracted by worldly things, as well as categories more
recognisable to the Roman criminal jurisdiction, namely magicians, adulterers, girls who lost their viginity before marriage 'unknown to their
parents', homosexuals and women who aborted their children (an especially wicked group).[80] Finally, yet more extreme tortures are revealed
in a well of fire, sealed with seven seals, and finally, the deniers of Christ
are shown, confined in a place of cold and snow.[81] All the damned
acknowledge the justice of God; they could have repented, when they had
the chance, but did not, and so deserved their fates.[82]

A distinction must be made, however, between the acceptance of
punishment by many Christians as being, in principle, good, and doubts
expressed by Christian bishops, such as Augustine, over the use of the
death penalty. Augustine, whose frequent dealings with the agents of the
state may have coloured his views, believed that the state's apparatus of
terror was necessary; 'the judge's power of life and death, the hooks of the
torturer, the weapons of the military escort, the rulers' display of *disciplina*
and the *severitas*, which even a good father must show', all were designed
with a purpose, to inspire fear, restrain the wicked and ensure that good
men could live unmolested among the bad.[83] Making use of these was a
different matter: Augustine asserted that judges would prefer to avoid
shedding blood, but were obliged by their job and the powers vested in
them to uphold public order by inflicting punishment.[84]

By the late fourth century, the agents of the state were themselves

---

[77] *Apoc. Paul.* 34.   [78] Id. 35.   [79] Id. 36.
[80] Id. 37. (usurers, blasphemers); 38 (magicians, adulterers); 39 (girls not virgins before
marriage; breakers of fasts; fornicators; homosexuals); 40 (abortions; failed ascetics).
[81] Id. 42 The passage influenced Dante's depiction of the lowest circle of Hell, where were
confined Brutus, Cassius – and Judas Iscariot.
[82] Although Paul's *intercessio* later results in a remission for the damned.
[83] Aug. *Ep.* 153.6.16; Nec ideo sane frustra instituta sunt potestate regis, ius gladii cognitoris, ungulae carnificis, arma militis, disciplina dominantis, severitia etiam boni patris.
Habent ista omnia modos suos, causas, rationes, utilitates. Haec enim timentur, et
cohercentur mali et quietius inter malos vivunt boni.
[84] Aug. *Serm.* 302.16, cf. Ambrose, *Ep.* 25.2, praising governors with a 'bloodless' record.

largely Christian, and therefore open to approaches from bishops, who backed appeals for leniency with the moral *auctoritas* inherent in their office. The former *iudex*, Ambrose, contrasted the *auctoritas* of the judge with the *misericordia* appropriate to a Christian. Reform, he told one governor, was the real aim of punishment. The convicted man, while still alive, could hope to improve; if unbaptised, he still had a chance through the sacrament of baptism and, if already baptised, he could perform penance.[85] Likewise, both in letters and sermons, Augustine drove home the point that Christians were obliged to love their enemies and not to inflict on them the supreme penalty, which would cut off hope of penitence or redemption in the life to come.[86] The Church as intercessor, he argued, had to coexist with the state as guarantor of the peace, in order to allow space for reform, as a further function of punishment, to take effect.[87] Indeed, according to Augustine, the interaction of the *severitas* of the state with the *intercessio* of the Church produced the ideal compromise, of benefit to society as a whole.[88]

Augustine did not develop these ideas only as a matter of theory. When a gang of Donatist Circumcellions confessed under torture to the murder and mutilation of two Catholic priests, Augustine seized the chance to advocate the qualities of mercy – while also showing magnanimity to his enemies. Writing to Marcellinus, the *tribunus et notarius*, Augustine rejected the philosophy of retaliation expressed in the *lex talionis*, 'an eye for an eye', but also insisted that he supported the principle of punishment as reform and trusted that a penalty could be found that would either bring the murderers to their senses, or at least give them something useful to do. The Christian judge, wrote the bishop, should conduct himself like a good father – as indeed he observed that Marcellinus had done in the *quaestio*, when he had gained a confession using beating but not the hooks. The state's exercise of its legitimate powers of exacting retribution might be carried too far, whereas the judge should seek rather to 'heal the wounds' of sin.[89] In a companion letter, to the proconsul, Augustine advanced similar arguments, but further elaborated on the theme that State and Church had complementary roles, relying, respectively, on fear

---

[85] Amb. *Ep.* 25.8.   [86] E.g. Aug. *Serm.* 13.8; *Ep.* 100.1.

[87] Aug. *Ep.* 153.6.19, ita formidabitur ultio cognitoris, ut nec intercessoris religio contemnetur, quia et plectendo et ignoscendo hoc solum bonum agitur, ut vita hominum corrigatur.

[88] Id. Prodest ergo et severitas vestra, cuius ministerio quies adiuvatur et nostra; prodest et intercessio nostra, cuius ministerio severitas temperatur et vestra. On Augustine and punishment in general, see Houlou (1974). Punishment as reform was occasionally acknowledged in imperial legislation, e.g. at *NTh.* 8 pr., ... legibus, per quas delinquentes pro qualitate criminum convenit emendari.

[89] Aug. *Ep.* 133. 3, nec in peccatorum atrocitatibus exerces ulciscendi libidinem; sed peccatorum vulneribus curandi adhibeas voluntatem.

and compassion.[90] The proconsul's discretionary powers over sentencing, acknowledged by both jurists and emperors,[91] but in practice exercised with discretion, were also adduced; would the proconsul concede less to the Church than he was allowed anyway, in cases to which the Church was not a party?[92]

Augustine consistently believed that, in the field of punishment, Church and State could be made to work towards the same goals. Ecclesiastics, he maintained, did not want to see the guilty let off and accepted the legitimacy of the state's emphasis on retribution and deterrence. Some offenders, it appeared, did survive condemnation in the secular courts for crimes like adultery. These still faced excommunication[93] and, if they failed to perform due penance, perhaps publicly,[94] as Christians, too, humiliated the guilty, there was little hope for them in the hereafter. Where Augustine differed from the traditional priorities of the Roman state was that he advocated the function of punishment as reform, and had therefore logically to reject the death penalty, not for its cruelty but because it denied the sinner the chance to repent, or salvation in the afterlife.

Augustine's views on punishment by the state therefore integrated a Christian concern for reform with more traditional ideas of retaliation. The need for reform did not preclude the necessity of punishment. However, it was possible to draw from the Scriptures a more radical repudiation of punishment as retribution. In response to an Arian outrage on a Catholic chapel in Constantinople in 379, Gregory of Nazianus, who was temporarily in charge, rejected the option of punishment altogether. He conceded that the offence was serious and that 'we believe it very important to exact retribution from those who have wronged us', and that punishment had the beneficial effect of forcing others to behave. However, 'it is greater by far ... to endure suffering passively. The former course curbs wickedness, the latter persuades people to be good, which is a far greater thing to achieve than not to be bad.'[95] Thus Gregory, while

---

[90] Aug. *Ep.* 134.2, sed alia causa est provinciae, alia est Ecclesiae; illius terribiliter gerenda est administratio, huius clementer commenda est mansuetudo.

[91] *Dig.* 48. 19. 42 (Hermogenianus, *Epitome*). Interpretatione legum poenae molliendae sunt potius quam asperandae; *Dig.* 50. 17. 155. 2 (Paul. *Ad Edictum* 65), In poenalibus causis benignius interpretandum est.

[92] Id. cur non flectas in partem providentiorem, lenioremque sententiam, quod licet iudicibus facere etiam non in causis Ecclesiae? For judges' discretion, see *CT* 29. 2 and above, p. 140 for references to 'alternative penalties' in imperial constitutions; *Dig.* 48. 19 for judges' limited discretion; and Symm. *Rel.* 49.4 for why judges might exercise caution in letting people off. [93] Aug. *Serm.* 351.10.

[94] Id. 9, in notitia multorum vel etiam totius plebis, agere poenitentiam non recuset, non resistat, non lethali et mortiferae plagae per pudorem addat tumorem.

[95] Greg. Naz. *Ep.* 77.5.

accepting the validity of the standard justifications of retributive justice and reform, also rejected them as inadequate for the Christian. The 'silent exhortation' of magnanimous self-restraint was, in his view, a more effective means of carrying out his mission in a manner compatible with Christian principles, principles which were themselves incompatible with the operation of the secular usages of Rome:

> Do not let yourself be fooled by the empty reasoning that no blame attaches to a just prosecution and handing over the transgressor to the laws. There are the laws of the Romans and there are our laws. The former are immoderate, harsh and bring about the shedding of blood; ours are good and kind to men and refrain from anger towards wrongdoers.[96]

While Gregory might be dismissed as a magnanimous idealist, incapable of coping with the harsh realities of competitive church politics, his arguments were nonetheless grounded in contemporary values and Christian belief. In particular, his distinguishing the *lex Dei* from the 'laws (*nomoi*) of the Romans' went to the heart of the justification both of a separate jurisdiction exercised by bishops over their own people, and of the right of bishops to intercede with judges and assert the humane values of the 'Christian law' against the harsher practices of the secular courts.

At no period prior to the fourth century were *iudices* in the Roman Empire liable to face concerted pressure from individuals, with a strong and permanent local power base, whose duty was to enjoin mercy on their rulers. This, and other factors already noted, suggest conclusions at odds with the traditional interpretation of the Later Roman Empire as a society of unprecedented harshness and 'savagery', at least in the area of punishment and attitudes to it. This is not to discount the reality of the pain suffered by the condemned who were 'burned to ashes' or those who endured the slower death of the mines or public humiliation. Nor should the social effects of the increased vulnerability of *honestiores* to cruel punishments be underestimated; the adherence of the elite to the Roman order was now compelled by fear, at the expense, perhaps, of more congenial inducements to loyalty, based on self-interest. What must be understood, however, about Late Roman society in general was that there was a measure of support for the values expressed in the jurisdiction of the state. The right of the state to punish the guilty, to exact legitimate retribution, to deter others by public torture and execution was taken for granted. Cruelty was indeed challenged – but on account of the innocence of those on the receiving end, not as a matter of principle. Exaction of retribution from the guilty was also the prerogative of the Christian God and the wicked could expect appropriately painful punishment,

---

[96] Greg. Naz. *Ep.* 78.6.

often in this world and certainly in the next. There was therefore a measure of social acceptance, at least among the elite, for what we would regard as 'cruel and unusual' punishment.

Acceptance of pain was a feature of Roman history. Where the Later Empire differed from previous centuries was that punishment would still be inflicted publicly to shame the offender and deter others, but would no longer be used in the context of the arena to entertain in the manner of the 'fatal charades' indulged in by the givers of early imperial public entertainments. No longer were criminals (or Christians) to be sent to the beasts on the Emperor's orders, as had been the fate of the martyrs at Lyon in 177 or Perpetua and her friends at Carthage in 203, nor were women subjected to rape by donkeys or robbers forced to take part in mythological or other dramas in the arena, which ended in their crucifixion and/or exposure to bears.[97] The abolition of exercises in the ingenious inflictions of pain, which had made death a bizarre spectator sport, is surely one of the more significant social changes in the direction of moderation and mercy to take place in Late Antiquity.

Moreover, due to the interaction of Christianity with overall shifts in moral values, imperial *clementia* expressed itself in new ways. General amnesties for criminals were proclaimed, to coincide with Easter.[98] When uncertainties arose, because of the time some proclamations took to reach their destinations, amnesties were made an annual event; governors did not have to wait for official notification.[99] However, the imperial indulgence did not extend to more serious crimes: no remission was granted to those guilty of treason, homicide, sorcery and magic, fornication and adultery, sacrilege, violation of tombs, abduction and the counterfeiting of money. Taking sanctuary had also to be sorted out. Certain categories of people, such as those whose work was necessary to the state, or Jews liable to criminal charges or debt,[100] were debarred or had their rights restricted, and the Council of Ephesus in 431 deliberated about where in the church and its precincts, those who sought sanctuary could be kept safe. As was perhaps inevitable, the Church's insistence on its right to protect the weak conflicted with the state's urge to control and, where necessary, punish. The result, in the case of sanctuary, was a set of regulations which, taken as a group, laid greater stress on restrictions imposed on the privilege than on the importance of the right as a refuge or, at the very least, a breathing space.[101] Imperial laws seldom laid stress on reformation: one exception was Gratian's refusal in 381 to extend the

---

[97] These and other examples are discussed by Coleman (1990).
[98] *CT* 9.38.3 (367); 6 (381); 7 (384); 8 (385).   [99] *CT* 9.38.8 (385, Milan).
[100] *CT* 9.44.1 (392, debtors to the fisc); 2 (397, Jews); 3 (398, slaves, decurions, procurators, collectors of purple dye fish, public accountants).   [101] *CT* 9.44.5 (432).

Easter amnesty to reoffenders, on the grounds that those who had been let off once had used the privilege, not to reform, but to indulge in their 'habitual criminal activity'.[102]

Although the interventions of bishops may not always have been effective, the existence of an 'alternative law' and bishops' articulate insistence on the values of compassion cannot have been without effect. The *lex Christiana* worked, not through the *ad hoc*, and therefore arbitrary, system of patronage by individuals, but on the basis of a coherent set of moral beliefs: 'You will decide'. wrote Gregory of Nazianus to a governor, 'not between men but between right and wrong; for it is these questions which should occupy the minds of men like you, who are virtuous and upright rulers.'[103] The unrelenting pressure exercised by bishops on the *iudices* of their cities and provinces had far-reaching social effects. One was that the operation of punishment would be kept under constant scrutiny and abuses publicised. A second was that sentences must sometimes have been less severe than the law enjoined, although a prudent *iudex* would be unlikely to publicise his infringement of the imperial monopoly on *clementia*. And, finally, the impression in the sources that Late Antiquity was a period of unprecedented judicial violence derives precisely from the fact that the activities of executioners (and torturers) were put under a critical spotlight, not only by bishops, but by other public figures, who also subscribed to the rhetoric of criticism and accountability indulged in by the elite, from the emperor downwards. Punishment and pain were open to question and challenge. Cruelty that is publicised may also be checked: it is (or was) silence that bodes worst for the oppressed.

---

[102] *CT* 9.38.6 (381). See also *NTh.* 8 pr. on the laws, per quas delinquentes pro qualitate criminum convenit emendari; and id. 11 pr. (on guardians, modifying an earlier, harsher law), nec enim utile est vel a iudicibus observandum, quod modum emendationis excedit.   [103] Greg. Naz. *Ep.* 146.7.

8 The corrupt judge

In the 380s, a Christian writer at Rome of modest literary attainments consoled himself for the bad state of things in this world with the contemplation of their reversal in the next. Why, he asked, did people flout the Law of God and get away with it?

'So why, here, are sinners kept free from fear by their power, while some make a mockery of the statutes, the poor are oppressed, accusations are framed against the righteous . . . wicked and corrupt men are held in honour, greedy and grasping men grow rich, and the judge is for sale? . . .' (In the next world) 'those who used their power to despise the statutes or made a mockery of the law by sharp practice in their pursuit of wickedness, so puffed up in these ways that they might have appeared to trample on justice itself, – they shall be brought low and overthrown and shall be subjected to torments . . .'[1]

The rhetoric of the passage is familiar: the villains are the powerful, the unworthy rulers, the greedy – and the corrupt judge. Similar generalisations were made by another Italian, Maximus of Turin (c. 400), who warned his congregation that they should not make false accusations, yet 'the abuse has grown to such an extent that the laws are sold, statutes corrupted and verdicts habitually venal',[2] while Zeno of Verona attacked the greedy, including, among others, judges who gained money by *gratia*.[3]

Venality and susceptibility to improper influence, *gratia*, such was the behaviour expected of judges in the writings of Christians, and pagans or neutrals could be similarly censorious. The anonymous author of the *De Rebus Bellicis*, writing in the Danubian region in c. 369, complained that the 'loathsome greed' of *iudices* was yet one more hardship to be endured by provincials and was the worse because the evil originated with those

---

[1] Ambrosiaster, *Quaest. Vet. Test.* 4.2, ut quid hic peccantes per potentiam securi sunt, alii leges inludunt, pauperes deprimantur, iustis accusatio componitur . . . iniqui et corruptores in honore sunt, avari et raptores locupletantur, iudex venalis est? Illi autem qui per potentiam leges contemperserunt aut tergiversatione inluserunt iniquitatem sectantes, sic gloriosi in his, ut ipsi iustitiae insultare viderentur, ut humiliati et confusi tormentis subiciantur.'

[2] Max. Taur. *Serm.* 26.103. For this, and other refs., see MacMullen (1988) 151–2.

[3] Zen. Ver. *Tract.* 1.10 (Migne *PL* 11.332–7).

expected to be its cure.[4] Ammianus complained of judges and advocates, who took bribes to fix cases in favour of generals and the powerful, once the restraining hand of the emperor (Valens) was removed,[5] and Zosimus, writing long after the events described but perhaps reflecting contemporary perceptions, accused Stilicho of dominating the courts and making justice subject to either money or improper influence.[6] From a Hellene turned Christian in Cyrenaica in the early fifth century, comes one of the most comprehensive attacks to be made by a provincial notable on a current governor; under the *praeses*, Andronicus, who had, allegedly, bought his office, 'banquets became the forum for false accusations, a citizen was destroyed as a favour to a woman, and he who avoided illegal accusation was condemned, provided that, before conviction, he had not already suffered the fate of the convicted' (by harsh treatment before the trial).[7] For a judge, or a judge's assessor, to resist pressure from the powerful was so infrequent as to be astonishing, and Augustine made much of his friend, Alypius', resistance to the social pressure, bribes and threats of a 'potentissimus senator', unnamed, who sought to use him to pervert the course of justice.[8]

Moreover, distrust of judicial venality and abuse of power was shared by those who drafted imperial laws. In 325, Constantine proclaimed from Nicomedia to all provincials that they were to bring all complaints against provincial governors or palatine staff directly to him.[9] Later, in a wide-ranging edict issued in November 331, he launched a general attack on the corruption of the system:

The judge's curtain shall not be up for sale; entrance (to his hearings) shall not be gained by purchase, the private council chamber shall not be made notorious by auction. The governor (*iudex*) shall not make his appearance only because he is bought; the ears of the judge shall be open to the poorest on equal terms with the rich.[10]

A similar open invitation to lodge complaints against judges for extortion, venality and injustice was issued by Theodosius I in 386,[11] three years after Gratian in the West had threatened judges who sold verdicts with the penalty established for *peculatus*.[12] In the late 360s, Valentinian I put governors in charge of the supervision of tax assessments and reminded them that, when holding their hearings, they were to avoid making their advent burdensome to anyone, as was the rule.[13] Stern moral condemna-

---

[4] Anon. *De Rebus Bellicis* 4.   [5] Amm. Marc. 30.4.2.   [6] Zos. *Hist. Nov.* 5.1.1.

[7] Synesius, *Ep.* 58.   [8] Aug. *Conf.* 6.10.16.

[9] *CT* 9.1.4, referring to officials who had acted without honesty or justice.

[10] *CT* 1.16.7 (with 1.16.6; 2.26.3; 3.30.4; 4.5.1; 11.30.16–17; 11.34.1).

[11] *CT* 9.27.6.   [12] *CT* 9.27.5.

[13] Giardina and Grelle (1983), 259, Inscr. vv. 10–13, rectores provinciarum quibus forma studioque postuletur nullus honorosus videri excurssus (sic.) . . .

tion, as well as a heavy fine, were the lot of judges guilty of improper delegation of powers, and judges were threatened further if they connived 'venally' at the delay of execution of a sentence or illegal appeals.[14] In the fifth century, judges were even held to account for the flight of decurions from their councils, although venal tax-collectors also incurred blame.[15] Because *iudices* could not be trusted to implement imperial laws, other responsible organisations were involved: prison conditions and the return of people enslaved or imprisoned abroad were made, in part, the responsibility of the Church, while decurions were brought in by Valentinian to enforce the law on tomb violations, encouraged by the connivance of venal governors.[16] And, to keep the rest in line, an example could be made of a corrupt official: in 382, a former *dux*, Natalis, was to be escorted to his former province by soldiers from the imperial bodyguard to restore fourfold what he and his staff had extorted, 'in order that the punishment of one person may inspire fear in many'.[17] Public punishment served the same purpose as the public threats issued in the imperial laws against corrupt judges; it proved that the emperor meant what he said.

The rhetoric of imperial laws on *iudices* mirrored that of those who attacked governors whom, for whatever reason, they disliked. In his general attack on prison conditions, Libanius argued that governors were in effect murderers, because they allowed helpless people to be arrested and imprisoned at the request of their powerful friends, and then forgot about them, allowing them to die in prison. The situation was also the result of judicial negligence and incompetence: *iudices* sat in their courts judging tax cases and trivial suits over small amounts of money or land, a slave, camel or donkey, or an item of clothing, and let the more serious cases slip.[18] When Libanius turned his fire on a specific individual, Tisamenus, his method of discrediting the governor was to claim that, as a *iudex*, he was guilty of cruelty, incompetence and negligence. He avoided holding hearings at all, if he could, and if he had to do his job, wasted time in waffling to the advocates, then sending them off, to come back another day. This reduced the litigants to despair, because of the extra cost involved, and left the advocates with nothing to do.[19] Further delays ensued when Tisamenus married off his daughter, suspending court hearings while he supervised the wedding arrangements.[20] His cruelty was demonstrated in his indiscriminate use of floggings on defendants, whom he then sent back to prison to die.[21] On the possible 'venality' of Tisamenus, Libanius conceded that the governor himself was innocent, but that he had allowed corruption and the subversion of the laws among

---

[14] *CT* 1.12.8 (400) imposing a fine of 30lb gold for improper delegation; 9.40.15 connivance with criminals.   [15] *NMaj.* 7.1 (458).   [16] *NVal.* 23.6.   [17] *CT* 9.27.3 (382).
[18] Lib. *Or.* 45.16–17.   [19] Lib. *Or.* 33.10.   [20] Id. 28.   [21] Id. 31.

his immediate family and entourage.[22] This attack, not just on corruption, but on the malfunction of the judicial system at Antioch because of dereliction of duty on the part of the governor, coincided with an apparent shift in the attitude of the state towards its *iudices* reflected in legislation of the 380s and 390s: the state's right to punish criminal conduct by judges was expanded to encompass punishments for inefficiency and governors found to be 'lazy, negligent or idle' were to be dealt with by their superior and a substitute appointed if necessary.[23]

Although most of what follows will concern itself with behaviour of *iudices* censured by the laws, for behaviour which affected the outcomes in both civil and criminal procedures, it is worth noting that cruelty in criminal trials, which was not often an issue for emperors, was nevertheless very much part of the image of the 'bad governor' in Late Antiquity, and may have contributed to the suspicion of provincial *iudices* felt on other grounds. Synesius' series of attacks on Andronicus in 411–12 focussed on the arbitrary cruelty of a man who imported into Pentapolis instruments of torture never seen there before, who subjected innocent men to assault because of his greed, and who was finally excommunicated by the Church, at Synesius' urging, because he fastened edicts to the doors of the church illegally denying to suppliants the right of sanctuary.[24] Whatever the truth behind Synesius' portrait (which he was later to admit may have been too harsh), the powers vested in the governor allowed for the use of pain, as we have seen, and the extension of its use up the social scale from the second to the fourth century may have been partly driven by the practice of the courts and the *iudices*' desire to get at the facts.

Moreover, this negative image would have been enhanced both by the paraphernalia of terror that accompanied the *iudex* on his rounds and the lurid portraits of persecuting judges in the Late Roman Christian martyracts. The concise expressions of faith recorded in some of the early Acta, based on court records, gave way in the fourth century to speeches by martyrs of sometimes unbelievable length; Romanus, for example, continued to address an ever more irritated *iudex*, after his tongue had been cut out.[25] On the receiving end of the martyrs' confessions were oppressive governors, whose main characteristics were sadistic cruelty in the invention of tortures, and a propensity to ungovernable rages: Asclepiades, for example, the torturer of Romanus, is labelled at the outset a 'tyrannus', by contrast with Romanus, who speaks 'ore libero', as a free man, and is later described as 'incensus' and 'furens', mad with rage and 'vomiting forth' his fury (after yet another long speech).

---

[22] Id. 38–40.   [23] *CT* 1.5.9 (389).   [24] Syn. *Epp.* 57–8, 72–3.
[25] Prudentius, *Peristephanon* 10, which is therefore by far the longest of the poems in the collection.

The portrait of the judge as an unbridled sadist is a feature of the fourth century which owes much both to the rhetorical fashions of the time, and in particular to the version of Christian history put forward by Eusebius, ably supported by Lactantius. The two Christian historians painted both the imperial authors of persecution and their agents in the blackest of colours. Among governors, Urbanus of Palestine was singled out by Eusebius for especial criticism. On his entering office, 'the war against us was waged more fiercely'; a Christian who broke through Urbanus' security cordon to try to convert him was beaten and subjected to frightful tortures; and later 'the same judge, being a terrible inventor of evil and a manufacturer of assaults on the doctrine of Christ, thought up unheard-of retaliation against the holy and condemned three men to fight, one-to-one against gladiators. Then he gave over Auxentius, a reverend and holy priest, to be eaten by the beasts and others, again, being of mature age, he castrated and condemned to the mines and others, again, after cruel tortures, he shut up in prison.'[26] Both historians of the Great Persecution attacked Sossianus Hierocles, the author of an attack on Christianity, who was governor of Bithynia in 303, before moving on to serious persecution of Christians in Egypt in 307.[27] In Eusebius, language varied with purpose; in his attack on Hierocles as persecutor, the governor is seen 'raving like a drunkard, and exceeding the bounds of right', whereas, in Eusebius' refutation of Hierocles' written attack, personal abuse was scrupulously avoided.[28] Lactantius' method was different; Hierocles' governorship of Bithynia is discredited by allegations that he corrupted his delegates, created obligations on false pretences, bribed them into giving corrupt verdicts and denying redress to the victims.[29] This is recognisable as the figure of the Corrupt Judge, enslaved to greed and dishonesty.

Yet complaints about cruelty seldom feature in the law, except by implication, for example when exemptions from torture are questioned. The figure of the cruel judge, unlike his venal counterpart, is largely the property of historians and rhetors. While this divergence of what interested the law from the concerns expressed by literary sources may prompt wariness over some of the rhetorical impressions created by the latter, particularly as regards the extent of the abuses chronicled, the silence of the law may also have another consequence. Perhaps it was precisely because the law took too little account of excessive cruelty on the part of

---

[26] Eus. *Mart. Pal.* 4.8; 7.4.
[27] See Barnes (1981) 22, 164–7, with refs. for Hierocles' career given at p. 165 n.4 (at p. 360), adding to refs. in *PLRE* I Sossianus Hierocles 4, p. 432.
[28] Eus. *Mart. Pal.* 5.3; for refutation, see F. C. Conybeare's edition of Eusebius' *Against Hierocles* in the Loeb Classical Library (Cambridge MA: 1912), 482–605.
[29] Lact. *Div. inst.* 5.2.3.

iudices that opinion-formers independent of the imperially controlled judiciary took the remedy into their own hands.

The fact that 'corruption' and 'venality' are assumed to be characteristic of the judicial system as a whole both by emperors, who were its guardians, and by its critics has, not surprisingly, given Late Roman jurisdiction a bad name. However, important though these perceptions of corruption are for the social and cultural history of Late Antiquity, other explanations may also be offered for the prevalence of criticism of an in fact vulnerable and heavily supervised judiciary. While not seeking to dismiss all allegations of corrupt activity as literary inventions, we may understand better the situation of both *iudices* and their critics, if the grounds for legal and literary representations of *iudices* as up for sale and subject to *gratia* are examined afresh.

Iniuria iudicis

Several times in their discussions of the complications of civil litigation, the jurists of the Early Empire referred to a court verdict as being reached 'iniuria iudicis' or 'per iniuriam', by a wrongful decision. The casual tone of these scattered references to judicial 'iniuria' has been interpreted as a reflection of a general expectation that judges would misbehave.[30] There are two grounds for caution. The first, to which we will return, is the meaning of 'iniuria'. The second is the nature of juristic speculation, which encompassed both real and possible situations. Even in a perfect legal system, judges, being human, were liable to make wrong decisions: these, under the Roman Empire, could be through genuine error, or for corrupt reasons.[31] Such mistakes, regardless of the motive, would have consequences, on which jurists should express an opinion. The more hypothetical the situation envisaged by the jurist, the less can any reference to judicial 'iniuria' be taken as reflecting the alleged prevalence of 'iniuria iudicis' in real life.

Most juristic references to 'iniuria iudicis' deal with the consequences for later transactions of an incorrect decision over the ownership or control of disputed property. Gaius, on the Provincial Edict, pointed out that, in lawsuits, a procurator must present his accounts in good faith and, in an action, must make over what he has obtained from a lawsuit, including what he may have obtained 'through the mistake or wrong decision of a judge'.[32] Also writing in the mid-second century, Pomponius

---

[30] E.g. Kelly, J.M. (1966) 102.
[31] Cf. Gaius, *Inst.* 4. 178, defining 'calumnia' as suing another wrongfully in the hope of winning through the 'error vel iniquitas iudicis'.
[32] *Dig.* 3.3.46.4 (Gaius, *Prov. Edict* 3), usque adeo ut et si per errorem aut iniuriam iudicis non debitum consecutus fuerit, id quoque reddere debeat.

pictured the situation of a slave freed by will on condition that he paid a sum of money to the testamentary heir; subsequently, the will was challenged and judgement went against the testamentary heir – to whom the slave had already paid the price of his freedom. Juristic opinion was divided as to whether the slave was free or not, but agreed that the question of the rightness of the judge's decision could be set aside; 'even if the rightful heir named in the will lost the case through the wrong decision of the judge, nevertheless he (the slave) had obeyed the condition by his payment and would be free'.[33] And their contemporary, Salvius Julianus opined that when a procurator lodged a just petition and the master (*dominus*) an incorrect one, the procurator should not be answerable if the master gained anything 'iniuria iudicis'.[34] Under Septimius Severus, Papinian turned his mind to what might happen if someone defeated in a suit 'per iniuriam' mortgaged the property he had claimed, and concluded that the creditor, whose claim could be no stronger than that of the debtor, would have no redress, because the ownership of the property was *res iudicata*, decided by law.[35] Nor could a father who went into hiding while a lawsuit was pending be deprived of his property, as he was entitled to receive a judgement, including a wrong one.[36] Two further problems relating to debt were considered by a later jurist, Tryphoninus, who first asked himself if property taken by a creditor, through a wrong decision given by a judge, not from the debtor, but from its rightful owner (*dominus*), should be restored, once the debt was paid, and, second, on the subject of the redemption of a mortgage or pledge (*pignus*) by oath or judicial decision, stated that even if a debtor was released by a judge 'per iniuriam', the decision had to stand.[37]

The jurists' concern was with the effects of an incorrect decision, not its

---

[33] *Dig.* 40.7.29.1, nam si iniuria iudicis victus esset scriptus verus heres ex testamento, nihilominus eum paruisse condicioni ei dando et liberum fore. The other view was that the money already paid to the defeated *heres* had to be paid to the victor, but that this need not affect the slave adversely, as his payment could be held as part of the inheritance and therefore passed to the victor with the rest of the property.

[34] *Dig.* 46.8.22.4 (Julian, *Digest* 56): Cum autem procurator recte petit, dominus perperam, non debet procurator praestare ne iniuria iudicis dominus aliquid consequatur: numquam enim propter iniuriam iudicis fideiussores obligantur.

[35] *Dig.* 20.1.3.1: Per iniuriam victus apud iudicium rem quem petierat postea pignori obligavit... Non plus habere creditor potest, quam habet qui pignus dedit. Ergo summovebitur (creditor) rei iudicatae exceptione... Modestinus' definition of *res iudicata* as being the ending of a dispute by the decision of the judge to condemn or absolve is at *Dig.* 42. 1.1.

[36] *Dig.* 15.1.50.pr. (Papinian, *Quaestiones* 19), nam et si in diem vel sub condicione debeatur, fraudationis causa non videtur latitare, tametsi potest iudicis iniuria condemnari.

[37] *Dig.* 20.5.12.1, et cum per iniuriam iudicis domino rem, quae debitoris non fuisset, abstulisset creditor quasi obligatum sibi, et quaereretur, an soluto debito restitui eam oporteret debitori, Scaevola noster restituendum probavit; id. 20.6.13 nam et si a iudice quamvis per iniuriam absolutus sit debitor, tamen pignus liberatur.

motive, but the terms of juristic discourse also imply that 'iniuria iudicis' did not, necessarily, imply a corrupt decision, but one which had been taken 'contra ius', 'unlawfully', that is, a decision which was legally incorrect. Ulpian, who often states first principles, contrasted *iniquitas*, the deliberate pronouncing of a wrongful or unjust decision, with *iniuria*, the 'being without' law or justice.[38] He made a crucial distinction between '*iniuria*' which was something done 'contra ius' and '*iniuria*', meaning insult, affront, or injury, which could be made the subject of an action for '*iniuria*'. In a discussion of the legal position of a man who kills a thief, when he might have arrested him, he insisted that *iniuria* should be understood not in terms of the action for *iniuria* as the equivalent of *contumelia*, insult, but 'something that was done not by law, that is against the law, that is, if someone kills culpably',[39] and, in his commentary on the Praetorian Edict, summed up the meaning in broad terms; '*iniuria* is so called because it is done against the law (*ius*); so everything which is not done according to law, is said to be done by *iniuria*. Thus the general meaning, but specifically *iniuria* means insult (*contumelia*).'[40]

The moral neutrality of a definition of *iniuria* as meaning no more than something done against the law, which could apply to any judicial error, without implying culpability is reinforced by the connection made in the third century of *iniuria iudicis* with appeal. A decision which was held to be 'contra ius' by a litigant could be appealed against, without automatically casting a slur on the moral character of the judge; in a rescript on trusteeship, Diocletian ruled that a trustee who had lost his case by an incorrect decision of the judge yet had made no use of his right of appeal, could not act under mandate.[41] As in many of the jurists' analyses, the fact that a matter was *res iudicata*, meant that it could not be set aside, even if the verdict was wrong. A wrong decision therefore, however it was reached, stood, with all that it might imply for subsequent transactions, unless an appeal was lodged. The mass of legislation in the fourth century and later on *appellationes* reveals imperial disapproval of slowness on the part of some judges to accept or forward appeals, due in part to inefficiency, but also to fear that the grounds of appeal might reflect on them.[42]

---

[38] *Dig.* 47. 10. 1. pr., iniquitas ... cum quis inique vel iniuste sententiam dixit, iniuriam ex eo dictum, quod iure et iustitia caret.

[39] *Dig.* 9.2.5.1 = *Coll. Mos. Rom.* 7.3.4, iniuriam autem hic accipere nos oportet non quemadmodum circa iniuriarum actionem contumeliam quandam, sed quod non iure factum est, id est contra ius, id est si culpa quis occideret.

[40] *Dig.* 47.10.1, iniuria ex eo dicta est, quod non iure fiat; omne enim quod non iure fiet, iniuria fieri dicitur. Hoc generaliter, specialiter autem iniuria dicitur contumelia.

[41] *CJ* 4.35.10 (293), cf. *Dig.* 49. 1. 1. pr. (Ulpian), that an appeal was necessary to correct 'iniquitatem iudicantium vel imperitiam...'

[42] *CT* 11.30.13; 25; 31. See above, ch. 5, 'In court', p. 113.

The liability of the judge

The development in language discussed above does not suffice to explain the omnipresence of the late antique assumption that judges were corrupt. Other trends also played their part. One already noted was the growth in the accountability of the administration in general, which inevitably generated a flood of imperial constitutions restricting abuses at every level. In the case of the judiciary, the holding of judges to account was not new.[43] From the time of the Twelve Tables onwards, the state had interested itself in the improper conduct of *iudices*. In the second century CE, Aulus Gellius asked himself whether the capital penalty exacted in the Twelve Tables from judges who took bribes was too harsh.[44] In the time of Cicero, *iudices*, who gave verdicts as a group (and are often therefore known, in this context, as jurors) were notoriously open to bribery, despite efforts by the state to control the abuse.

By the second century BCE, a second form of liability had been recognised, the liability of the *iudex* to the plaintiff: judges 'made the case their own' ('litem suam fecerunt'), if they turned up late, or not at all, to a hearing, and the plaintiff could then claim damages equivalent to the value of the suit from the judge.[45] Liability of judge to plaintiff continued under the Empire and was expanded. Judges were liable, on procedural grounds, not only if they failed to attend the hearing, but also if they exceeded the limits set by the formula (which defined the nature of the case), or failed to adjourn, when required, and, in a broader sense, they could answer to litigants if they fraudulently reached a decision which was against the letter or spirit of the law.[46] In the time of Constantine, the liability of the judge to the litigant was still a reality. In a law of 318, addressed to Felix, governor of Corsica, Constantine issued a reminder of the rights of litigants where judges had acted improperly. If a wrong verdict was reached, through bribery or favouritism, or if a case ran out of time, due to the judge's negligence in face of repeated reminders, then the penalty would be that the *iudex* must pay to the plaintiff from his own resources the value of the amount in dispute,[47] and, if bribery was proved, the judge was faced with *infamia*. Little other evidence survives from the fourth century, however, of litigants gaining redress for themselves and, by the end of the century, the state had become the prime, if not the sole, enforcer of its own justice.

[43] For discussion of judges' liability down to the third century, see MacCormack (1982).
[44] Aul. Gell. *Noctes Atticae* 20.1.7.
[45] Speech of C. Titius in 161 BCE against drunks who turned up to conduct trials, quoted by Macrobius, *Saturnalia* 3.16.5: 'inde ad comitium vadunt, ne litem suam faciant'.
[46] *Dig.* 5.1.15 (Ulpian). The precondition was that the decision was reached fraudulently, 'dolo malo', and was not a genuine error, made in good faith.   [47] *CT* 1.16.3 + 2.6.2.

In fact, instances of a judge being made to 'call a case his own' are rare in any period, because of the difficulty of enforcement,[48] and the expansion of the state's responsibility in this area was predictable. Increasing concern on the part of law-makers with the behaviour of judges expressed itself through the amplification of the ancient statutes on criminal law, authored by the Dictator Sulla, Caesar and Augustus. Judges who resorted to the laying of false information or took bribes to secure a conviction, when a man's life or fortunes were at stake, were liable under the expanded remit of the Sullan Lex Cornelia *de sicariis*, even if a conviction was not secured, and, by the fourth century, could face exile and confiscation of property.[49] The liability was reinforced by the evolution of further sanctions under the Lex Julia on extortion (*repetundae*), which stipulated penalties for bribery and extortion by judges in both civil and criminal suits, with the added risk that a judge might be held to account for an unjust verdict, if 'impelled by anger'.[50] Liability under the Lex Julia also extended to the 'companions' of judges, their *consilium* and, by extension their office staffs.[51] Proper deference for imperial constitutions was an inevitable requirement; judges who ignored imperial constitutions, which had been read out to them or brought to their attention, would be punished.[52] They were not, however, expected to defer to irrelevant imperial pronouncements, nor did they have to hunt them down for themselves.

Under the Later Empire, jurisdiction became the main responsibility of the lowest rank of provincial governor, hence the frequent references to him as *iudex*. Under the system of line-management established by Diocletian and refined by his successors, the provincial *iudex* became answerable to his immediate superiors, as well as to the more distant emperors. His life was also made more difficult in the 380s and 390s (if not earlier) by the assimilation of 'negligence, laziness and idleness' to other judicial malpractices; if convicted for these faults, he was to be dealt with by his superior and a substitute appointed, if necessary.[53] By then also, the mechanism of appeal had come to replace other forms of individual redress sought by litigants from judges and, in 385, the emperors ruled that, if a litigant could prove that he had been denied a hearing or his case

[48] Kelly (1966) 102–17.
[49] *Dig.* 48.8.1 pr. and 1 (Marcian, *Institutes*); 48.8.4 pr. (Ulpian, *De Officio Proconsulis* 7); for the fourth century, Paul, *Sent.* 5.23.11 (10): Iudex qui in caput fortunasque hominis pecuniam acceperit, in insulam bonis ademptis deportatur.
[50] *Dig.* 48.11.3; 7 pr. and 3 (Macer, *De Iudiciis Publicis*), vel licet non acceperint, calore tamen inducti interfecerint vel innocentem vel quem punire non debuerant? See also *CT* 11.7.3 (320); 12.1.61 (324).
[51] *Dig.* 48.11.5 (Macer, *De Iudiciis Publicis*): In comites quoque iudicum ex hac lege iudicium datur.   [52] *Dig.* 48.10.1.3 (Marcian, *Institutes*); Paul, *Sent.* 5.25.4.
[53] *CT* 1.5.9 (389, to Tatianus, praetorian prefect).

had been deferred by the 'arrogance' or 'favouritism' of the judge, the judge would pay the value of the sum in dispute, not to the litigant, but to the fiscus, and the head of his office staff would be deported.[54]

Gratia

Iniuria, as we have seen, is discussed by jurists because mistakes were always possible and had to be allowed for. Their discussions imply nothing as to whether judges often made mistakes or why they made them. But if *iniuria* could be read as morally, but not legally, neutral, *gratia*, favour, had clearly no place in a just system. However, when, under Severus and Caracalla, *gratia* first appears in the jurists as a potential source for judicial malpractice, the discussion is conducted, principally by Ulpian, in terms, again, of what might happen, not what did happen. Judges, as we have seen could be made liable to litigants if they delivered a verdict against the law by deliberate fraud (*dolo malo*), which was defined by Ulpian as clearly proved *gratia*, bias towards the defendant, *inimicitia*, enmity, or *sordes*, corruption,[55] and matters could be restored to their original condition (*restitutio in integrum*) if a magistrate failed to give a lawful ruling 'through favour or corruption'.[56] Problems with *gratia* were not confined to judges: tutors and curators might be found guilty of deliberately damaging a property in their charge through 'corruption or demonstrable favouritism',[57] a tutor might purchase a poor estate 'through corruption or favour',[58] the wishes of the deceased expressed in a will might be set aside, 'through excessive friendly feeling', without money having changed hands,[59] witnesses in a court case might be relied on, provided that they were free 'from the suspicion of friendship or enmity'.[60] All these situations could arise; the jurists make no judgements about how often they actually did.

In describing the workings of *iniuria* or *gratia*, the early imperial jurists wrote as lawyers, not social historians. However, although it may be argued that third-century jurists made no comment as to the actual prevalence of *gratia* in the judicial system and could have used *iniuria* in a morally neutral sense, a different interpretation could have been made by later generations of imperial lawyers. *Iniuria* was something done against the law, therefore illegal, and, despite the distinction drawn by Ulpian, it also carried connotations of inflicting harm. In the ferociously moral

---

[54] *CT* 2.1.6.   [55] *Dig.* 5.1.15.1(Ulpian).   [56] *Dig.* 4.6.26.5 (Ulpian).
[57] *Dig.* 4.4.7.8 (Ulpian), nisi aut sordes aut evidens gratia tutorum sive curatorum doceatur.
[58] *Dig.* 26.7.7.2 (Ulpian): Competet adversus tutores tutelae actio, si male contraxerint, hoc est si praedia comparaverint non idonea per sordes aut gratiam.
[59] *Dig.* 29.4.4 pr. (Ulpian), quamvis non pecunia accepta, sed nimia gratia collata.
[60] *Dig.* 22.5.3.1 (Callistratus); 22.5.21.3 (Arcadius Charisius).

world of the fourth-century imperial constitutions, what had been simply
'contra ius' in the second century acquired a rhetorical gloss, which
enabled emperors to exert moral pressure on judges, whose wrong decisions had to be ascribed, not to ignorance (as a rule), but to the possibili-
ties of perverting justice available to all judges, venality and *gratia*. In the
language of imperial power, the phrases favoured by the jurists reappear,
with rhetorical embellishment, not to describe potential but to denote
fact; Constantine, for example, referred to those who 'will have given
wrong judgements, having been corrupted ('depravatus') for a price or by
favour',[61] Valentinian and Valens condemned judges influenced by favour or collusion[62] and Arcadius drew yet closer to the jurists' acceptance
of human fallibility, when he allowed that justice might be suppressed
'through the error or favour shown by the judge'.[63] Thus a legal discourse,
conducted by the jurists in terms of what might happen, was reworked by
the late antique drafters of constitutions so that it appeared to reflect a
'real world' in which judicial (and other) malpractice was common.

Selling a verdict or helping a friend were both violations of the rules and
perverted the course of justice, therefore both were censured by legislators, whose aim was to prevent all infringements of the rules. However,
moral distinctions could be made between receiving a bribe and friendly
co-operation with a respected associate – such as a bishop – concerned to
receive justice for his client. Gregory of Nazianus, in many ways the least
worldly of clerics, cultivated the governor, Olympius, ascribing to him the
power to arbitrate in spiritual matters and restore the public good and
adding that Olympius had no gold wrongfully acquired, nor did he show
anger. He then discussed *gratia* in terms which reveal the difficulties
confronted by contemporaries in discussing a morally ambivalent concept. According to Gregory, Olympius' practice with regard to 'favour'
was in a slightly different category from his other policies; the governor, in
this respect, was flexible, which was, wrote Gregory, a criticism, but only
because he imitated the philanthropy of God, and could therefore be
expected to be more merciful and generous than the occasion might
warrant.[64] In other words, this was *gratia* to be exercised in a manner
parallel to the emperor's exercise of *clementia*. Later letters of Gregory to
the same governor put the doctrine into practice, but only, it should be
noted, with regard to the punishment for an offence, not the trial or
verdict. The citizens of Diocaesarea had misbehaved and the city was

[61] *CT* 1.16.3, qui pretio depravatus aut gratia perperam iudicaverit.
[62] *CT* 9.42.7 (369), per gratiam atque conludium; 12.1.77 (372), per gratiam aut conivente
iudice.
[63] *CT* 11.30.57 (398), per errorem vel gratia cognitoris oppressa putatur esse iustitia. For
other refs., see *CT* 1.28.2; 6.18.1; 11.10.1; 11.30.51; 13.8.8.2.
[64] Greg. Naz. *Ep.* 140 (382).

threatened with destruction; Gregory intervened on its behalf.[65] A former priest, Leontius, was guilty of an offence – yet Gregory begged that his punishment should not be too severe.[66] From the standpoint of governor and bishop, this was traditional *intercessio*; a legal rigourist might also have called it *gratia*.

Was *gratia*, then, in the eye of the beholder, given that any intervention, however well-intentioned, with the course of justice might be construed, especially by the opposing party, as improper influence?[67] The reaching of a decision due to *gratia* was easy to allege and hard to prove, and there were strong motives for powerful or disgruntled litigants to claim discrimination on those grounds. Ulpian is one of the few writers of antiquity to acknowledge openly that people would resort to allegations about *gratia* – if they lost a case: on the liability of a substitute *heres*, heir/executor to the legatees, he commented that no-one could be mad enough to launch a legal challenge over *gratia* against a verdict given in his favour.[68] It was therefore the more important that 'suspicion' of *gratia* should be avoided as far as possible, which was why governors, according to Ulpian, should give guidance on points of law to their judges but not advise on points of fact which might influence a verdict, and provide grounds for allegations of improper influence and corruption.[69]

On the other hand, interceding with judges, or men who might influence judges, was part of a patron's activity, and was presumably expected to have some effect. The language of such interventions shows a careful avoidance of anything that might be construed as pressure to break the law. Symmachus, in particular, showed a proper caution, combining the assertion that his client's case was in accordance with law with the effect of his own intervention in 'tipping the scale' of the judge's favour.[70] Nor were recommendations of clients to judges neutral. The case of the client was always just, and the client himself, or herself, was often the victim of an unscrupulous opponent. Like other, less elevated petitioners, Symmachus resorted to the moral maxim to back his case: 'It is voiced by law

---

[65] Id. 141–2.   [66] Id. 143.

[67] Cf. Synesius, *Ep.* 2, to one Cledonius, on behalf of his kinsman, asking that he be given ownership of his father's pottery shop, according to his father's will and the governor's ratification and that, despite 'the accusation' (unspecified) the hearing be hastened. The opposing case, which could be undermined by this intervention, is not allowed for.

[68] *Dig.* 4.6.26.5 (Ulpian, *Ad Sabinum* 34), nec enim tam improbe causari potest secundum se iudicatum per gratiam.

[69] *Dig.* 5.1.79.1 (Ulpian, *de Off. Procons.* 5), haec enim res nonnumquam infamat et materiam gratiae vel ambitionis tribuit.

[70] Symm. *Ep.* 1.69 to Celsinus Titianus, *vicarius Africae*, asking that the case of his client's brothers be heard by Titianus rather than the *consularis* of Numidia, 'quare si et illius apud te grande momentum est, et a legibus causa non discrepat, et interventus meus libram tui favoris inclinet...' Cf. Synesius, *Ep.* 42 'it is in your power to gratify both myself and the laws'.

and statutes that a contract entered into in good faith cannot be broken' –
yet this was, allegedly, what his client's opponents had done. Exploitation
of the rhetoric of victimisation was available to the powerful, as well as to
the genuinely oppressed and clients of the elite are often represented as
being themselves victims, either of oppression by the other side, or false
accusations. Thus Symmachus lined up the two powerful brothers Petronius, *vicarius* of Spain, and his brother Patruinus in support of the
harrassed Caecilianus, allegedly the victim of spitefully renewed legal
action, while Basil of Caesarea lobbied friends of the Prefect on behalf of a
widow, who, he maintained, was entitled to a longer period to pay a debt
than the written agreement allowed (the creditor had agreed orally to
extend the time) and also to remission of the interest on her debt, having
paid the principal.[71] Libanius, of course, was no less active, both on his
own behalf and that of others. While enlisting the *comes rei privatae* in
support of his claims to the disputed inheritance of his uncle Phas-
ganius,[72] he was also twisting the arms of governors and military leaders to
the benefit of his friends, and the confounding of their enemies. He
suggested, in one case, biassed witnesses who would, he said, supply the
'truth',[73] and accused opponents of themselves making false claims,[74]
even suggesting they be given a full hearing to make allegations about his
friends' rapacious activities, as they will so obviously be untrue.

Gratia iudicis, therefore, was a concept which faced two ways, and
epitomised the problems both of operating in the Late Roman judicial
system and of assessing the extent of corruption within it. On the one
hand were the laws, which insisted on impartiality and fairness, and,
while allowing some scope for discretion, also condemned departures
from the rules which might be accounted for by improper pressures
exerted on the judge. On the other, was the fact that the exertion of such
pressures by a patron on behalf of his client were traditional, widespread,
and (within limits) socially acceptable. Moreover, even if a trial had not
been hastened, or a verdict influenced, or a sentence ameliorated by
bribery or the intervention of a patron, the losing side might suspect as
much and criticise the governor as venal and susceptible to *gratia*. But
such allegations are not fact, and we may suspect that the system within
which he worked and the *potentes* with whom he had to deal, and who
controlled the record, ensured that the corruption of the Late Roman
governor was far more often asserted than proved.

[71] Basil *Epp.* 177–80.   [72] Lib. *Ep.* 57, to Evagrius, *'comes rei privatae'* 360–1.
[73] Lib. *Ep.* 105.4, to Gaianus, governor of Phoenicia. The 'reliable' informant, Hermeias,
was connected to the family of Libanius' clients.
[74] Lib. *Ep.* 106 defends a zealous recruiter of decurions against the numerous (slanderous)
accusations he anticipates and asks Rufinus, *comes Orientis* to delay a decision till his
return.

The accountability of the *iudex*

Given the problems with the evidence suggested above, the quantification of the real extent of judicial corruption in Late Antiquity as compared with the Early Empire may be an impossible task. What is clear is that a judgement must be reached on the basis of how the system worked, rather than by attempts to quantify complaints made against it. As we have seen, the imperial state did all it could to control its judges, and we should not assume that such controls were ineffective. In addition to the laws, the universal right of appeal was an important check, when taken in conjunction with the nature of the records, which had to be produced as part of the process. Those records were, from at least Diocletian onwards, probably verbatim transcripts of what was actually said. It was therefore easy to detect bias or improper conduct by the *iudex*, simply by reference to the transcript. As the appeal would go straight to the governor-judge's superiors in the provincial hierarchy, the corrupt judge could expect to be called to account to some effect, both by the aggrieved party and a superior, whose disfavour could adversely affect the delinquent's chances of future promotion.

Some comparisons may also be drawn between the situations of early and late imperial provincial governors in relation to the people to whom they were answerable, the provincials and the emperor. These will suggest that, while the potential for abuse of power was real, the opportunities available to late Roman *iudices* for misbehaviour were restricted by imperial, provincial and episcopal vigilance. The Late Antique provincial *praeses*, as already observed, was on the lowest rung of the career ladder; above him were *vicarii* and praetorian prefects, who acted for the emperor in supervising his activities. Unlike his Early Imperial predecessor, who governed a province inhabited largely by non-citizens, and who was answerable to the emperor directly, the provincial *iudex* of Late Antiquity governed a smaller province, inhabited almost entirely by Roman citizens, every one of which had the right of appeal to a higher authority, a right which, if considerations of cost were excluded, was, in formal terms, easily exercised. Nor was he the most eminent person in the province, and as a mere *vir clarissimus*, he was obliged to take account of the views of the powerful men on the spot. In extreme cases, he might find his authority subverted by a local notable claiming superior status; in 441, Theodosius II had to intervene to support his governor against an alleged honorary *vir illustris* of Emesa, who took over the governor's court hearings and used a band of slaves to disrupt tax-collection.[75]

---

[75] *NTh.* 15.2.

The corrupt governor under the Early Empire[76] was protected, to some extent, by senatorial solidarity with its own members, which could have inhibited convictions of any governor brought to trial before the Senate, although this effect might in turn be counteracted by competition within the elite. Summoning *iudices* to account in Late Antiquity was more difficult. The system of fines for malpractice made *iudices* accountable for numerous abuses and derelictions of duty, but it is not clear from the constitutions how the fines due to the fiscus were collected, or how often charges of venality against governors could be proved. However, emperors in the fourth century still legislated on the gubernatorial crimes of extortion (*repetundae*) and peculation, stipulating loss of status as well as fines for those convicted and, in the case of peculation, increasing the penalty from a fine to capital punishment.[77] In a more delicate case of abuse of power, Theodosius I had to set the governors and *vicarii* to watch over each other; women and their families under pressure to marry an imperial official, governor or *vicarius* were removed from the jurisdiction of the culprit and placed under the power of a different authority, which in extreme cases could be the praetorian prefect himself, for as long as the oppressor was in office.[78]

Central to the effectiveness of the system of bringing bad governors to justice was access either to the emperor or to a competent authority. Complaints from provincials that emperors were 'shut away' were reinforced by the occasional scandal, which revealed how little the emperor knew about the provinces he governed. Valentinian I's mismanagement of the developing crisis in Africa in the early 370s was a prime example: the Tripolitanian city of Lepcis Magna, having appealed in vain to the corrupt *comes Africae*, Romanus, for protection, despatched an embassy to Valentinian in Trier to complain of Romanus' incompetence. However, their access to the emperor was prevented by Romanus' equally corrupt relation, Remigius, the *magister officiorum*, and the delegates from Lepcis suffered further misfortunes in the course of their vain search for justice. Only after further officials had been suborned by Romanus and parts of the province were in open revolt, did the truth begin to come to light and Romanus and his wicked confederates suffered justice, albeit belatedly, at the hands of Valentinian's trouble-shooter, the *comes* Theodosius.[79]

[76] See Brunt (1961) for refs. Pp. 224–7 list 40 prosecutions attested down to Trajan, with outcomes.
[77] *CT* 9.27: Ad Legem Iuliam Repetundarum; 9.28.1 (392), penalty for peculation increased.
[78] *CT* 3.11.1 (380). Such approaches were not grounds for sacking the offending official.
[79] E.g. for Romanus and Remigius 'rapinarum particeps' see Amm. Marc. 27. 9. 2; 28. 6. 8; 29. 5. 2; 6; 50.

The problem of access was partly dealt with by the delegation of imperial powers to act to the praetorian prefects, who served also as, in theory, the final courts of appeal. The disciplining of *iudices* seems, therefore, to have become the responsibility of the praetorian prefects,[80] although emperors did on occasion intervene with requests that complaints from the provincials be forwarded directly to them for action. Under the Early Empire, hopeful provincial prosecutions had sometimes been hampered by divisions in provincial councils,[81] caused by rivalries between cities and individuals hoping for the governor's patronage, if they frustrated an accusation against him.[82] In Late Antiquity, petitions from provincial councils were more tightly regulated. Constantine's law stating that decrees of provincials were not to be forwarded to the imperial court without being vetted by the governor could be interpreted as permission for the governor to suppress unfavourable reports on his governorship. However, the concern of Constantine for accountability expressed by that emperor elsewhere suggests that his intention was that the governor be allowed, as was proper, to express his view, but not to prevent the forwarding of the decrees;[83] similarly, when decrees were passed by municipalities, they were to be forwarded to the praetorian prefect unchanged.[84] The condition that governors should vet decrees was still operative in the mid-fourth century,[85] but, in 392, Theodosius I ruled that, when an extraordinary meeting of the provincial council was called, its delegates could by-pass the governor.[86] Increasingly emperors laid stress on the representative authority of provincial delegations; municipalities were not to send separate delegations but were to pool their resources and send three men to represent the province as a whole,[87] delegates were to come equipped with letters and decrees,[88] the council's meetings were to be held in public and special provision was made for consulting the most eminent provincials.[89] The delegation of authority to the Prefects should not be assumed to have had a detrimental effect on provincials' representations of their cases. When the emperor was ineffective or a child, it can only have reassured doubting provincials when an imperial edict to the praetorian prefect instructed him carefully to consider the submissions of provincial delegations and refer to the emperor those requiring

[80] E.g. *CT* 12. 1. 173 (409, east) on tax assessments and receipts.
[81] As in Bithynia in 106, over the prosecution of Varenus Rufus: Plin. *Epp.* 5.20; 6.5; 6.13; 7.6; 7.10.
[82] *CIL* 13.3162 (Thorigny). T. Sennius Solemnis successfully resists a proposal to prosecute the former governor, Claudius Paulinus, who shows his appreciation.
[83] *CT* 1.16.2 (?331).   [84] *CT* 12.12.4 (364, referring to a law of Constantine, now lost).
[85] *CT* 12.12. 3 (364); 8 (382).   [86] *CT* 12.12.12.   [87] Id. 7 (380).   [88] Id. 11 (386).
[89] Id. 12 and 13 (28 July and 10 Sept. 392).

'agreement and indulgence' for the benefit of oppressed people everywhere.[90]

Governors were in fact vulnerable, socially and politically, in Late Antiquity.[91] Their relative inferiority of status, which made them more susceptible to pressures from their social superiors, also created opportunities for provincials to strike back, especially if their target lacked influential protectors. Even when he did have powerful senatorial connections, as was probably the case with the younger Nicomachus Flavianus, proconsul of Asia in 382-3, complaints from the influential could cause his removal; Flavianus was sacked for flogging a decurion.[92] Moreover, there were a number of strategies available to oppressed or aggrieved provincials, especially if the governor had unwisely offended the Church. Synesius of Cyrene, who spoke favourably of some other local officials and was no enemy to Roman government, launched a concerted attack on the *praeses Libyae*, Andronicus, whom he had known in youth, with the aim, not of having him convicted in court, but of removing him from office. To this end, he began with the assertion that Andronicus should not be in office at all: he had broken the rule that locals were not appointed to serve in their province of origin – clearly by bribery.[93] He then enlisted both Church and State in his support. Andronicus was denounced to the local bishops for being 'the first' to import unspeakable instruments of torture (possibly a literary reminiscence of Eusebius' Persecuting Judge), for posting illegal edicts, denying the right of sanctuary, and threatening the clergy in the manner of a tyrant.[94] Andronicus was duly excommunicated and, although he tried to demonstrate repentance – a sign either of the effectiveness of episcopal power or a less 'tyrannical' character than was alleged – Synesius continued to take a hard line.

At the same time, Synesius' representations to Anthemius, the great praetorian prefect, via a friend, show how much a governor had to fear from provincials with illustrious connections. Through his associate, Troilus, Synesius argued that Anthemius was himself responsible for seeing the laws undermined: 'are you not guilty of undermining the law, for imposing a new fashion on the ancient statutes, even while the laws threaten harsh penalties for those who fraudulently become ruler of their own province of origin? Why do you not censure those who contrive to overturn your decrees? If they were not unknown to you, you act unjustly; if unknown, you are guilty of neglect . . .'[95] It was therefore right, Synesius argued, that those who 'trampled the laws underfoot' should be thrown

---

[90] Id. 14 (408), addressed to the Prefect Anthemius, effectively by himself. Arcadius had died earlier that year and Theodosius II was eight years old.
[91] See the pertinent observations of Corcoran (1996): 234–53.   [92] Lib. *Or.* 28.5.
[93] Syn. *Epp.* 58; 72.   [94] Syn. *Ep.* 58.   [95] Syn. *Ep.* 73d.

out of office, and be replaced by law-abiding magistrates who would give judgements according to the facts, not by whim. Andronicus had treated litigants atrociously – and had even tried to frame the previous governor for *peculatus*. On these grounds, Synesius petitioned Anthemius, in accordance with the laws, 'whose antiquity makes them worthy of respect (for this is the reverence due to law) or, if more applicable, more recent decrees, which, one might say, proclaim the still living power of imperial rule'.

Whether Andronicus was in fact as corrupt as he was painted is of less importance than Synesius' demonstration of the power of the influential provincial over a governor's career and reputation. The public face of the *iudex*, the judge in the court of first resort, the representative of the state, who wielded its power and terror, and who had the ability to deliver in court what verdicts he chose, was a potent distraction from the weakness behind the mask. The reputation of the *iudex* in general had little chance when confronted with the prevailing discourse in both laws and the rhetoric of powerful provincials on corruption and accountability. Earlier juristic analyses of the potential for corruption on the part of governors translated easily into the moralistic language of imperial law, castigating venality and *gratia*, not as potential but as fact. In the provinces, public speakers, from the sophist Libanius to the bishop in his church, thundered warnings against the general abuse of power by *potentes*, which included *iudices*, (while of course exempting individuals from their strictures). As patrons, including bishops, did constantly seek to influence judges on their clients' behalf, suspicions of *gratia* were inevitable and doubtless often well-founded; lowly *iudices* needed powerful friends. Such was the way the system had worked, throughout Roman imperial history. The difference in Late Antiquity was not that judges were more corrupt but that emperors, provincials and the ever-critical Christian Church were more often prepared to say so.

9 Dispute settlement I: out of court

Resort to law was one among several methods of handling or settling disputes between individuals or groups. Although it has come to be recognised that disputes in early mediaeval Europe were settled in a variety of extra-legal ways,[1] alternative means of dispute handling[2] and resolution under the Later Roman Empire have received little systematic attention. Yet a number of methods for 'finishing' disputes existed, of which the law took limited, or no, cognisance. These may be listed as force, arbitration, and mediation or negotiation. In cases of public violence, the agencies of law-enforcement became involved only when the situation got so out of hand that the imperial majesty itself was threatened. Formal arbitration involved the law to the extent that a settlement might require enforcement through the state's courts, in the event of a breach of the terms by one or more of the parties, and rules were laid down for some aspects of arbitration, because 'the praetor' was required to ensure that the decisions of an arbiter were honoured.[3] Arbitration, however, could also consist of an informal agreement brokered by an adjudicator, without introducing the legal formalities required of a formal process (although legal redress might then be harder to come by). Settling a dispute through mediation by a third party or negotiation between the parties themselves was, by definition, extra-legal. The written law is, naturally, silent on informal and legally unenforceable agreements. This did not, in practice, mean that informal agreements were less binding. Adoption of mediation or negotiation by the parties implied a predisposition on the part of both to reach agreement by these means and abide by it thereafter.

The under-representation even of arbitration in the legal texts, which

---

[1] See the important collection of studies in Davies and Fouracre (1986).
[2] Not all disputants seek a settlement, and rules about 'handling' are no less significant than rules about 'resolution'. Arguably late Roman legal procedure, especially appeals, connived at the prolonging, rather than the resolution of disputes. The Archive of Sakaon shows underlying tensions between family members in Theadelphia, in Egypt, extending from the reign of Diocletian to 343, which periodically erupted in petitions over abductions of women and the forcible seizure of land.   [3] *Dig.* 4.8; *CT* 2.9.

accounts for the neglect of alternative forms of dispute resolution by legal historians, can be corrected from other sources. Insights on how disputes were conducted are increasingly to be found in the papyri of Late Roman Egypt, a province which, thanks to the combined efforts at standardisation of Septimius Severus (in Egypt, 199–200), Diocletian, and the cumulative effect of the increased use of Roman law after the universal conferring of citizenship in 212, now had more in common with the rest of the Roman world than at any previous time in its recorded history. Through use of these texts, the real complexity of the handling and settlement of disputes has become more apparent.

The attractions of alternative forms of dispute resolution should not be underestimated. Litigation in court could be an expensive, unpredictable, perhaps risky and often futile indulgence. To take an opponent through all the formalities of bringing suit, plus appeals, required by Roman law, would have been beyond the power of many Roman citizens, who might have described themselves as being, like Isidore of Karanis, 'men (or women) of moderate means' (*metrioi*).[4] Apart from the expense and risk involved, litigation between members of small communities was divisive, whatever the outcome. Therefore, as we shall see, it was preferable that the potentially damaging effects of quarrels between neighbours be controlled by a mutual willingness to compromise, or at least to neutralise the situation before it got out of hand. Intervention by others or negotiation between the parties enabled the resolution of disputes in ways not acknowledged by, because irrelevant to, the written laws.

Arbitration, or other forms of dispute resolution, such as mediation, negotiation or violent self-help, were not used simply as alternatives to going to court. Disputants or people with a grievance asked themselves certain questions: could s/he do better by going to law? Or, if poor, or lacking connections, or otherwise disadvantaged, were there devices to hand which might compel or put pressure on an ostensibly more powerful person to reach agreement? Involving the state by threats of legal action or the launch of petitions to powerful people were among several modes of action, incorporated into complex strategies aimed at forcing a disputant to settle through arbitration, or to gain some other practical or psychological advantage. What mattered about the resolution, or handling, of disputes was the overall context within the family or community, which conditioned the activities of the disputants. Most extant documents reveal no more than one stage in what was, in many cases, a protracted struggle for supremacy or settlement.

One crucial decision had to be made by disputants. Who decided the

[4] *P. Cair. Isid.* 68.

outcome? The legal anthropologist, Philip Gulliver, has maintained that dispute settlement can be analysed in terms of two main models, adjudication (judicial decisions, arbitration) and mediation/negotiation and that the distinction is based on the locus of the decision-making. Adjudication 'is essentially characterised by the fact that decision-making and the outcome of the issues in dispute are controlled by a third party exercising some degree of accepted authority', and the disputants therefore address themselves to him. In negotiation, the disputants are 'interdependent in the absence of authority', they interact and reach a joint decision, which both are morally obliged to accept, while the mediator is 'a facilitator but not an adjudicator'. The choice of method could have important implications for the criteria used to reach a resolution. Adjudication is likely to be based on 'concern for values and a definition of disputes in terms of values', norms would be applied, and attention given to acts rather than actors, excluding the wider context. While the adjudicator would expect to apply the rules, mediation/negotiation allowed for 'a definition of disputes in terms of interests ... and a concern for the personal qualities and dispositions of the disputants, for the future of their and others' rights and relationships...'.[5]

Although, on Gulliver's argument, the cultures of the two forms of settlement were widely divergent, nothing precluded the use of both methods in the course of settling a dispute over a period of time. Nor are the two cultures mutually exclusive. As Gulliver conceded, the distinction between arbiter and mediator could break down, in that 'occasionally mediators virtually take control and make effective decisions'.[6] In the Roman system, much could hinge on the role of the adjudicator. Romans, like Seneca,[7] recognised that a judge had to play strictly by the rules, while arbiters, although expected to be consistent with Roman law, could also take other factors into account. Even in formal trials, as we have seen, adjudicators took account of the social status and character of witnesses, when reaching a verdict, and even of the litigants themselves.

All this affects one of the most distinctive forms of dispute resolution to operate in late antiquity, the episcopal 'hearing', or 'court', to be discussed more fully in the next chapter. The relevance of arbitration procedure to the operation of *episcopalis audientia* was asserted by the drafters of imperial laws in the late fourth and fifth centuries[8] and has been recognised by analysts since. However, Christian ecclesiastical procedure has tended to be discussed in isolation from the wider social context in

---

[5] Gulliver (1979) 20.   [6] Id. 209.
[7] Sen. *De Beneficiis* 3. 7. 5, arguing that a formal trial was better than arbitration, if one had a good case, because judgement by a *iudex* was in accordance with statute and justice, and not unpredictable things, like *humanitas* and compassion.
[8] *CT* 1. 27. 2; *NVal.* 35. Below, ch. 10, pp. 201–3.

which the bishop operated. Just as more than one strategy might be employed by a petitioner to a governor, so bishops too might use a number of methods to sort out a delicate situation and, indeed, were expected to do so. One outcome of this, as we shall see,[9] is an over-estimation of the effectiveness of imperial legislation in defining episcopal powers of adjudication.

Arbitration

Most uses of the word arbiter in Latin imply the authority of the adjudicator, not the conciliating or enabling role of the mediator, although there were exceptions.[10] The decision of the arbiter, like that of a judge, represented the adjudication of a person whose authority was accepted by the disputants either because, as judge, he was authorised by the state, or because, as arbiter, they had chosen him and thus signified their consent to whatever award he might make. The connection between the two as adjudicators went back to the Twelve Tables; the 'iudex arbiterve' were equally competent to deliver a judgement that would conclude the case. A further similarity, also dating from the early Republic, was that the *iudex*, like the arbiter, was 'given' ('datus') by the praetor in response to the wish of the parties to have their business settled, in the expectation that they would abide by his ruling. Even under the Early Empire, it could still be said that the arbiter undertook the 'functions of the *iudex*', and nobles accustomed to adjudicating disputes between clients and tenants used the words interchangeably.[11] Two distinctions were drawn. One was that the arbiter concluded the case,[12] whereas judges' rulings might be open to appeal. The other was that the *iudex*, according to Seneca, was bound to give judgement according to the law (therefore a strong case should go to court), while arbiters could adjudicate how they liked.[13] Some eight hundred years after the Twelve Tables, the paths of *iudex* and arbiter had

9 See below, ch. 10.
10 E.g. Aug. *In Psalm.* 103.4.8, commenting on Job's plea for an arbiter (= mediator) employed a broad definition, 'quid est arbiter? medius ad componendam causam', invoking Christ as the ultimate arbiter/mediator, without whom the way of pity would perish. Even here, however, the onus for resolving the conflict rests with the 'medius', not the parties.
11 E.g. Pliny, *Epp.* 5.14.8; 9.15.1; 7.30, 'non desunt enim qui me iudicem aut arbitrum faciant. Accedunt querelae rusticorum, qui auribus meis post longum tempus suo iure abutuntur.' See MacMullen (1974), 39–45, 121, 257 n. 208.
12 *Dig.* 4.8.13.2. Recepisse autem arbitrium videtur (in Pedius Book 9) qui iudicis partes suscipit finemque se sua sententia controversiis impositurum pollicetur.
13 Sen. *De Ben.* 3.7.5, 'ideo melior videtur condicio causae bonae, si ad iudicem quam si ad arbitrum mittetur, quai illum formula includit et certos, quos non excedat, terminos ponit, huius libera et nullis adstricta vinculis religio et detrahere aliquid potest et adicere et sententiam suam, non ut lex aut iustitia suadet, sed prout humanitas aut misericordia inpulit regere'.

moved further apart. The state, whose jurisdiction was represented by the *iudex* in his court, had taken responsibility for what happened in its own *iudicia*, where, as we have seen, the *iudex* was increasingly held liable (along with his office staff) to the state, not to the litigant, whose consent to be present in the court was no longer assumed. The arbiter, however, was left relatively free of state interference, apart from interventions to strengthen adherence to his decisions by having them written down and guaranteed by oath.[14] He therefore retained his traditional status of an adjudicator, largely independent of the law, and responsible to the parties whose agreement authorised him to settle their case.

Roman law, based on the praetorian Edictum Perpetuum, as expressed and refined by the jurists and in the constitutions of emperors, took an interest in arbitration because of the praetor's duty to ensure that the litigation was indeed ended by the arbiter's decision, a principle echoed in an imperial law of the early fourth century[15] and also applicable to the awards made by bishops in their hearings.[16] This was fair, because resort to arbitration could not happen without the co-operation of both parties. However, a number of preliminary issues of definition had also to be sorted out, such as what the arbitration should be about, how and when a decision should be reached, what should happen if a party to the dispute or the arbiter himself was absent, the number of arbiters and their status and whose decision should be valid, or whether, in the event of the death of one party, their heirs could continue in the arbitration till a conclusion was reached.

Life was not always as complicated as the jurists made it, but such problems as these were expected to be anticipated in the drafting of the all-important preliminary agreement to go to arbitration, the *compromissum*, which the jurist Paulus, in his Commentary on the Edict, declared should be drawn up in the manner of a document to be presented in court and should guarantee that the dispute would be ended.[17] The subjects in dispute should be specified clearly in the *compromissum*, where it should also be explained whether there was one dispute to be resolved or several and whether an award was to be made by the arbiter for all the cases at once or for each separately.[18] The *compromissum* could state the number,

---

[14] Justinian (*CJ* 2.55.4, 30 Oct. 529): arbitrations agreed 'cum sacramenti religione', on oath, are to be written down in some form, so that no 'licentia' should be given to treacherous people to get out of agreements, 'definitiones iudicum eludere'.

[15] *CT* 2.9.1 (the section on arbitration), 'Litigia sententiis vel transactionibus terminata non sinimus restaurari.'

[16] Cf. Aug. *Ep.* 33.5, 'et homines quidem causas suas saeculares apud nos finire cupientes . . . submisso capite salutamur, ut dissensiones hominum terminemus . . .'.

[17] *Dig.* 4.8.1, compromissum ad similitudinem iudiciorum redigitur et ad finiendos lites pertinet.   [18] *Dig.* 4.8.21.

identity and status of the arbiters and whose opinion should be valid, an especially important provision if the arbiters included a slave;[19] it should also set a time limit, within which the arbiter should reach a decision, although this could be extended under certain conditions.[20] If there was no mention of an heir, or reference by only one of the parties, the arbitration was broken off by the death of any party; questions of succession had not been considered when the arbiter first undertook his work.[21]

No-one could be compelled to act as arbiter[22] but once he had accepted the job, he was obliged to finish it, to avoid disappointing the disputants; prospective arbiters were entitled to make preliminary enquiries, before finally committing themselves. The arbiter could not be forced to give an award in the absence of a *compromissum*, as that document was a precondition of the whole settlement,[23] nor could he exceed the terms laid down in it.[24] There also existed general restrictions on who could act as arbiters. Although slaves were not debarred, wards in guardianship (*pupilli*), the mad, the deaf and the dumb were excluded.[25] Likewise, none of the excluded categories could act as parties to a dispute, because they were not capable of showing understanding of the arbiter's award; in particular, Ulpian, following Salvius Julianus, believed that a judgement affecting a ward should be delivered in the presence of the guardian.[26] On minors, Gaius further opined that an arbiter was not obliged to make an award at all, if a ward had referred a matter to arbitration without the guardian's consent; the irresponsible *pupilli* could not be held liable, if they lost, or broke the terms of the arbitration.[27]

Arbitration was binding, on moral grounds: the parties had chosen the procedure and agreed on the arbiter. But, if the moral sanction proved

---

[19] *Dig.* 4.8.8 and 17.

[20] *Dig.* 4.8.14; also *CT* 11.30.63, where the emperor specifies time-limits for arbitrations in near or distant provinces in the East, a signal that individuals' discretion over time-limits, agreed by them with the arbiter, was being usurped by the state.

[21] *Dig.* 4.9.1; 4.27.1.

[22] *Dig.* 4.8.3.1, 'tametsi neminem praetor cogat arbitrium recipere quoniam haec res libera et soluta est et extra necessitatem iurisdictionis posita'. [23] *Dig.* 4.8.11.

[24] *Dig.* 4.8.32.21.

[25] *Dig.* 4.8.9. Ulpian also thought that priests should not be expected to act as arbiters, unless they received a priesthood after agreeing to take a case. His pious justification, that priests should be free for their divine duties, anticipates that of Constantine for privileging the clergy: 'id enim non tantum honori personarum sed et maiestati dei indulgetur, cuius sacris vacare sacerdotes oportet'. He would doubtless also have disapproved of bishops acting as arbiters, on similar grounds.

[26] *Dig.* 4.8.27, 'item coram pupillo non videri sententiam dictam, nisi tutor praesens fuit'.

[27] *Dig.* 4.8.35. Relevant to this is Constantine's failure to think through the consequences of his granting of permission to minors at *CS* 1.3 to take disputes to *episcopales audientiae*, leaving the bishop and his opponent with no obvious means of enforcing the judgement. See below, pp. 196–7.

inadequate, adherence to the terms of the *compromissum* and the final outcome was enforced by the fixing of a penalty (*poena*), which could be expressed as money or in some other way and could, theoretically, exceed the value of the objects in dispute. The jurisdiction of the state could therefore become involved at the point at which forfeiture of the *poena* by a party became a possibility, because the procedure had broken down due to actions by the arbiter or his clients. The jurists therefore spent much effort on picturing situations in which the arbiter might repeal, or be unable, to make his award, such as if one party was declared bankrupt and could therefore neither sue nor be sued.[28] They also had to anticipate occasions when one or more of the parties might break the terms of the *compromissum* 'with impunity', that is, without forfeiting the *poena*. They did not always agree. What should happen to the *poena* if, for example, one party decided to abandon the arbitration and take the case to court? Paulus, whose opinion was, by implication, endorsed by Tribonian by virtue of its inclusion in the *Digest* held, against others, that the *poena* was forfeit and could be recovered by application to a judge in the normal way, because, if the *poena* were not forfeit, it would enable someone who regretted his acceptance of a *compromissum* to escape the conditions to which he had signed up.[29] That principle was still observed by the emperors of 381, who ruled that either an arbitration agreement should be honoured, or the *poena* should be exacted, before the formal civil hearing took place.[30] Still less could the parties abandon their first choice of arbiter and try another; as Paulus observed, if that happened, a case could be prolonged indefinitely.[31] However, the *sententia* of the arbiter could be overturned, if deliberate fraud could be proved against him by one of the parties; in a case involving a mother and daughter, Diocletian and Maximian allowed the exemption on grounds of 'sordes vel evidens gratia', corruption or blatant bias, although they also urged the parties to sort out their differences independently.[32]

---

[28] *Dig.* 4.8.17, 'cum neque agere neque conveniri possit'.

[29] *Dig.* 4.8.30, 'sed si hoc obtinuerit, futurum est ut in potestate eius quem paenitet compromisisse sit compromissum eludere', cf. *CT* 11.31.9 (23 March 423), which envisages appeals from arbitration.

[30] *CJ* 2.4.40, 'Ubi pactum conscriptum est atque Aquilianae stipulationis vinculis firmitas iuris innex, aut gestis secundum legem adcommodandus est consensus aut poena (una) cum his, quae data probabuntur, ante cognitionem causae inferenda est.'

[31] *Dig.* 4.8.32.16. This prohibition applied, of course, only to arbitrations recognised by the law. If parties colluded in time-wasting by resorting to a string of informal arbiters, without recourse to the law, that was their business.

[32] *CJ* 2.55.3 (11 Jan 290/93), 'Arbitrorum ex compromisso sententiae non obtemperans, si sordes vel evidens gratia eorum qui arbitrati sunt intercessit, adversus filiam tuam agentem ex stipulatu, exceptione doli mali uti poteris. Sed et ex doli clausula, quae compromisii stipulatione subici solet, filiam tuam convenire non vetaberis.' Like petitions, to be discussed below (pp. 184–7), the mother's appeal to the emperors and threat of

The jurists' guidelines sought to ensure that arbitration did its job, that it finished the case. However, as they also acknowledged, the law's interest in it was carefully circumscribed. In practice arbitration was flexible and not bound by the constraints of normal jurisdiction. How it operated in practice therefore depended entirely on the conventions accepted by the parties, which could be shaped by local customs, consistent with the minimal Roman rules but with characteristics of their own.

Egypt, as so often, shows a local system in operation. By the third century, the setting up of an arbitration in Egypt required two written documents. The first was the agreement between the parties to choose an arbiter and abide by his decision (*pactum compromissi*). The crucial sections of this document declared the existence of a dispute, the intention of both parties to employ an arbiter, their agreement to observe his judgement and penalty clauses and/or an oath, along with the formula of stipulation and the signature of the *notarius*. Other details, recommended for inclusion by the Roman jurists, also sometimes appear: the date of the hearing, the date of the judgement or the making of the award, and the naming of the witnesses.[33] The second was less formal but also essential, the written agreement of the arbiter to act (*receptum arbitri*). Approaches to the arbiter could be made by one or both parties, asking him to initiate proceedings and explaining their reasons for wishing him to act. In third-century Theadelphia in the Arsinoite nome, one Heroninos wrote to Aurelius Heracles, asking him to act as arbiter in a dispute over an ass and to summon his opponent Pesuas to a hearing; this would avoid resort to court proceedings before the *strategos* or local judge,[34] a motive also advanced by two female disputants from Euergetis in AD 300, whose suit over 3000 drachmas was arbitrated by two priests, again to avoid court proceedings.[35] Once procedures and arbiter were agreed, the arbiter formally summoned the defendant to appear (as Heracles was expected to summon Pesuas), the parties argued their cases, perhaps employing more articulate or legally trained friends as advocates, and evidence was produced in the shape of documents, witnesses and experts, as would have happened in a formal trial. Then, or on a later occasion, the arbiter made his award.

If no further hitches occurred, the dispute was formally concluded with the drafting of yet another written document by one or both parties, the *dialysis*, which recorded what had been agreed and how the agreement had been reached. Modrzejewski's dismissal of the *dialysis* as 'a superflu-

---

challenge on grounds of *dolo malo* could be strategies to force a more favourable settlement.   [33] On all this, see Modrzejewski (1952) 241–3.   [34] *P. Giss. Univ.-Bib.* 3.27.
[35] *P. Berl. Möller* 1, although one party, Didyma, had already petitioned the Prefect of Egypt, probably as part of a strategy to force her adversary to settle.

ity characteristic of the Byzantine legal style, the written or even tacit acceptance of the decision bringing the same legal consequences'[36] does scant justice to the social workings of small-town litigation, or to the deviousness of disputants prepared, at need, to falsify the record – if no such record existed. A written document, properly drafted, could help to preclude the reopening of a dispute later by interested parties or their heirs, who could ignore or 'forget' the original decision.[37] Moreover, the creation of the *dialysis* is significant for the expansion of a culture of the written word beyond the confines of the imperial bureaucracy; the activities of the creators of records and archives in Constantinople were being imitated by the small-town litigants of the provinces.[38]

Most documents relating to the handling or settlement of disputes, such as petitions, or requests for arbitration, give only a part of the history of a dispute, and do not reveal how, or if, it was concluded. *Dialyseis,* because they record the course of the dispute, as well as its settlement, are the exception. We meet the parties, who were often members of the same family, perhaps children of the same father in dispute over the division of the inheritance; three brothers, for example, Aurelii Horion, Eudaimon and Eulogios, all sons of Dionysios, agreed in 326 to end their dissension and share out their father's property in lots, which are clearly specified in the *dialysis.*[39] Women are prominent in these documents, opposing each other or taking on male opponents with equal gusto. Such women could act for themselves, if *sui iuris,* 'by the right of three children, according to Roman law',[40] or through agents, often their husbands.[41] The arbiters in the papyri were men prominent in the community: a deputy *epistrategos* acted over a disputed sale at Oxyrhynchus;[42] in the late third century, two senators of Oxyrhynchus ruled in a dispute over recovery of a bequest; and the case in Euergetis between two women, Aurelia Didyma and Aurelia Heracleia, was brought to a hearing before two identically named priests, both called M. Aurelius Besarion, but in charge of different shrines. In the sixth century, we find a *scholastikos,* Mark, involved in sorting out a dispute between a mother and son.[43] Given that invitations to act as arbiters were a form of recognition of social status, it was inevitable that bishops and other clergy would also become involved – with confusing consequences. Bishops had long acted as dispute-settlers

---

[36] Modrzejewski (1952) 255.
[37] On the attempt of the daughters of Kopres to quarrel with an agreement over land, to which they had given written consent, see below, p. 186.
[38] For parallels in early mediaeval England, see Clanchy (1993).
[39] *P.Princ.* 2.79, containing the first use of *diaeresis* for this form of settlement.
[40] *P. Berl. Möller* 1. Although all litigants in Egypt were now Roman citizens, the phrase, which is formulaic, conveys a continuing sense of the exotic 'otherness' of Roman law.
[41] E.g. *P.Oxy.* 36.2768.   [42] *P.Oxy.* 12.1562.   [43] *P.Mon.* 6 (AD 583).

for their own flocks, in a manner of little interest, because irrelevant, to the outside world, but, as they acquired greater social prominence, the familiar identity of the arbiter, or *mesites*, which could mean mediator or arbiter, would come to be conflated with the equally traditional but, until the fourth century, peculiarly Christian role of the bishop as the adjudicator or reconciler of the disputes of Christians in the context of the *episcopalis audientia*.[44] That other form of Christian adjudicator, the St Antony-style holy man, is conspicuous in the papyri – by his absence.

Augustine's observation of his own disputatious fellow-citizens at Hippo, that their worries were for 'gold, silver, farms and herds'[45] could be applied with equal truth to Roman Egypt. Didyma and Heracleia of Euergetis were in dispute over a sum of money allegedly owed by one to the other,[46] as also, nearly two hundred years later, were members of the clergy at Lycopolis in 481.[47] Inheritances,[48] the recovery of property,[49] the ownership of moveable goods, such as clothes, pillows or linen, or the contents of a house[50] are recorded subjects of arbitration. The fine detail required of these documents by the late fifth century is illustrated by the inventory of the wardrobe and linen cupboard of Theophilos the deacon, recovered through arbitration: 'a man's sleeveless tunic, one Egyptian cloak, one Egyptian cape, one rose-white tunic, two damask pillows, one dark-coloured mattress, one honey-coloured dalmatic, one ... blanket, two small heavy drapes, five embroidered tunics, one mallow-coloured garment, one plain tunic for a man, two linens for men, seven napkins and towels from Scinepoeis, one small cushion from Scinepoeis, one Damasus shirt, ten scarves, two suitcases, one large sheet from Scinepoeis, one ... from Scinepoeis, one napkin, one carpet bag (?), three new "linens", two other linen-wool blends, one woman's embroidered face-cloth (etc.)'.[51] Theophilos, who must have kept a careful record of his own of the misappropriated goods, was to insist on the last detail of his rights.

The path to arbitration was often rough, and the *dialysis* documents are perhaps at their most revealing of the social mechanisms of the handling and settling of disputes, when they record the complex manoeuvres engaged in by a party to force the issue. When Myronous, also known as Ptolema, acting through her husband, Theon, took on the brothers Harsiesis and Harsas, sons of Petosiris, late in the third century, her first move was to take her case to the *archidikastes* for investigation; only after this did all parties agree to go to arbitration and reach a settlement, in

---

[44] See below, pp. 192–5. For bishops as arbiters or mediators, see *P. Lips.* 43 = *M. Chr.* 98 = *FIRA* III pp. 174–6; *P. Oxy.* 6.903; *SB* 7449 = *Lond. Inv.* 2217.

[45] Aug. *Ep.* 33.5, see below, p. 204.   [46] *P.Berl. Möller* I.   [47] *SB* 7033 = *P. Princ.* 82.

[48] *P. Princ.* 2.79; *PSI* 12 1256.   [49] *P. Oxy.* 36. 2768.

[50] *P. Lips.* 43 = *M. Chr.* 98 = *FIRA* III, pp. 174–6.   [51] *SB* 7033 = *P. Princ.* 82.

which Myronous was awarded one talent and five hundred drachmas of silver.[52] Similarly Aurelia Didyma took her complaint against Aurelia Heracleia before the Prefect of Egypt; this was enough to force the other side to come to terms 'without taking the matter to a court of law'.[53] Late in the fifth century, too, the socially and economically weak could still bluff a superior with a threat of legal action combined with scandal: the deacon Theophilos of Lycopolis had promised to arrest his bishop, Cyrus, and bring him before a judge, unless Cyrus paid him the money he owed first.[54]

The Lycopolis *dialysis* of 481 is one of the longest and fullest to survive,[55] although part of its impressive length is owing to its habit of using three words where one would do. The course of the two disputes dealt with in the document was complex, and the outcome, a victory for the apparently weaker party, is perhaps surprising, given prevalent assumptions among historians about the advantages in such conflicts enjoyed by the wealthy and powerful. The document is virtually complete and all the features expected of the arbitration procedure are present.

Theophilos, deacon of Lycopolis, pursued two suits simultaneously, the first against bishop Cyrus, for a debt of money, the second against two priests, Daniel and Areion, who were brothers in a secular as well as a religious sense, for the return of clothes, linen and other moveable property, which the two had disposed of, or sold, to an unnamed third party. Neither bishop nor priests were initially prepared to co-operate, so Theophilos, undaunted by their superior clerical rank, announced his intention of taking the priests before Makarios, *synegoros*, collector of the taxes in the Thebaid, probably formally as a judge, and Cyrus, under arrest, to a formal court. The priests were the first to crack and agreed to go before Makarios, not as a *iudex*, but as arbiter, and an agreement was drafted, resembling a *pactum compromissi*, in which were specified a time-limit and a penalty for non-compliance. All this left the bishop stubbornly isolated. Goaded by 'sharp reminders' from the deacon, Cyrus 'humbled himself' to accept whatever award was made by the arbitrators, Makarios and, a new figure, Sabinus.

Theophilos' determination paid off. The arbiters' award seems to have gone in his favour on both counts. Cyrus undertook to pay 'sixteen (16)' gold pieces in settlement of his debt and the two priests agreed to hand back Theophilos' clothes, sheets, blankets, napkins and pillows, as specified. On these conditions, all possibility of the parties' bringing any suit

---

[52] *P. Oxy.* 36. 2768.   [53] *P. Berl. Möller* 1.   [54] *SB* 7033 = *P. Princ.* 82, pp. 78–80.
[55] For full text and discussion, see Dewing (1922), with modification of opening lines of text (1934).

against each other was ended. The agreement was tied up, with statements from the arbiters, that this ended the dispute; from the parties, that
they had no further claim against each other; and agreement to a supple-
mentary penalty clause, referring, not to the procedure but to the award
itself, that anyone who broke the agreement would pay 'thirty-six (36)'
gold coins to those who adhered to it, a punitive sum, more than double
the debt owed by Cyrus to Theophilos. The parties were formally asked
for their assent and agreed. All the participants then signified their assent
in writing, but that of Theophilos was not in his own hand: one Claudius
Heracleides wrote Theophilos' acceptance in his presence and at his
dictation, 'as he is illiterate'.

Behind the formal, ornate and occasionally turgid record of this *dialysis*
can be glimpsed a conflict in which social status, public reputation and
attempted abuse of power all had a part. Theophilos' just claims were at
first resisted by three men who were his superiors in the church hierarchy
and who could, potentially, frustrate his further advance in the church.
They were also his betters educationally; they could write, he could not.
Bishop and priests seem to have colluded to shield each other and deprive
a weaker associate of his rights; while Cyrus' debt was legally incurred and
his failure to pay one of omission, the priests must have engaged actively
at some point in the removal of property not their own. All three only gave
way when Theophilos proved by his threats of legal action that he set
greater store by his property than any pressures they might exert; significantly for the reputation of late Roman justice, so often maligned,
Theophilos, despite his relative poverty, could have some hope of a just
outcome. He was also capable of moral and social blackmail. A bishop's
influence with his congregation depended on his moral authority and a
bishop in court (and in the wrong) would have counted for little with his
congregation thereafter. Indeed, Cyrus seems later either to have regretted his initial obstinacy, or to have been seriously alarmed that the affair
would damage his reputation. He therefore, of his own accord, offered a
further sum of money to the third parties in whose hands the garments of
Theophilos, abstracted by the priests, now were. This generous act,
praised as such in the *dialysis*, may well have been hush-money, delivered
to the third party, either as compensation for a purchase made in good
faith, or as a silencer to hide the fact of dealings with receivers of stolen
goods.

For the historian of Late Antiquity, the whole affair has a salutary
message. It was possible, given the right combination of character and
circumstances, for a dispute between a relatively poor man and richer and
more powerful adversaries to have a just outcome. This comprehensive
defeat of the rich(er) by the poor(er), the social superiors by the social

inferior, the powerful and literate by the relatively helpless and illiterate illustrates the real complexity of small-scale social conflicts. Power, wherever it was dependent on a reputation for fairness, could not be abused arbitrarily, without being itself diminished, and the social expectations, the so-called 'consensus universorum', which underpinned the authority, especially of a bishop, within the community, limited the degree of freedom with which that authority could be exercised – or abused.

Petitions and disputes

As we have seen in earlier chapters, petitions forwarded to the emperor, or, more accurately, the central administration, could generate rescripts enabling a case to proceed to trial and sometimes offering a ruling on a point of law. However, the aim of the small-town, or village, petitioner was not primarily to contribute to the reform or refinement of the *ius civile*. Indeed, he or she may have hoped not to end up in court at all. Where extensively used, as in Roman Egypt, petitions were clearly one means among many for seeking an advantage in a dispute with neighbours or family. A declared willingness to go to law might act as a form of pressure to bring the other side to negotiate, rather than litigate, and thus conclude the dispute by informal means, sooner than incur the expense and risk of a legal hearing.

Petitions were therefore generated by often complex local situations and transmitted to administrators with no knowledge of the context in which they originated. Handling petitions and issuing rescripts was the never-ending job of the imperial and provincial secretariats, and experience of the deviousness of some petitioners would have suggested caution. Many petitioners therefore received a reply which did no more than refer the case to a lesser court, without offering any legal ruling. What the bureaux could not do was comment on the accuracy of the facts as presented, nor could officials be aware of the overall context of disputes, (although it may be assumed that they were well aware that they did not have the whole picture). The job of the administration was limited to stating the rules, where applicable, and moving the official judicial process forward, although it was then up to the petitioner to decide whether or not to take the matter further.

As evidence for the nature of disputes, petitions by supposedly wronged individuals addressed to people in authority are highly suspect. Isolated from their wider context in disputes, of which the reader is ignorant, the texts of petitions resemble one detail in a painting, of which the rest is lost. How did the dispute originate? We may have the petitioner's account, but how accurate is it? What case might be advanced by

the other side, at a hearing or through counter-petitions?[56] What was the
context of the petition in the course of the dispute as a whole? Was it an
opening gambit? A device resorted to in order to force a settlement by
other means? A last, desperate attempt to win justice? What was the
outcome? A decision by the addressee? A referral to another adjudicator
for trial or arbitration? Was the matter dropped? Or pursued by other
means? The absence of answers to most of these questions limits the value
of these documents for the history of dispute resolution. However, they
are richly informative as to the strategies adopted by the petitioner at the
stage when the petition was sent. Among those strategies is a second
reason for caution – the exploitation of highly coloured rhetorical language and stereotypes by the petitioner (or petitioner's advocate) to
further his or her cause and blacken the reputation of his/her opponent.
Facts, it was calculated, could be improved on by the insertion of moral
arguments and platitudes, a practice of which the emperors' and prefects'
edicts were such distinguished examples. The petitioner, therefore, was
invariably honest, hardworking and oppressed by the powerful (who
could be equated with the next-door neighbour); his opponents were
violent, greedy, unjust, 'totally evil'.[57] Naturally, therefore, the aggrieved
complainant fled to the protection of the magistrate and the laws; 'the
laws', wrote Isidore of Karanis, citing the wrongdoers by name, 'forbid
actions resulting in the ruin and flight of us, the reasonably well-off, and
now I myself, a man of moderate means in every way, suffer violence and
lawlessness at the hands of Heron, Pasios, Horian and Achillos...'.[58]
Isidore also claimed to be victimised by tax-gatherers, whom he (like the
emperors) believed were accountable to their superiors: 'often is it laid
down in the laws that no-one should be oppressed and extorted from ...
and Acotas has done this, not to collect taxes efficiently, but to dislodge
me from my property against the divine (= imperial) laws, having no fear
of my lord the eminent Sossianus Hierocles...'.[59] Similar indignation is
voiced by the redoubtable Taësis, daughter of Kopres, about a row
between her and her aunt and cousins: 'having endured violence and
lawless assault, and having been deprived of my goods by my father's
brother, Chaeremon, from the same village of Karanis, being unable to
put up with this, I have come to the protection of the laws ... they
attacked me with blows, [dragged] me around by the hair, tore my
clothing to pieces and left me lying on the ground...'.[60] Such language

---

[56] Cf. *P. Oxy.* 31. 2597 (late 3rd/early 4th C.), a letter from Cephalion in Alexandria to his
brother about his business; 'Your adversary is tireless in making petitions and so am I in
making counter-petitions.'   [57] *P.Cair. Isid.* 62.   [58] *P.Cair. Isid.* 68, 3–9.
[59] *P. Cair. Isid.* 69, 3–7. At id. 70.6. Acotas receives further unfavourable mention as
'lawless and reckless'.   [60] *P. Cair. Isid.* 63.

was universally employed and the reader, perhaps predisposed to believe in the oppressiveness of tax-collectors or other corrupt characters, should not be inveigled by the vehemence of the language of petitions into accepting uncritically the claims of their authors.

Female helplessness was another rhetorical topos, of great benefit to female petitioners. In the late 290s, young Taësis of Karanis, sometimes in the company of her sister Kyrillous, conducted a sustained campaign of petitions against her wicked paternal uncle, Chaeremon. At about the time of the accession of Diocletian, her father, Kopres, had died, leaving his property to his daughters, who were then minors. The girls were brought up by their mother's brother, Ammonios, while their father's brother, Chaeremon, cultivated the land and retained the moveable property and animals belonging to Kopres. On coming of age, sometime after 20 November 296,[61] Taësis submitted no less than three petitions about the inheritance to the *beneficiarius*, Gordianus. In the last of these,[62] she alleged that Chaeremon had stolen her inheritance and that there had been two orders of restitution issued by officials in response to her previous requests; now she had also been assaulted by Chaeremon's wife and daughters, from whom she had been rescued by two named villagers (who could also be cited as witnesses). In *c.* 298, Taësis was still going strong as, with Kyrillous, she requested from the *strategos*, Heron, the return of the moveable property left by her father, consisting of '61 full-grown sheep, 40 full-grown goats, 1 grinding mill, 3 silver talents, 2 artabas of wheat, and 2 slaves, of which he has sold a female one',[63] pointing out that Chaeremon had already ignored one previous order to hand the goods and animals back.

While the sisters may have had right on their side, they were far from destitute; the grazing lands required for the support of sixty-one sheep (not, of course, the original sheep of fifteen years before, but replacements) and forty goats would have been considerable. Nor may Chaeremon have been the villain he is painted. Taësis' petition to Heron concedes that Chaeremon did return their land, but implies that they were tricked; 'he handed over grain-bearing land to us, who are women and unable to pay the taxes on the land'. Tricked or not, Taësis and Kyrillous, or their guardian, had not objected to a deed of agreement, which also survives, between Chaeremon, its author, and the girls, then minors represented by their uncle Ammonios.[64] The facts behind it were that in 283/4, Kopres had left one aroura of land to his brother, the other to his daughters. For thirteen years, Chaeremon had cultivated both his share and that of his nieces, rent-free but with liability to tax. In 296, he

---

[61] *P. Cair, Isid.* 104, of that date, refers to the two sisters as still minors.
[62] *P. Cair. Isid.* 63.   [63] *P. Cair. Isid.* 64.   [64] *P. Cair. Isid.* 104, 20 November 296.

agreed that 'Taësion' and Kyrillous should cultivate the two arouras, his and theirs, for a further thirteen years on the same basis, after which his aroura would be returned to him; a formal note of agreement was drawn up, and Chaeremon signed it. This may have been followed by further negotiations on moveable property, as three days later a further agreement between five family members was drawn up, explaining who owned shares in two mortars, and all five signified their consent.[65]

Taesis' spirited occupation of the moral high ground should not obscure the real difficulties confronting all parties dealing with an inheritance bequeathed by its testator (assuming there was a will) some thirteen years before. Chaeremon's settlement with Ammonios as guardian over the land and the mortars seems to have been an intended final sorting-out of the estate, preparatory to the girls' coming of age, and could have been made in good faith. The ownership of the property not accounted for in Ammonios' settlements, the sheep, goats and other moveables, claimed by Taësis on her coming of age, may have been in dispute; Kopres' final disposition of his farm animals is not known and, in the extant petition, Taësis and Kyrillous did not cite the will as grounds for their claim. Neither party may have foreseen the (alleged) consequences for the grain-bearing arouras, if the women remained unmarried, but it was not in Chaeremon's long-term interest that the land should go out of cultivation, as he was due to take half of it back in 309. Whatever the final outcome, he, and his supportive womenfolk, must have welcomed the marriage of Taësis, a few years later, with another prosperous landowner, Heras, brother of Isidoros of Karanis,[66] through whose archive the documents pertaining to Taësis' struggle for justice were preserved.

Negotiation

Negotiation can usually be defined as private talks between parties aimed at reaching a mutually beneficial settlement. Such activities as the approaches made by Augustine to Donatists seeking to set up public negotiations on theology in the form of debates with opponents can therefore be set aside;[67] although his overtures were often couched in negotiatory

---

[65] *P. Cair. Isid.* 105. Of the five, only Chaeremon subscribes in his own hand; the other four are illiterate.

[66] Hence the survival of the documents relative to the Kopres inheritance. *P. Cair. Isid.* 6. 244, the Land Register for Karanis for 300 refers to 'royal' land of Heras, held by virtue of his wife, Taësis. They held or owned land at Ptolemais and Kerkesoucha, both villages dependent on Karanis. Later, in 316 (*P. Cair. Isid.* 59. 1–8, 33–43), Heras and Taësis together and Taësis separately acquire receipts for money paid for transportation on sea-going ships and other related charges; the same finds Kyrillous with lands in Ptolemais as an *epinemesis*, a cultivator of unoccupied land.   [67] See above, ch. 3 p. 73.

language, and contained many apparent preliminary concessions on venue, rules of debate and such, Augustine aimed, not to compromise, but to win. The law had no formal part in negotiations between parties, where agreement was reached by mutual consent, but it could be invoked at a later stage, if negotiations failed, or used as a bargaining tool. For negotiation was not necessarily an amicable or gentle process. The initiator of negotiations could appear to weaken his position by indicating a willingness to talk, which might be exploited by the other party. Therefore, it was important to the initiator to emphasise that he was negotiating from strength and, among other devices, the threat of legal action could be used to pressurise the other party into talks.

One example of such tough talking is a little-known letter from a North African landowner, addressed to one Salvius, who had laid claim to *coloni* employed on the author's estate.[68] Both disputants were advocates,[69] who had frequently conflicted with each other in the courts and had together picked up the kinds of law and procedures required to pursue their case over their disputed *coloni* .[70] For much of the letter, the author takes a tough line. Salvius was terrorising the author's unfortunate *coloni* by threatening to lodge a *petitio* for their restoration to him and, apparently, 'exhibit' them in court.[71] In spite of the *necessitudo*, (kinship or informal agreement) which bound the two together, Salvius was prepared to ignore the ties betweeen them and proceed as he chose; was there, then, the letter-writer asked, one law for advocates in post, and another for those retired from the bar, 'one law for Rome, another for Matari?'.[72] The author indicates his determination to resist and brings further pressure to bear, by introducing a complication over the control of part of the estate in dispute. The ownership of this part of the estate depended on complex dealings, involving the now deceased former owner, one Dionysius, a

---

[68] The *Ep. ad Salvium* is preserved among the *Spuria* of Sulpicius Severus in *CSEL* 1 (ed. Halm). This was drawn to my attention by A.J.B. Sirks, and , for a recent discussion in print, see Lepelley (1989).

[69] Africa was known for its advocates in antiquity, cf. Juvenal 7.148, nutricula causidicorum Africa. Cf. Aug. *Ennar. in Ps.* 136.3.

[70] *Ep. ad Salv.* 2 fateor, dum nos campus exciperet, me saepe armis eloquentiae tuae fuisse conterritum, sed frequenter, ut poteram, recidiva vulnera reponebam. Tecum sane condidici quo iure coloni quove ordine repetantur, cui conpetat actio, cui non conpetat exitus actionis.

[71] *Dig.* 10.4 is devoted to the *actio ad exhibendum*. The legal problem with this is that *coloni* were not slaves, therefore not moveable property eligible to be 'exhibited' in court. The law of Constantine of 332 (*CT* 5.17.1) allows *coloni* who are planning flight to be chained 'in the manner of slaves', but this provision does not seem to apply to those who have fled already, who are to be returned to their place of origin.

[72] Id. et is qui..mihi antiqua necessitudine sis copulatus, correpturum te homines meos, conventione neglecta temere minitaris. Quaero de insignia prudentia tua utrum ius aliud habeant advocati aliud ex togatis, an aliud aequum Romae sit, aliud Matari?

navicularius, along with a minor government official, Porphyrius, for whom the author had acted as *defensor* and advocate in a paternity suit against Porphyrius' alleged father, Zibberinus. This sub-plot, the details of which are obscure, saw the author active for his client both in court and before Zibberinus' family council. Clearly, family members were, as so often, using various legal and extra-legal means to achieve their goals, and, again as so often, the outcome was a compromise; Zibberinus allowed Porphyrius some 20 *iugera* of his land in settlement of his claim. Quite how Salvius was involved is not clear, but the informal deal was to his advantage. The drawback was that informal deals were vulnerable to legal challenge, and the author was clearly prepared to see it come unstuck, if Salvius would not agree to settle.

The letter, which is couched throughout in a difficult and rhetorical style, begins and ends with arguments favouring reconcilation after strife. At the outset, the author reminds his correspondent of the fact that advocates, charioteers and soldiers all seek rest and retirement after their exertions. These reflections pave the way for the main point of the letter, a concluding request to reach agreement through negotiation, out of court. Addressing Salvius as 'frater', (brother), the author urges him to join in a 'private conversation' ('privatum . . . colloquium'), and, in the meantime, to stop frightening his *coloni* or showing off. Lest Salvius delude himself that the author seeks negotiation because he has a weak case, this is explicitly denied; the author is not defenceless and knows his law. A final mention of the messenger, Maximinus, serves as a reminder that negotiation will not be confined to the text of the letter; the bearer also has a role to play in bringing Salvius round.

Brief and often allusive as this letter is, it encapsulates a variety of means of handling and resolving an accumulation of problems. No less than five people are involved in the possession and/or ownership of the estate and its *coloni*: the author, Salvius, the late Dionysius, Zibberinus and his questionable son, Porphyrius, and their exact relationship to each other and the estate is unclear. The author had acted as *patronus*, in both senses of the word, to Porphyrius in his long-running efforts to get something out of his father, both in the family council and before the state's *iudex*; the final outcome had been agreed, but could still be overturned, a reminder that agreements binding under Roman law had their advantages. The author's position of strength is emphasised: he is, or was, an advocate, he has stood up to Salvius in the past, he knows his law and will resist Salvius in the courts if need be. Throughout runs the moral tone characteristic of late antique communication. Salvius is guilty of frequent outbursts of anger ('frequenter iratus'), and of terrorising 'unhappy' *coloni*, which do not belong to him, and has exhibited 'iactantia' (empty shows of strength) and 'superbia' (arrogance). By contrast, the author exhibits both modesty – Salvius had frightened him too – and restraint, while acting as patron of the weak in a just cause. Whether or not the letter, plus the good offices of Maximinus the bearer, achieved the desired effect, is unknown. However, one may suspect that the letter itself, with its mannered style and moral tone, was not designed only for the recipient. Like the moral outpourings of the Egyptian petitioners, the letter of the African advocate was yet one more device to gain advantage in the conduct of a dispute.

Not all human relationships, then, which might have had a legal dimension, were governed by the written law of the state. The jurists knew that the law had its own frontiers and defined one such when they laid out the rules on arbitration and the extent of the state's involvement in an otherwise extra-legal settlement. There is no evidence that legally non-binding agreements were any less successful than those reached by due process of law. Indeed, the reverse may have been the case. Settlements concluded because all parties wished to reach agreement were more likely to last than arrangements imposed by one party on another through resort to the courts. A further incentive to resort to alternative methods of dispute resolution, apart from cost, was that a greater degree of compulsion existed in the state's processes than had been the case hitherto. The long-standing blurring of the distinction between the two forms of adjudicator, the *iudex* and the *arbiter*, both originally appointed with the consent of both parties, still underlay much of late Romans' dealings with each other. However, the assimilation of the *iudex* to the power of the state, was bound to widen the gap between the two, and make litigants less prone to accept the verdict of a judge imposed from outside rather than chosen by themselves.

Finally, it should be recalled that many disputants aimed to 'handle' their disputes to achieve maximum advantage for themselves, rather than reach a settlement. For outsiders who became involved, this was frustrating. Thus, while members of small communities devoted their energies to outmanoeuvring opponents, the energies of others – judges and arbiters in particular, but also serious negotiators – were devoted to the 'finishing' of disputes. While the law allowed limitless scope for ingenious delaying tactics (despite efforts to the contrary) both before and after the judge's decision, the great attraction of arbitration was that the arbiter's decision was supposed to end the matter. This, too, was the outcome expected from the new-style adjudicator, (who might also act as mediator), the Christian bishop.

Ancient lawyers and modern historians alike have found episcopal hearings difficult to categorise.[1] Because Constantine influenced the course of the history of Christianity in so many ways, the temptation has been, from Late Antiquity onwards, to ascribe especial importance to all aspects of his legislation, as it affected the Church, in particular to his two surviving laws on *episcopalis audientia*, which appear to give to bishops as judges powers superior to those of their secular counterparts, in that there could be no appeal from a bishop's verdict. But bishops were not only judges, who resembled their secular counterparts in that they tried to adjudicate in accordance with Roman law; they were arbitrators and mediators as well. Constantine's lack of sensitivity to the internal dynamics of Christian communities, as evidenced in other spheres, such as his failure to deal with schism and heresy,[2] was, it will be argued, equally apparent in his infliction on bishops of powers, which it would have been a social embarrassment to wield in the crudely authoritarian fashion envisaged by his laws, and for which, in their extreme form – the imposition of an inappellate verdict on reluctant litigants – there is no significant evidence in the sources at all. Indeed, what is significant about Constantine's legislation on episcopal hearings (to use the term the ancients used themselves), is that, as an attempt, either to empower or to regulate, it was of limited effect in the short term, not because bishops were to fail to take advantage of their powers as adjudicators over time, but because the laws were largely irrelevant to the daily operation of episcopal jurisdiction within the Christian community, as it functioned in the first part of the fourth century.

Part of Constantine's problem was that he seems to have had little understanding of how Christians had operated their internal systems of self-regulation before his time. Christian wariness of secular institutions

---

[1] For Valentinian III's attempt to do this in his Novella 35 of 452, see below, p. 202.
[2] Both the Donatist schism and the Arian heresy, the latter arguably the majority opinion in some parts of the Empire in the fourth century, originated under Constantine, and flourished for many years after his death.

had apostolic authority.[3] Bishops, once established as heads of their sees, clearly required powers to discipline their own clergy, and this remained true under Constantine and his successors. Distinct from that was the bishop's traditional role as a mediator and a reconciler of disputes between members of his congregation. In the third-century *Didascalia Apostolorum*, reworked in the fourth century, probably in Syria, as the *Constitutiones Apostolorum*, there were set out, among other matters, rules about how bishops should behave when trying to handle disputes between the Christian faithful. The language employed is that of healing, not judgement. The bishop is the physician of his flock and, if disputes arise, the bishop's first task is to act as mediator or go-between, and seek to reconcile the conflicting parties,[4] a role, as we have seen, to be sharply distinguished from that of judge, or even arbiter. Only if his negotiations and warnings against the dangers of anger had no effect, was the bishop to allow the case to go to him as judge. His authority extended, of course, only over Christians and his powers to enforce a decision concerning a dispute over, for example, property or some other 'civil' matter depended on the consent of the disputants, who, as members of his congregation, had implicitly accepted his right to hand down decisions on such matters. The sanctions open to him in disciplinary hearings were limited and effective only because regarded as serious by Christians themselves: these were, for the clergy, relegation and, for laymen, penance or, at worst, expulsion from the group (excommunication), a penalty regarded by believing Christians as worse than death, and described by Cyprian as execution by 'the sword of the Spirit'.[5]

Christian powers of jurisdiction over each other were confined to the clergy. A layman could not judge a cleric because that was not his job; 'for the burden of this responsibility rests, not with the laity but with the clergy'.[6] The exertion of episcopal authority in matters technically subject to his jurisdiction would have varied with the individual. Already, in the third century, some bishops could be accused of tyrannical behaviour, 'imitating officials and terrorising the poor'[7] but others prudently sought general agreement, at least for decisions that might create precedents; Cyprian of Carthage, when asked for his verdict on three misbehaving clergy, insisted that he should first consult his own clergy and whole congregation.[8] However Cyprian also asserted a bishop's right to control the membership and moral conduct of his congregation[9] and to use the

---

[3] Matt. 18.15–17 (disputes among followers of Christ to be settled without aid from secular institutions); I Cor. 6.1–8 (the 'saints' are better judges than the unjust).
[4] *Did./Const. Ap.* 2.41.3–9; 46; 53–4.   [5] Cyprian, *Ep.* 4.4, spiritali gladio.
[6] *Did./Const. Ap.* 2.37.2.   [7] Origen, *Matt.* 16.8.   [8] Cyprian, *Ep.* 34.4.
[9] Cyprian, *Ep.* 2, on a converted actor, whose membership is made conditional on his renunciation of his immoral profession.

full 'power of his office' to discipline those who challenged his authority.[10] This affirmation of clerical privilege, the right to judge in its own cases, was to prove of greater concern to bishops, in a post-Constantinian context, than their power to adjudicate over reluctant pagan, as well as Christian, laity. The separation of powers, initially motivated by Christian distrust of public *iudicia*,[11] was accepted down to the early fourth century by an indifferent state but acquired far greater significance when emperors began to regard the concerns of Christians as being also their own.

In the actual hearings of the pre-Constantinian Christians addressed by the author of the *Didascalia*, contemporary legal formalities were underpinned by a distinctively Christian ideology of reconciliation. If an episcopal hearing could not be averted by preaching at the disputants or by mediation, it was to be held on a Monday, so that objections to the bishop's verdict could be heard and the bishop negotiate further with all parties and reconcile them in time for the next Lord's Day.[12] Once the hearing had been convened, with the priests and clergy acting as the equivalent of the imperial or secular judicial *consilium*, the bishop should still seek to preserve *caritas* between litigants, although they should not be addressed as 'brothers', until peace had been restored between them.[13] The two parties should then be cross-examined, with much depending on their general moral characters. This focus on character, rather than the rights and wrongs of the cases advanced, is characteristic of the secular approach to justice; Aulus Gellius, the second-century author and former judge, and Callistratus, the Severan jurist, attached importance to the general character of litigants and witnesses, when assessing the strength of a case.[14] As in a secular court, witnesses were summoned and, in line with Roman practice, more than one was required to establish a point. However, whereas Roman trials could proceed in the absence of one of the parties, the Christian practice was that defendants should not forfeit their cases unheard, while the inward-looking nature of Christian 'hearings' is highlighted by the prohibition against testimony from pagans against 'one of us'.[15]

When proceeding to judgement, the bishop was to observe the care taken even by secular judges, whose practice is held up as a model to imitate: 'we make a clear distinction between the sacred and the things of this world. However, we do say; look, our brothers, how when murderers

---

[10] Cyprian, *Ep.* 3.3, fungeris contra eum potestatem honoris tui, et eum vel deponas vel abstineas.
[11] *Did./Const. Ap.* 2.45.1, advising bishops to do all they can to avoid the secular courts of the pagans ('gentiles').   [12] *Did./Const. Ap.* 2.47.   [13] *Did./Const. Ap.* 2.49.
[14] Aul. Gell. *NA* 14.2; Call. at *Dig.* 22.5.3.   [15] *Did./Const. Ap.* 2.45.2.

(adulterers, poisoners, tomb-robbers and brigands) are brought to trial by the power of the state, the judges conduct themselves with care, they ask questions and make enquiries about what they have done, and then again they say to the wrong-doer, "Is this so?" and, even though he confesses and admits the crime, they do not rush into sending him off to execution but over many days conduct a further enquiry about him, and, with the access curtain drawn, discuss the matter together and deliberate at length.'[16] Having taken his time, the bishop announced his decision and did his best to get the parties' agreement to it. The proceedings, obviously, carried more credibility if the bishop took account of the danger of false accusations which brought trouble on the innocent and affected the congregation as a whole. The risks to the Christian community posed by such trouble-makers were taken seriously; false accusers were to be excommunicated temporarily, until they proved the sincerity of their repentance, after which they were to be readmitted, with a warning. After a second offence there could be no return.

Although the *Didascalia* was pre-Constantinian, the reworking of the text in the fourth century serves to remind that Christian communities were not totally revolutionised by the imperial conversion but remained, in some respects, assertive of an ideology which was explicitly dissociated from that of the state and which established a religious and moral framework for the entire inner workings of the group, including its controls on its members' behaviour. Although some aspects of episcopal jurisdiction, such as the *consilium* of priests and deacons, multiple witnesses and the emphasis on character, echo practices in the Graeco-Roman world as a whole, the bishop's role as judge was to defy categorisation in Roman legal terms. He was clearly not strictly a *iudex*, in a secular juridical sense: he was not obliged to use Roman, or any other system of law; his judgements, even in 'civil' disputes, could not be enforced by any form of state authority, and the range of formal sanctions available to him was limited. Nor could he be defined as an arbiter in the senses recognised by the jurists, in that no formal agreement, *compromissum*, was required as a preliminary to set out the terms of the arbitration or stipulate a *poena* for non-compliance. Nor can his role be fully assimilated to that of a mediator. The bishop did mediate in the sense that he often handled disputes in which the law took no interest, by furthering negotiations between disputing parties till they agreed a settlement. This interpretation of his role is also consistent with the rhetoric of reconciliation employed concerning disputes by the leaders of the Church. However, in many, although not all cases, the source of the final decision over a dispute was not the parties concerned, as is required of mediation in its strict sense, but

[16] *Did./Const. Ap.* 2.52. The different types of criminal (adulterer etc.) are specified only by the *Constitutiones* and reflect the standard fourth-century hit-list of capital crimes.

the bishop himself, nor was it appropriate that the mediator should be supported by so much of the apparatus of a formal legal hearing, the set day, the advisers, statements, cross-examination, witnesses, deliberations, and the issuing of a binding decision, taken by himself as adjudicator, not by the disputants themselves.

For Christians before Constantine, these problems of definition were irrelevant. The system worked in practice as did many extra-legal forms of settlement. Where the Christians differed from others who picked arbiters or mediators to help them was that the bishop's role was institutionalised and his right to adjudicate or mediate derived from his office. Ultimately, however, the bishop's effectiveness in his hearings, as elsewhere, depended on the respect accorded him and his office by his congregation and the consequent pressure exerted by the group on individuals to accept his decisions. Thus the difficulty of placing the bishop in any one of the accepted categories of dispute-settler became a problem only when the law of the state began to interest itself in the hitherto effective but extra-legal practices of the Church.[17]

Of the two extant Constantinian laws on *episcopalis audientia*, one is in the Theodosian Code, but excluded by Justinian, whose collection of constitutions on the subject began with Valentinian I. This constitution, the rubric and text of which are corrupt,[18] instructed the provincial *iudex* to allow an appeal to the 'episcopale iudicium', the episcopal court, from anyone wishing to refer a civil suit (*negotium*) to adjudication by the *lex Christiana*, a phrase best understood as judgement on Christian principles. This was to be permitted even if the secular trial had already started and the bishop's judgement was to be binding, but it was not (apparently) open to any one party to make a unilateral and unauthorised approach to the bishop or sabotage the proceedings supervised by the secular *iudex*.[19] The language of the constitution, insofar as it survives intact, is elaborate (as one might expect) and, perhaps because of damage in transmission, obscure. No distinction is made between court jurisdiction (*iudicium*) within the legal system and the less formal procedures of arbitration, in which the law took, as we have seen, a limited interest. Constantine's legal draftsman uses the words interchangeably, referring to both episcopal and secular lay jurisdiction as 'iudicium' and the decisions reached by both as 'arbitrium'.

---

[17] For discussion of textual points and legal status of *episcopalis audientia*, see esp. Selb (1967), Vismara (1987).

[18] *CT* 1.27.1 was 'given on 23 June at Constantinople' (i.e. not before the city's foundation in 330) in the consulship of 'the Augustus and Crispus Caesar', i.e. before Crispus' execution in 326, perhaps 318.

[19] The text is not easy here: ita tamen, ne usurpetur in eo, ut unus ex litigantibus pergat ad supradictum auditorium et arbitrium suum enuntiat. Iudex enim praesentis causae integre habere debet arbitrium, ut omnibus accepto latis pronuntiet.

This example of imperial fudging of two related but distinct procedures has been faithfully echoed by historians of Constantine from Sozomen to the present. Sozomen, writing *c.* 440 in Constantinople, used a full version of the Theodosian Code, which may have contained a constitution, now lost, but similar to that preserved now as Sirmonidian Constitution 1, to be discussed below. Relying on its authority, Sozomen stated that Constantine, 'permitted litigants to refer their suits to judgement by the bishops, if they wished to appeal from the secular judges, that their verdict should prevail and be superior to that of other judges, as if it were delivered by the emperor himself, and that their officials should put the judgements into effect'.[20] MacMullen, despite warnings against fuzziness delivered elsewhere, is equally sweeping; 'episcopal courts were soon authorized to hear any civil case, by change of venue from other courts and without right of further appeal. They became, that is, courts of last instance.'[21] Given the use of such terminology by the ancients themselves, we should not perhaps worry about when or if to refer to episcopal 'courts' or 'judgements'. However, the danger in so doing should be evident from what has been said above about the versatility of the bishop's role in dispute resolution; the bishop was not only a 'judge', despite the legal paraphernalia of his 'court'. Moreover, a consequence of implying too close a parallelism with the jurisdiction of the state is that, inadvertently, concepts may be imported into our view of what bishops were actually doing as adjudicators which applied to the state's *iudicia* and *iudices*, but which are inappropriate for the actual workings of bishops' hearings or the religious framework within which they functioned.

It may, however, have been true that Constantine, perhaps unintentionally, did assimilate episcopal to secular *iudicia*, without appreciating the likely consequences. To redefine episcopal jurisdiction as equivalent to that of secular judges, at this early stage in the conversion of the Empire, would have raised a host of practical problems. What sanctions could the *lex Christiana* impose on recalcitrant pagan litigants, for whom excommunication held no terrors? What would happen if bishops took to issuing rulings, from which there could be no appeal, which contravened Roman law and, in particular, imperial constitutions? Blithely indifferent to these snags, the Christian emperor pressed on, even though his own Christian supporters may have had their doubts. The first Sirmondian Constitution is a characteristically brusque response to a question from Ablabius, Christian Praetorian Prefect of the East, about whether he had correctly understood Constantine's policy. It refers to a previous edict, part of which may have been in the Theodosian Code as seen by Sozo-

---

[20] Soz. *HE* 1.9.   [21] MacMullen (1972) 160.

men, which declared that the verdicts of bishops could not be challenged. Anyone could take an action to a bishop, even a minor. Ablabius was to enforce their decisions. A case could be referred to a bishop, if only one of the parties requested it, even if the other did not. Appeal from a bishop was not allowed. Moreover, if a bishop offered testimony as a witness, his evidence should be decisive, 'for it is backed up by the authority of truth'.[22] The tone is assured, but Ablabius' doubts are understandable. Minors could not be held liable, if they acted independently of their guardians; how, then, could a bishop (or any other judge) make an award against them? Secondly, the ruling that enabled referral of a case at the wish of only one of the parties ran counter to the principle fundamental to all forms of arbitration, that the arbiter was able to act because he had the consent of both parties. Thirdly, the privileging of the single witness of a bishop violated the accepted rule, that more than one witness was required to substantiate a case, a principle shared in common by Roman law[23] and, as we have seen, the rules followed by bishops' hearings – and which was to be reaffirmed by Constantine himself soon after.[24] Even without these faults of detail, the law as a whole was flawed. The ageing emperor's good intentions were undermined by his limited understanding, not only of legal principle but also of the constituency the legislation was designed to benefit. The response from the Empire at large was silence. The law had very little immediate effect, doubtless because it intruded on existing ways of dispute settlement which operated effectively within the Church and which accorded with its ideology of not imposing its will (in this area, at least) but of mediation and reconcilation. Because Constantine's law was at odds with the way bishops conducted their affairs, they may simply have ignored it.

Searches, therefore, for significant examples of mixed pagan-Christian hearings before bishops in the decades following Constantine's law to Ablabius are unproductive. One fourth-century example of an episcopal hearing, perhaps early, recorded on a papyrus from Hermopolis,[25] finds a nun, Thaësis, in dispute with characters of unspecified religious persuasion, described as the 'tenants of Besarion'. The dispute concerned, among other things, the contents of a house, which, on the order of the bishop, Plusianon, were split between the two parties. There is no indication that the tenants were pagan or that, if they were, they had opted for the bishop as arbiter under duress. For 'arbiter' he clearly was, not

---

[22] *CS* 1.2, *illud est enim veritatis auctoritate firmatum.*   [23] *Dig.* 22.5.12.

[24] *CJ* 4.20.9 (of 334).

[25] *P. Lips.* 43 = *FIRA* III, pp. 574–6. L. Mitteis, the editor of *P. Lips.* 43, pp. 147–8, linked the text with *CS* 1, as extending episcopal jurisdiction to the laity. Given the 'mixed' consilium of the bishop and arbitration procedures already in use in Egypt, this is too legalistic a view.

'judge'. The dispute is labelled by the rare Greek word *diaite* (spelled in the papyrus *diete*), meaning arbitration, the arbitration award made by Plusianon is also described as such, *to dietetikon*, and the group in whose presence the hearing was conducted consisted, predictably, of a deacon, but also of a lay local councillor, Dioskorides. There is clearly a Christian context to the hearing – the nun, the bishop, the deacon, the location of the hearing in the outer court of the local church – but, even without Constantine's legislation, the bishop would, in many communities, have been a prominent figure, to whom local people may well have resorted, informally, for resolution of their disputes with neighbours.

It should also be remembered that Egyptian villagers conducted their lives according to their own far from simple rules and changed only slowly. Thus bishops' determination to discipline their own people might have come as news to the two petitioners who denounced a priest to a local Oxyrhynchite senator.[26] The priest, allegedly, had taken possession of the petitioners' house and land, while they had been absent as fugitives. When 'with good reason we asked him to hand them over, he refused', and the senator (not the local bishop) is requested to exert his authority and order the squatter to move out. Even members of the clergy, in the 340s, did not invariably resort to their, or a, bishop for redress. A deacon, Zoilus, from Theadelphia, whose family's dealings with his fellow-villager, Sakaon, have already come to our notice, was the alleged victim of a series of violent acts by Sakaon, including the kidnap of his daughter-in-law, assault on his son and the theft of livestock. Instead of resorting to a bishop, Zoilus at first took no action, 'intending to avail myself of the proper course of the laws', then, on 6 April 343,[27] petitioned the *praepositus pagi*. His choice may, of course, have been due to his wish to raise the stakes by involving officialdom and to nail Sakaon on a criminal charge, an area in which his bishop could do little, but the sidelining of the bishop, in a case where a deacon's rights were, apparently, at stake, suggests that he was not, as yet, accepted as a universal troubleshooter, even by his own clergy.

Instead of a revolution in judicial procedures, traditional preoccupations continued to prevail. The Catholic Church in Africa in the mid-340s still concerned itself with its internal jurisdiction over clerics and lay Christians. At a Council in Carthage in 345 or 348, Gratus, the bishop of Carthage delivered, to the unanimous agreement of his fellow-bishops a series of rulings. What took up the attention of the African bishops were martyrs' graves (canon 2), the cohabitation of consecrated celibates with anyone other than a close relation (canons 3 and 4), restrictions on the ordination (canon 5) and the business transactions of clergy (canons 6, 8), and the prohibition of one bishop taking over the congregation of another

---

[26] *P. Wash.* 20, pp. 4–5. The unspecific, fourth-century date leaves open the slight chance that the incident predates Constantine's laws.   [27] *Archive of Sakaon* no. 48.

(canon 10). Laymen were forbidden to employ clerics as agents or managers of their property 'in violation of the imperial constitution' (canon 9), and neither clerics nor laymen were to take communion in a church other than their own (canon 7). In cases of serious disrespect to superiors or a dispute, a system of collective jurisdiction was to be employed, which safeguarded bishops from the awkwardnesses which could result from being judges in their own cases; a deacon would be judged by three neighbouring bishops, a priest by six[28] and a bishop by twelve (canon 11). This last, cautious provision, while conducive to greater fairness, was hardly symptomatic of an episcopate with the collective will to take on, as individuals, the civil and praetorian lawsuits of all-comers, as envisaged by Constantine. Nor were the penalties prescribed other than those traditionally available to a bishop dealing with his fellow-Christians: clergy who disobeyed the rules would be deprived of their office, laymen would perfom penance or be excommunicated. Thus the African church in the decades following Constantine was in spirit still that of the pre-Constantinian era, concerned for *ecclesiastica disciplina*, as applied to the Christian faithful, but with no apparent ambition to impose their jurisdiction, even with imperial backing, on the secular world.

While, as has been argued, the long-term importance of Constantine's laws on episcopal hearings may have been overestimated, the significance of the emperor Julian's repeal of all the laws giving judicial powers to bishops has not been appreciated at all. As we have seen, the fact that there existed already satisfactory systems of dispute resolution which could involve bishops, the potential for legal chaos present in the first Sirmonidian constitution, and the lack of any substantial evidence for its implementation along with counter-indications from Egypt and Africa, all invite the conclusion that Constantine's laws were not so much disobeyed as ignored. Morever, the repeal of the laws by Julian and their subsequent replacement by less sweeping and better reasoned legislation would suggest that the ultimate exclusion of Constantine's legislation from Justinian's Code[29] was no accident.[30] The motivation for Julian's

---

[28] Cf. Aug. *Ep.* 65, referring the case of the presbyter Abundantius to a council of 6 bishops, on grounds of immoral conduct on the Sabbath. The initiating bishop could make his view clear in advance; Augustine observes that the council may decide as it pleases but that he, personally, will now be reluctant to entrust a congregation to a man with a bad reputation.

[29] The section in the *CJ* on *episcopalis audientia* and related matters (*CJ* 1.4) begins with laws of Valentinian I and Valens.

[30] Their inclusion in the Theodosian Code (*CT* 1.27.1 and the law behind Soz. *HE* 1.9) could result from the intention expressed by the compilers of the Code, at *CT* 1.1.5 of March 429, to include past laws, whether valid or not, for their historical interest. Although I suspect this intention had been largely abandoned by 435, a number of laws do seem to have been included in the Code's collection of Christian legislation for their historical interest.

abolition of episcopal powers was straightforward. Whether activated or not, the existence of such powers was incompatible with Julian's notion of the place of Christian bishops in his new, non-Christian, Empire. Julian's abolition of Constantine's laws granting various powers to bishops was no empty gesture, and his justification, as delivered in a letter to the citizens of Bostra, was that these powers had been abused.[31] Responding to protests about violent disturbances in the city caused by the clergy, Julian reminded the Christians that his new law had rescinded the powers of those who 'have acted like tyrants..' and who now, 'yearning for their previous power, because it is not permitted to them to act as judges and to write wills and appropriate to themselves other peoples' inheritances and to allot everything to themselves,..they lead the people into conflict'. It is immaterial that Julian's rhetoric on bishops' abuse of secular judicial powers is not supported by independent evidence. Julian's intention was to remove the powers themselves, to weaken the Church overall, and his justification was their alleged abuse. Because, short-lived though he was, he was a legitimate emperor, the legislation of the Apostate was valid unless repealed (or lapsed because, in practice, ignored). He thus presented his successors with, in legislative terms, a clean sheet and a number of options. Valentinian and Valens could reinstate the legislation of Constantine, they could afford Julian's reversal of Constantine's laws tacit recognition, by doing nothing, or, also by doing nothing, allow it to lapse. Inaction, however, was seldom viable in practice, because of the Romans' habit of testing the policy of their legislators, especially on controversial matters. Valentinian and Valens, with whose legislation the section in Justinian's Code on episcopal hearings begins, were therefore obliged to take a stand.

In his summary of Valentinian's career and character, Ammianus Marcellinus praised the emperor for his neutrality on religious matters, and the tenor of his legislation on Christian matters in general bears this out. Where, for example, women were at risk from clerical legacy-hunters, Valentinian lent support to their kinsfolk in protecting them from unwanted intruders, and, on the question of the obligations of clerics who had fled from the baker's guild, he ordered that they should be recalled at any time, 'since the privilege of Christianity has been abolished'.[32] There is no evidence that Valentinian or his brother went out of their way to restore Constantine's contentious laws on episcopal hearings, a course that would surely have been viewed as gratuitously partisan. Instead, Valentinian followed a policy of upholding the traditionally separate quality of episcopal jurisdiction, ruling in a rescript, preserved

---

[31] Julian, *Ep.* 435D–38C.   [32] *CT* 14.3.11.

for polemical purposes by Ambrose, that like should judge like: 'in cases of faith or of any ecclesiastical rank, he who is neither unequal in office nor dissimilar in legal right should judge'.[33] This established the parameters of debate for the following decades. Gratian's law of 376 ruled on the place for the hearing of cases pertaining to religion and issued a reminder that, while Roman civil law and custom were to be observed in ecclesiastical hearings (not, incidentally, Constantine's nebulous *lex Christiana*), criminal cases were always to go to the secular courts to be heard by *iudices* or the courts of the praetorian or city prefectures ('illustres potestates').[34] The right of cases involving the clergy to be heard by bishops was also reaffirmed, perhaps in 384.[35]

By the end of the fourth century, more sustained and systematic attempts are found to assimilate episcopal hearings to the traditional frameworks of Roman judicial procedure. The drafter of Theodosius' constitution of 384 still believed in the complete segregation of episcopal from secular judicial procedures. The clergy had their own judges, he said, 'and nothing in common with public law – only insofar, however, as pertains to ecclesiastical cases which, it is proper, are decided by episcopal authority'.[36] This was not good enough for the increasingly professional lawmakers of Arcadius and Honorius. By 398, it was argued that episcopal jurisdiction could be assimilated to the procedure of arbitration.[37] Jewish courts, long recognised by the Roman state, provided a useful analogy and, in the same year, the emperors ruled[38] that if litigants agreed to go to the Jewish court and conduct their case using a *compromissum*, as required in cases of arbitration, they could do so 'in the manner' (*ad similitudinem*) of an arbitration, and the provincial *iudices* would enforce the awards, as if the 'arbitrators' had been assigned by the decision of a *iudex*. All this suggests that similar thinking was taking place

---

[33] Ambr. *Ep.* 21.2. Citation of this rescript to Valentinian II justified the bishop's contention (21.4) that, in matters of faith, bishops could judge concerning Christian emperors, but not vice versa.

[34] Symm. *Ep.* 3.36 to Ambrose strongly implies that the bishop was, in Symmachus' view, attempting to expand the scope of his jurisdiction illegally.

[35] *CS* 3, of Theodosius, date uncertain, addressed to Optatus, Praefectus Augustalis (of Egypt). Part of the law handles problems peculiar to the province, in particular that a judicial enquiry on 'Christian holiness' should be referred to the metropolitan bishop at Alexandria.

[36] *CS* 3, 'nomen episcoporum vel eorum, qui ecclesiae necessitatibus serviunt, ne ad iudicia sive ordinariorum sive extraordinariorum iudicium pertrahatur. Habent illi iudices suos nec quicquam his publicis commune cum legibus – quantum ad causas tamen ecclesiasticas pertinet, quas decet episcopali auctoritate decidi.'

[37] *CJ* 1.4.7, to Eutychianus, 27 July 398: 'Si qui ex consensu apud sacrae legis antistitem litigare voluerint, non vetabuntur sed experientur illius (in civili dumtaxat negotio) arbitri more residentis iudicium. Quod his obesse non poterit nec debebit, quos ad praedicti cognitoris examen conventos potius afuisse quam sponte venisse constiterit.'

[38] *CT* 2.1.10.

about episcopal hearings and, in 408, the idea was expressed again. The 'iudicium episcopale' was to be valid for all who agreed to be heard by *sacerdotes* (priests, bishops). As with arbitration, the agreement was essential. As private individuals could 'give a hearing' to consenting litigants, 'without the knowledge of the judge', it followed that bishops also could do so.[39] However, the second part of the constitution betrays continuing confusion over the relationship of bishops' hearings to *arbitria*, or *iudicia*. Episcopal decisions were inappellate, it seems, because they were to be held equivalent, not to the award of the arbiter (the authority of which derived from the agreement of the parties to go to him in the first place), but to the jurisdiction of the Praetorian Prefects from whom, as *vice sacra iudicantes*, appeals were not (in theory) allowed.[40]

If the conceptual thinking was, on occasion, confused, the trend towards assimilation of episcopal procedures to their secular equivalent was clear enough. Accusations brought against the clergy and heard before a bishop were to be supported by witnesses and documentary evidence, as in secular courts, and the same standards of proof were to apply.[41] But the parallel with arbitration procedures also remained plausible and, in 452, Valentinian III, with his Empire crumbling round him, made explicit the connection between episcopal hearing and arbitration by insisting on the preliminary formality of a *compromissum*, before clergy confronted each other in the presence of the bishop. The same was to apply to lay disputants, if they agreed, but, if they did not, then the bishops were unable to act as *iudices* at all, 'as it is agreed that bishops do not operate by our laws ('forum legibus non habere') and cannot conduct hearings except on religious matters'.[42] The impact of Valentinian's law is unknown. Three years later he was assassinated and bishops had more to worry about than the fine print of *compromissa*. Even had it achieved some status as an enforceable *lex generalis*, the formalities may have been beyond many disputants, although, as was seen in the Lycopolis dispute,

[39] *CT* 1.27.2.
[40] Id. 'episcopale iudicium sit ratum omnibus, qui se audiri a sacerdotibus elegerint eamque illorum iudicationi adhibendam esse reverentiam, quam vestris referre necesse est potestatibus, a quibus non licet provocare. Per iudicum quoque officia, ne sit cassa episcopalis cognitio, definitioni exsecutio tribuatur.'
[41] *CT* 16.2.41, extracted from *CS* 15, 3 December 412.
[42] *NVal.* 35. pr., 'Itaque cum inter clericos iurgium vertitur et ipsis ligatoribus convenit, habeat episcopus licentia iudicandi, praeeunte tamen vinculo compromissi. Quod et de laicis, si consentiant, auctoritas nostra permittit; aliter eos iudices esse non patimur, nisi voluntas iurgantium interposita, sicut dictum est, condicione praecedat, quoniam constat episcopos [et presbyteros]forum legibus non habere nec de aliis causis secundum Arcadii et Honorii divalia constituta, quae Theodosianum corpus ostendit, praeter religionem posse cognoscere.'

arbitration before a secular authority between a group of clergy could be preceded by something resembling a *pactum compromissi*. Moreover, the flexibility of the bishop as adjudicator or mediator would have allowed the formalities to be circumvented in practice. If the law had any effect, it would have been to undermine the effectiveness of the *audientia* in favour of less formal methods of dispute resolution, to which bishops, as mediators, were no less committed.

What all these attempts to legislate for episcopal hearings had in common, apart from interventionist zeal, was a hazy awareness on the part of the imperial lawyers that the versatility of the episcopal hearing had somehow to be constrained by regulations, which, while protecting bishops' authority, would also, in a sense, absorb the bishops' jurisdiction into a coherent overall system for the administration of justice, based on categories long observed and operated by the state. The failure of successive legislators to do so effectively resulted, not from their lack of sophistication, but from the uniqueness and individuality of the episcopal system of dispute resolution, which incorporated elements from the adjudication of both *iudex* and *arbiter*, but then combined them with patterns of behaviour based on ideals of reconciliation and mediation and rooted in the communal self-regulation of the pre-Constantinian Church.

Also rooted in the early history of the Church and fundamental to the ideal of the bishop as judge was the Church's duty towards the poor. In bishops' hearings the considerations which influenced secular judges – improper influence (*gratia*), power, wealth, standing and office – should (in theory) have had no effect. That principle could be expressed even in the imperial capital, where wealth and power were most concentrated. Ambrose' treatise on the duties of the clergy contrasted the values expected of the episcopal judge with those of his secular counterpart. In bishops' hearings, *gratia*, wrote Ambrose, had no place, the outcome would depend on the strength of the case, the clergy must not prefer the strong to the weak, or convict an innocent man because he was poor, while letting off a guilty party because he was rich. Yet he also acknowledged that pressures exerted by the powerful might be hard to resist. People in general (he said) were frightened of the resentment of the eminent, if convicted, but if that worried priests, they should not take on a case in the first place. True, a cleric might preserve a tactful silence, consistent with a fair outcome, where only money was involved, but where the interests of God were at issue, concealment was a heavy sin.[43] This is the voice of a man aware from his daily experience of dealing with

---

[43] Ambrose, *De Officiis* 2.24.125.

imperial courtiers that compromises on matters of principle had sometimes to be accepted. However, he could not have violated his stated
ideals too openly in his own court without forfeiting his credibility and
with it the trust of the Milanese 'poor of Christ'.

Reference to their various attempts to resolve disputes among their
clergy and congregations is not lacking in the correspondence of the
Fathers of the Church. Possidius claimed for Augustine that he worked so
hard in his court hearing cases brought to him by Christians and non-
Christians alike that he sometimes went for an entire day without food.[44]
Augustine himself, in a letter designed to calm the ruffled feelings of his
correspondent, described the men who wanted him to settle ('finish')
their secular cases, and how, each day, he was greeted respectfully by men
hoping for a favourable settlement and how it was his job to make them
live in earthly harmony with each other; 'not about gold, nor silver, nor
farms nor herds, on account of which things I am greeted daily with
bowed heads, that I may settle the quarrels of men, but about our very life
is this so shameful and destructive quarrel between us'.[45] Bishops also
remained responsible for the conduct of their clergy, and, among other
things, their relationships with each other. When Gregory of Nazianus
discovered that one of his deacons had tied up and punched a man whom
he claimed had injured him, Gregory ordered another deacon to investi-
gate, in the presence of both, and report back. The offender would be
invited to justify his assault but had also to accept punishment, 'for I will
not tolerate such disgraceful behaviour, virtually before my very eyes'.[46]

Although bishops often had to act as disciplinarians, the language of
mediation, intercession and reconciliation permeates the reports of Augustine and others on disputes in which, for one reason or another, they
took an interest. Both the flexibility inherent in the bishop's role and the
late-antique habit of employing a number of different strategies for the
handling of disputes permitted resort to more than one type of intervention. In a case already noted, when Faventius, *conductor saltus Paratianen-
sis*, was arrested, after seeking asylum with the church at Hippo, Augustine reacted by issuing a forceful reminder to the official responsible that
Faventius had a right to questioning by the municipality and a respite of
thirty days.[47] On learning that his client had already been removed to face

---

[44] Possid. *Vit. Aug.* 12.
[45] Aug.*Ep.* 33. 5: 'Non de auro, non de argento, non de fundis et pecoribus, pro quibus
rebus cotidie submisso capite salutamur, ut dissensiones hominum terminemus, sed de
ipso capite nostro tam turpis inter nos et perniciosa dissensio est.'
[46] Greg. Naz. *Ep.* 149 (as bishop, 382–3).
[47] Aug. *Ep.* 113, to 'brother' Cresconius, asking him to find out the whereabouts of
Faventius and paraphrasing laws protecting him, for which see *CT* 9.2.6 (21 Jan. 409),
plus earlier law on 30 days, *CT* 9.2.3 + 9.3.6 (30 Dec. 380). *Ep.* 114 is to the arresting

trial before the proconsul, Augustine communicated to the bishop, For-
tunatianus, in whose city the trial would take place, that the real reason
for his insistence on the delay of thirty days was that time might be bought
for an amicably mediated settlement.[48] Therefore, in order to create space
for the mediation to happen, Augustine asked that the hearing of Faventius' case be postponed, on grounds that the law had been broken, 'so that
by these means we can conclude the business with his opponent'.[49]

The personal authority of bishops encouraged them to behave more
like arbiters, in that as adjudicators they offered solutions, rather than
conducting themselves strictly as mediators by allowing the parties concerned to come up with solutions for themselves. However, even the most
assertive of bishops could be found confining themselves to mere good
wishes, in letters designed to encourage the parties to talk, rather than
litigate. Ambrose, for example, exploited a change in the tenancy of the
praetorian prefecture to urge one Tatianus, (whose case the change
favoured) to reach a negotiated settlement of a family dispute over a
marriage.[50] A number of reasons were put forward: negotiations were less
psychologically damaging than a court hearing; his correspondent, being
now in a stronger position, could offer negotiations out of family feeling
(*pietas*) not fear; the other side could no longer rely on the patronage of
the judge; his correspondent would rightly be influenced by ties of kinship, not the provocation of injury; and he would enhance his reputation
by being the first to offer negotiations. In the world of high politics, in
which Ambrose moved, his arguments may have had less significance
than the fact that it was he who wrote the letter.

Whatever their formal powers, in their capacity as mediators and
negotiators, bishops were often unwilling to impose settlements and
some, at least, understood that the aggrieved had to be reconciled.[51]
Thus, when Gregory of Nazianus was informed that a slave of a noble
member of his congregation had been forcibly ordained a priest by
inhabitants of a country district, and that the owner, Simplicia, had
lodged a protest, he had to take on the role of mediator, seeking to
reconcile Simplicia with the *fait accompli* and avoid her resorting to legal
action.[52] Gregory's letter on the matter had three aims. One was to allay

---

officer, Florentius, citing the law and ensuring he receives a copy. For this as evidence for
disobedience and enforcement, see above, pp. 92–3.

[48] Aug. *Ep.* 115, id utique existimans, quod per ipsos dies possumus fortasse causam eius
amica disceptatione finire...

[49] Aug. *Ep.* 115, 'ut per hoc possumus cum eius adversario rem finire'.   [50] Ambr. *Ep.* 52.

[51] See also Aug. *Epp.* 62 and 63 for his techniques in soothing the feelings of clergy after one
of their number has dithered disastrously over which of two bishops to serve; 'partem
obiurgando, partem monendo, partem orando correximus' (62.1).

[52] Greg. Naz. *Ep.* 79 (after early 374).

the anger of Simplicia, by admitting himself and others to have been wrong, but blaming Simplicia also for her lack of real charity. Secondly, he sketched out a negotiating position; Simplicia could join Gregory, if she wished, as a judge of the case, if any complaint was to be made, or else could accept a hearing in her absence. Thirdly, Simplicia was urged to avoid a confrontation before the law; 'do not despise our laws and flee to the laws of the world outside, do not confront us but forgive us, if we have taken short cuts through the freedom of our charity...' Here the episcopal mediator was not, of course, impartial. His aim was to have the ordination recognised and to avoid trouble with a wealthy patron. However, a mediator does not have to be impartial and, in deploying the arguments of charity and forgiveness, and opposing Christian values to those of the secular world, as well as by offering a form of redress through his own hearings, Gregory's core aim is clear; it was to end the dispute between Simplicia, the country people and her slave by reconcilation of the parties concerned.

Nor was Gregory expected to be impartial on another occasion, when asked by the governor, Olympius, to arbitrate over a father's insistence that his daughter should divorce from a husband she loved. Gregory shrewdly suspected that Olympius had passed him the case in order to get the result he wanted; 'I imagine your Generosity does not support the divorce as you entrusted the enquiry to me.' But, although Gregory and Olympius could act within the law to enforce Gregory's ruling, that the daughter remain with the husband, it nevertheless was also incumbent on the bishop to reconcile the father, Verianus, if he could, particularly as the father's rights under the 'laws of the Romans' were unclear.[53] However, reconciliation was no soft option and Verianus was left in no doubt where he stood:[54] Gregory would not accept a divorce, as his task was to forward union and friendship; he was backed by the governor; he would not condone the father's taking 'the worse course' and insisting on the divorce; the girl was too frightened of her father to speak freely. Although ostensibly designed to persuade, Gregory's letter to Verianus was not, this time, that of a negotiator. No compromise is offered, and there is the implication that Gregory, moved, perhaps, by having witnessed for himself the fear of the young wife, was prepared to counter the father's stubbornness with intimidatory tactics of his own.

Where situations became too delicate to be handled locally, bishops opted for referral of sensitive cases to outside authorities. This could be institutionalised, as in the decision of the Council of Carthage (345/8) to refer contumacious clergy, who could not be dealt with by their own

---

[53] Greg. Naz. *Ep.* 144. 4. Divorce was incompatible with 'our laws' (i.e. those of the Church) 'even if those of the Romans judge otherwise'.   [54] Greg. Naz. *Ep.* 145.

bishop, to boards of three, six or twelve bishops,[55] but it could also be individual choice. Gregory of Nazianus, for example, referred to bishop Theodore of Tyana, the case of Euprepia, asking that her rights to her grandmother's inheritance should be honoured[56]and, during a bout of illness, requested the same bishop's help in protecting a group of noble women from the 'tyranny and oppression' of powerful men, by conducting an impartial investigation.[57] In neither case, does Gregory claim to be impartial and the reasons for referral seem to spring from Gregory's inability to enforce his decisions unaided (his poor health ensured that he was never bishop anywhere for very long).

A bishop might also become incompetent to handle a dispute because of earlier failures on his part, though few would have been honest enough to admit their error. Augustine is an exception. His decision to refer the case of the apparently corrupt suffragan bishop Antoninus of Fussala to the Bishop of Rome stemmed in part from the complexity of the case, which had progressed through no less than five hearings in Africa, and the number of allegations made against Antoninus (who had allegedly terrorised the neighbourhood with a gang of cronies consisting of a renegade *notarius* from Augustine's monastery, a *defensor ecclesiae*, a veteran and various watchmen). The main motive, however, was Augustine's own embarrassment at a series of misjudgements on his part, which had led to a loss of confidence in him on the part of the congregation at Fussala. Augustine, having illegally consecrated the under-age Antoninus, as an emergency measure, in the first place, without testing him in the lower clerical grades first, had then ordered Antoninus to restore what he had stolen – which he did. However, the congregation at Fussala still refused to accept Antoninus as their bishop, thus putting Augustine on the spot, as Antoninus could not be transferred. Various compromises were suggested and blocked by the locals, and successive judicial enquiries by local bishops, supported by a papal delegation, failed to resolve the problem thanks to obfuscation and delaying tactics on the part of Antoninus. A dispassionate overseas arbiter was better placed to establish the facts and win the trust of the parties.[58]

Equally dispassionate (and guaranteed to be right) was a saint, at whose shrine truth might be tested and oaths taken. This could provide a way of escape for a bishop reluctant to adjudicate in delicate situations. Recalling the detection of a thief at the *memoria* of the martyrs at Milan, Augustine informed his congregation at Hippo that he was referring a dispute between two of his priests, Bonifatius and Spes, to a final decision, again overseas, at the shrine of St Felix, at Nola. As he did so,

[55] Conc. Carth. (345/8), can.11.   [56] Greg. Naz. *Ep.* 160.   [57] Greg. Naz. *Ep.* 162.
[58] Aug. *Ep.* 209 + *New Letter* 20. For full narrative see Frend (1983a) and (1983b).

Augustine likened his own caution to that of secular judges, whose duty in a doubtful case was not to issue a preliminary judgement (*praeiudicium*) but to refer it to higher authority.[59] Such voluntary abdications of power may have been the exception rather than the rule; letters would tend to deal with the problem cases and ignore the many routinely dealt with by the bishop in public *audientiae*. But the fact remained that the bishop's Christian duty to further reconciliation would often be incompatible with strict enforcement of his powers of jurisdiction. Mediation, negotiation, reconciliation were more effective means of holding a community together than a reliance on the formal legal powers conferred by the Christian State.

On rare occasions, we are able to witness a bishop engaging in all the forms of handling disputes open to him. A long-running dispute between a North Italian bishop, Marcellus, his brother Laetus, a *vir clarissimus* (a senatorial layman, therefore worth conciliating) and their sister, a widow, had reached the court of the Praetorian Prefect.[60] The object of dispute was an estate owned by Marcellus, who, as bishop, was entitled to own property independently. Marcellus' wish was to donate the estate to the sister, for her support during her lifetime, on condition that she in turn passed it to the local church, on her death. Laetus challenged his right to do this[61] and took the case as far as the court of the Prefect, where it began to run out of time. Only when the practical disadvantages of resorting to the secular courts became apparent did it occur to the disputants that resort either to *episcopalis audientia* or a less formal version of arbitration might be desirable. The advocates therefore sought a delay, to enable the case to be referred to an outside investigator. The parties went along with this, expressing a number of grievances with the secular procedure, and chose Ambrose of Milan. The bishop's response was characteristically opportunist, although perhaps with a touch of irony. Ignoring his own admissions as to the disillusion of the parties with the secular courts and the long delay before they recognised the superior attractions of the ecclesiastical system, Ambrose made the most of their final choice – 'so

[59] Aug. *Ep.* 78. 4, 'ne divinae potestati, sub cuius examine causa adhuc pendet, facere viderer iniuriam, si illius iudicium meo vellem praeiudicio praevenire. Quod nec in negotiis saecularibus iudices faciunt, quando causae dubitatio ad maiorem potestatem refertur...'

[60] Ambr. *Ep.* 2.82 (Migne *PL* 16, 1276–9). The dispute was 'veternosum iurgium', perhaps indicating that it had dragged on through the lower courts and reached that of the Prefect on appeal, but see Martroye (1929), 300–11, citing *CT* 12.1.172; 16.2.23; 16.11.1.

[61] Cf. the more celebrated case of the sell-up of the estates of Valerius Pinianus, husband of the younger Melania, which was challenged by his brother Severus and enabled by the personal intervention of Serena, the wife of Stilicho (*Vit. Mel.* (Gr.) 8).

great was their eagerness as Christian men that a prefect should not act as judge in the case of a bishop'.[62]

Having recalled Pauline advice to Christians about judging their own disputes,[63] Ambrose accepted the commission, not as *iudex*, but as *arbiter*, on the grounds that acting as a *iudex*, and imposing a decision, would cause offence to the parties who felt they had not been treated properly.[64] While Ambrose saw his role in a quasi-legal guise – he refers at the end of the letter to the arbitral *poena* – his intention was to merge the job of arbiter with the role of mediator and to allow, if he could, the solution to emerge from the offers made by the two parties. He therefore immediately moved into mediation mode. Reminding both of useful Biblical maxims, such as that it is better to give than to receive, in order to prepare the ground for compromise, Ambrose investigated the negotiating positions of the two sides. The first offer came from Marcellus, behaving (wrote Ambrose) almost like an arbiter himself: he would cede the estate to his brother, provided that the sister had the use of part of it in her lifetime.[65] Ambrose, acting as go-between, put this offer to the brother, who welcomed it (Ambrose said) but pointed out that women were incapable of running estates properly and that he was afraid that it would deteriorate.[66] Everyone was impressed by this point, according to the bishop, who now reverted to his arbitral function and expressed, to unanimous agreement,[67] his *sententia* as adjudicator. Laetus was to get the estate, but pay a stipulated amount of the produce to the sister annually for her mainte-

[62] Ambr. *Ep.* 82. 2, 'cum iam conclusi essent dies, et paucarum horarum superesset spatium, quibus tamen alia audiret praefectus negotia; petierunt causae patroni prorogari paucorum dierum tempora, ut ego residerem cognitor. Tantus ardor erat christianis viris, ne praefectus de episcopi iudicaret negotio. Aiebant praeterea nescioquae gesta indecore, et pro suo quisque studio iactabat, quae episcopo potius iudice, quam praefecto examinari oporteret.'   [63] I Cor. 5.12 and 6.4.

[64] Ambr. *Ep.* 82.3, 'recepi cognitionem, ita tamen ut compositionis essem arbiter'. While the contrast with his role as *iudex* may have a specific reference to his formal *audientia*, it is more likely that Ambrose wished to lay stress on the consensual nature of his role; as arbiter, with the consent of the parties, he would seek to persuade them to agree, rather than enforce a judgement. His usage of arbiter is also therefore milder than the legal equivalent; Ambrose did not intend resort to a *compromissum* or *poena*.

[65] Id. 7, 'tu enim obtulisti, quasi arbiter litis, ut soror in diem vita suae possideret partem praedii, post obitum eius fratri cederet omnis possessio. Neque quisquam eum vel tuo, vel Ecclesiae conveniret nomini; sed sibi haberet, si ita mallet, ut nihil dispensaret Ecclesiae.'

[66] Id. 7, 'quemadmodum enim femina, et, quod est amplius, vidua possessionem regeret tributariam? Quid sibi profuturum, quod sibi iura possessionis cederes, si maiora ex incultu agri subeunda sibi damna arbitraretur?'

[67] Id. 8, omnium conspirante assensu, the standard rhetoric for legitimising a decision. Many women, of course, did own and run estates, although the complaint (above, pp. 186–7) of Taësis and Kyrillous against Chaeremon, that they, as women, could not run the lands ceded to them shows there could be practical problems for small-scale landowners.

nance. Thus everybody would be happy, Laetus, because he had won ownership of the estate, the sister because she was guaranteed maintenance, regardless of whether the harvests were good or bad – and Marcellus did best of all, as he had behaved like a good brother to both, while Marcellus' church was none the worse, charity being a gain to Christ, not a loss. In conclusion, further exhortations were offered to Marcellus, who, in reconciling his family, had in effect acted as joint arbiter with Ambrose himself.[68]

The case of Laetus vs. Marcellus encapsulates the operation in practice of episcopal dispute settlement. Ambrose could have acted as a *iudex*, as he had the consent of the parties for so doing. Realising, however, that the arrogation to himself as an individual of powers as a *iudex* in a sensitive case, involving another bishop, could cause difficulties of other kinds, he refused the role. Instead, he chose to act as arbiter, but, even then, avoided importing more of the secular ideology of arbitration than was required for his purpose. No formal mechanisms, therefore, were needed to enforce his decision, which was to depend on the consent of the parties. Moreover, the decision would rest, not only on the consent, but also on the active participation of the parties in a negotiating process, skilfully guided by the mediator, Ambrose. Even after Ambrose had delivered his award as arbitrator, the contention that the disputants in fact made the decision for themselves was reinforced with reference to Marcellus, who was designated by Ambrose as 'joint arbiter' with himself, because he first 'gave shape' to the final decision.

The functioning of bishops as judges, arbiters, or mediators, within or beyond the confines of *episcopalis audientia* was only partly dependent on the goodwill of emperors, whose laws could provide little more than a framework for a set of complex interrelationships between bishops and congregation, bishops with each other and with their clergy, bishops and the intervention of an often well-meaning but also heavy-handed secular arm. Ecclesiastical preference for conducting community relations by its own rules did not prevent the clergy from co-operating with the state, even on strictly church matters, such as heresy, on which Christian emperors and Church councils alike were active legislators.[69] However, much of bishops' activity in sorting out quarrels among their flock over 'gold and silver, farms and herds' continued to depend, as it had done since well before Constantine, on the consent of the faithful. The author-

---

[68] Id. 11. Christo ergo auctore et duobus arbitris sacerdotibus, te, qui formam prior dedisti, me qui sententiam prompsi, facta pax non diiudicabit; quando tanta fidei convenerunt suffragia, ut perfidia non possit esse sine poena.

[69] Heresy could also be handled as an internal disciplinary matter. Aug. *Ep.* 236 concerns a sub-deacon, Victorinus or Victorianus, who was proved to be a Manichee and expelled from the city; 'eum coercitum pellendum de civitate curavi'.

ity of the bishop, initially dependent on his position in his city church, was enhanced in the fourth century by his adoption, as required, of the roles of *iudex*, and arbiter. The former endowed him with the jurisdictional authority of the state, the latter allowed him to adjudicate between non-Christian, as well as Christian, disputing parties, as a figure of authority acceptable to both. But the prevalent ideology of the handling of disputes by bishops remained that of mediation and reconciliation, not only because the bishops were true to Christian doctrine but for practical reasons, that they had to govern, for life, the congregations, whom they taught as well as judged. While *iudices* served for a short time, then departed, and arbiters delivered judgement only on a single case, bishops were a fixture, and their *auctoritas* was dependent on tried and tested rules laid down, not by emperors, but by the Gospels and St Paul.

Conclusion

Interpreting the history of Late Antiquity from its laws is an enterprise fraught with risk. The legal texts which survived through the imperial codes are extracts, largely divorced from the context in which they were created and the rhetoric by which they were justified. Each 'general law', despite the generality of its application, may originally have been evoked by a single incident; they are, therefore, for the historian, no more than a form of anecdotal evidence, and are no guide to the extent or severity of the problem addressed. Even repeated laws do not demonstrate that a difficulty was serious, still less that previous legislation was ineffective; frequency of evocation establishes that citizens were interested in knowing about and, probably, enforcing legislation on that matter. Repeated laws were laws that worked.

Legal texts are multi-layered and contain within them some cultural tension. All imperial laws, whether complete or, as is the case with most, excerpted are an uneasy merger of statute with imperial political broadcast. They are the expression of two cultures, the legal and the imperial. The rhetoric of the laws may distract from, but seldom entirely submerges, a long legal tradition, which shaped the distinctive intellectual discipline, of which the great Severan jurists were the most eminent exponents. The priorities of emperors and lawyers were not the same. The latter sought (ideally) to expound, discuss, educate; it was not, usually, their job to tell people what to do. Emperors, on the other hand, were not lawyers and the source of the legal advice available to some, notably that great reformer, Constantine, is obscure; their main interest was the public assertion of their power, through the language of their legislation. Whatever the quality of the advice available, legal advisers advised, emperors decided. Their decisions, while taking account of legal precedents, if drawn to their attention, were assertions of power.

Tensions existed also between the ideology of unfettered imperial rule and the restrictive impact on imperial discretion of imperial codification of laws. Both Theodosius II and Justinian envisaged their systematisation of Roman Law as the ultimate affirmation of their own status as legislators and their control of the legislative process thereafter. While Theodosius put in place mechanisms for the recognition in East and West of future Novellae, Justinian went further; not only the imperial, but also the juristic tradition, as mediated through the *Digest*, would henceforward be in the emperor's sole charge. Emperors, however, were unlikely to admit publicly that law-codes could also prove an effective device for limiting their own discretionary powers; these could not be abolished altogether, nor, given the benign effects of, say, *clementia*, was their complete removal desirable. But it was no coincidence that the first code of constitutions called after an emperor was the product of an emergent bureaucracy, which from the late fourth century, had evolved concepts of 'generality' in law which helped to discredit and then marginalise the exercise of discretion through the rescript system. Thus, paradoxically, while Theodosius II vaunted his Code as an assertion of his authority in East and West, and the Roman Senate put on record its acclamations of the great work (along with its dislike of arbitrary *ad hoc* decisions),[1] his officials were quietly aware that the Code was in fact a reaffirmation of the principle expressed by the western quaestor of 429, that imperial power consisted of submission of the *principatus* to the *leges*.[2]

Through the language of power, in which laws were expressed, 'universal' consent for the laws was sought or compelled. In part, that consent was achieved through the consultation process by which the laws were created. Emperors were quick to seize the high moral ground and deplore the iniquities of those who ignored or disobeyed the imperial fiat, but they could only know of such delinquencies from the often self-interested representations of those requesting laws in the first place. While it was always open to emperors to ignore representations from outside, the fact remained that the formulation of policy depended heavily on the quality of information available. The content of the response, however, did not depend solely on what the emperor and his consistory were told by one delegation; other representations, existing policy, precedent, legal conventions all played their part. Moreover, the response to a delegation might take the form of a specific ruling combined with 'general' legislation applicable to wider concerns. While, therefore, *suggestio* was central to the prompting of imperial laws, their content was determined by numerous considerations. What a law might say could not always be predicted by those who evoked them. Nor can the imperial government, despite its responsiveness, be described simply as passive. 'Spontaneus motus' had also its part to play.

[1] *Gesta Senatus* 5: Ut ad preces nullae leges promulgentur, rogamus.
[2] *CJ* 1. 14. 4. Not present in the surviving versions of the Theodosian Code, which are seriously deficient in the early books.

Where the texts of laws followed, perhaps uncritically, the versions of events offered to the emperor from outside, the voice of the proposers can be heard alongside that of the emperor and his quaestor. Suppliants were not slow to manipulate the system for their own advantage. Laws which appear to signal oppression of subjects by the emperor can often more plausibly be read as permission for subjects to oppress each other. Thus decurions desperate to maintain the numbers on their councils would be quick to blow the whistle on fellow-decurions seeking a way out by asking for a reaffirmation of what they knew the law to be; Christians in conflict with pagans or their own heretics knew well how to exploit imperial religious preferences to further their cause. Laws which bore down hard on those who fled their responsibilities in guilds or councils, or which outlawed sacrifice or other forms of religious deviance, were indeed a reflection of imperial policy, but their timing and addressees may be determined by local factional conflicts, in which the emperor was implicated and his known opinions exploited by the parties for their own ends.

Viewed from the centre, and from the perspective of emperors themselves, power and authority, and the imposition of the imperial worldview on the governed through the moral rhetoric of laws and the ferocious apparatus of law-enforcement bulk large. But the functioning of law must also be viewed from the periphery, the standpoint of the recipients. Roman citizens were neither passive nor stupid, and many played the system to suit themselves. Both the law-making process and the laws themselves were 'used' by the ostentatiously loyal citizens of the Empire. Imperial rhetoric of respect for law and condemnation of evildoers was played back regularly in the language of petition; the emperor (and his officials) were to be held to their word. That word could also be observed in practice. Laws which upheld the rights of, for example, prisoners or those awaiting trial could be, and were, invoked by vigilant patrons, especially bishops, thus mitigating the effects of arbitrary power.

Imperial ideology, as expressed through imperial law, was also assimilated into conflicts and rivalries of other kinds. While emperors exerted themselves to stifle dissent and create a harmony based on 'simple' law and religious orthodoxy, from which ambiguities and unprofitable disputation had been excised, the response from the powerful of the provinces and the Church was to acclaim the emperor's policies in language similar to his own, and to seek to impose a corresponding conformity on their own dissidents. To this end, it was necessary to sound loyal and much is made of acclamation as a demonstration of loyalty to emperor, city or local notables. But acclamation, even when it could in practice be guaranteed, was also available for exploitation, because public endorsement through supportive shouting could always, in theory, be withheld. Thus acclamations, once offered, became a form of contract, the *consensus universorum* was placed on the written record, and both parties would be held to what was 'agreed'. Moreover public demonstrations could be negative and, through the reporting to the centre of unfavourable slogan-shouting, governors could be held to account and their future prospects ruined by those they governed. Far from being the passive victims of an oppressive autocracy, the citizens of the Empire knew well how to assert and exploit their power to withhold consent, as well as to offer it.

Imperial rule therefore was both autocratic and populist. As imperial rule became more overtly autocratic, so, increasingly, the emperor became the avowed champion of the *populus*, who had once vested authority in him, – against his own servants. The rhetoric of emperors, designed to ensure the accountability of his own officials, was echoed by critical voices among the governed. Widespread, but usually highly generalised, suspicion of corruption in the judicial system was symptomatic, not of a greater degree of wrongdoing than hitherto, but of a concern that justice should be properly administered and an alertness to abuses. That concern was manifested in the ever-closer involvement of the state as guarantor of the judicial process and increasingly tight regulation of every stage of civil and criminal court actions. Yet this increased awareness coexisted with the continued exertion of *gratia* by powerful men, hoping to influence, or expedite, the judicial process for the benefit of clients, and governor-judges remained, as they had always been, vulnerable to pressures from provincials and others more powerful than they.

The increased presence of the state in the judicial process may have encouraged an increased use of other forms of dispute resolution, although there is no certain evidence that this was the case. The sharpening of the distinction between the two forms of adjudicator, the state *iudex* and the privately chosen *arbiter*, which had been blurred in earlier centuries, could have made the state's process less responsive to the needs of some disputants. Also, the attractions of episcopal hearings, which were inappellable and designed to 'finish' disputes, would have been strong, not only for professed Christians but for all seeking a quick and binding outcome. Yet the readiness of Egyptian petitioners to play the official system, as part of their complex strategies for dealing with their neighbours, suggests that, in practice, many relatively humble disputants continued to have confidence in the Roman system – at least to a point.

Where the integrity of the legal process was most under threat was in areas where the operation of rules, which bound all alike, was subverted by the continued, and legitimate, exercise of patronage. The emperor's attachment to his discretionary powers was only to be expected; the autocrat should have the right to bend the law, to the benefit of subjects, as many, including his own judges, might insist. It was also inevitable that patrons throughout the empire, bound by the honourable traditions of centuries, would continue to use connections to help their clients, and that these might include dubious litigants – or even escaped *coloni*, whose labour, in areas where tenants were in short supply, might be of substantial economic benefit. The difficulty for emperors in dealing with the threat from patronage to the integrity of law was that the threat was omnipresent, and that he himself was a prime offender.

The impression of heightened conflict between law and patronage may be also the outcome of the increasingly confident self-assertiveness of the centre in the regulation of matters hitherto outside its remit. No precedent, for example, existed for the systematic imposition of right religious belief through law, or of legal disabilities on those who thought wrongly. Similarly, the imperial lawyers' attempt to categorise *episcopalis audientia* as purely a *iudicium* or an *arbitrium*, with *compromissum* attached, was a bold attempt to assimilate the jurisdiction of bishops into the evolving imperial system, even though it was to founder on the complexity in practice of the bishop's role as a settler of disputes. But, for all its drawbacks, the determination of the bureaucracy at Constantinople from the late fourth century onwards to impose order, generality and system on all the diversities of Empire was far from futile or ineffective. Professional, co-ordinated and largely independent of the imperial figure-head, the lawyers of Theodosius II and, especially, Justinian, through their systematisation and codification of law, affirmed the subjection of the *principatus* to the *leges*, and, in the process, created the monuments of law that would transmit the intellectual heritage of Roman jurisprudence to future generations.

Bibliography

NOTE ON ABBREVIATIONS

The following are the main legal sources cited:

Dig. Digest (Pandecta) of Justinian ed. Th. Mommsen and P. Krueger (1868). Berlin; translated by Alan Watson and others (1984), Pennsylvania

Gaius, *Inst. Institutes of Gaius,* ed. E. Seckel and B. Kuebler (1903). Teubner; translated with commentary (1946) by F. Zulueta, 2 vols. Oxford; text and English translation (1988) by W. Gordon and O. Robinson. London

CJ Codex Justinianus ed. P. Krueger (1895). Berlin; no reliable English translation

CS Constitutiones Sirmondianae ed. in Mommsen's edition of the *CT*: 907–921; translated by C. Pharr, *The Theodosian Code* (1952). New York

CT Codex Theodosianus ed. Th. Mommsen (1905). Berlin; translated into English by C. Pharr (1952). New York

Const. Deo auctore on the composition of the *Digest* was addressed by Justinian to Tribonian on 15 December 530; *Const. Imperatoriam,* 'to all the young enthusiastic for the laws' prefaces the *Institutes* of Justinian and is dated 21 November 533; *Const. Omnem* (16 December 533) to the commissioners of the *Corpus Iuris Civilis* celebrates completion of the whole legal project; *Const. Tanta,* the confirmation of the *Digest* is addressed, on the same day, to the Senate (of Constantinople) and 'all peoples'

FIRA Fontes Iuris Romani Anteiustiniani (2nd edn. 3 vols.1940–43) S. Riccobono and others eds. Florence

FV Fragmenta Vaticana at *FIRA* vol. 2: 463–540

ABBREVIATIONS

Abbreviations of periodicals follow the conventions of *L'Année Philologique,* but some perhaps less familiar legal journals and papyrological collections are noted below:

BASP Bulletin of the American Society of Papyrologists. New York

BIDR Bullettino dell'Istituto di Diritto Romano. Milan

IURA IURA. rivista internazionale di diritto romano e antico. Naples

JJP Journal of Juristic Papyrology. Warsaw

RHD Revue d'Histoire du Droit (also *Tijdschrift voor Rechtgeschiednis*). Leiden

RHDFE Revue historique de droit français et étranger

RIDA Revue internationale des Droits de l'Antiquité. Brussels
SDHI Studia et documenta historiae et iuris. Rome
ZSS RA Zeitschrift der Savigny-Stiftung für Rechtsgeschichte. Romanistiche Abteilung.
   Graz

MAIN PAPYROLOGICAL COLLECTIONS USED

Meyer, *Jur. Pap.* = Meyer, P. *Juristische Papyrologie.* Munich
P. *Abinn.* = Bell, H. I., Martin, V., Turner, E. G. and van Berchem, D. eds.
   (1962) *The Abinnaeus Archive. Papers of a Roman Officer in the reign of
   Constantius II.* Oxford
P. *Berl. Möller* = Möller, S. ed. (1929) *Griechische Papyri aus dem Berliner Museum.*
   Göteborg
P. *Cair. Isid.* Boak, A. E. R. and Youtie, H. C. eds. (1960) *The Archive of Aurelius
   Isidorus.* Ann Arbor, Michigan
P. *Col. VII* = Bagnall, R.S. and Lewis, N. (1979) *Columbia Papyri VII. Fourth
   Century Documents from Karanis.* American Studies in Papyrology 20. Mis-
   soula
P. *Fam. Tebt* = van Groningen, B. ed. (1950) *A Family Archive from Tebtunis*
   (Papyrologica Lugduno-Batava 6). Leiden
P. *Lips.* = Mitteis, L. ed.(1906) *Griechische Urkunden der Papyrussammlung zu
   Leipzig.* Leipzig
P. *Lond.* = Kenyon, F. G., Bell, H. I. and Skeat, T. C. eds. (1893–1974) *Greek
   Papyri in the British Museum.* London
P. *Mich.* = Edgar, C. C. and others eds. (1931 – present) *Papyri in the University of
   Michigan Collection.* Ann Arbor
P. *Oxy.* = Grenfell, B. P., Hunt, A. S., and others eds. (1898 – present) *The
   Oxyrhynchus Papyri.* London
P. *Princ.* = Johnston, A. C. and others eds. (1931 – present) *Papyri in the Princeton
   University Collections.* Baltimore and Princeton
P. *Sakaon* = Parassoglou, G. M. ed. (1978) *The Archive of Aurelius Sakaon.* Bonn
P. *Thead.* = Jouguet, P. ed. (1911) *Papyrus de Théadelpbie.* Paris
SB = Preisigke, F. and others eds. (1915 – present) *Sammelbuch griechischer Urkun-
   den aus Ägypten*

SECONDARY WORKS

Acland, A. F. (1995) *Resolving disputes without going to court.* London
Angliviel de la Beaumelle, L. (1992) 'La torture dans les Res Gestae d'Ammien
   Marcellin', in M. Christol and others eds. *Institutions, société et vie politique
   dans l'Empire romain au IVe siècle ap. J.-C.* Coll. de l'Ecole française de Rome
   159: 91–113. Rome
Arce, J. J. (1974) 'El historiador Ammiano Marcelino y la pena de muerte',
   Hispania Antiqua 4: 321–44
Archi, G.G. (1976) *Teodosio II e la sua Codificazione.* Naples
Arjava, A. (1996) *Women and Law in Late Antiquity.* Oxford
Arnaoutoglou, I. (1995) 'Marital disputes in Greco-Roman Egypt', *JJP* 25: 11–28

Aru, L and others eds. (1971) *Studi in onore di Edouado Volterra*. 6 vols. Milan
(= Studi Volterra)

Bagnall, R.S.(1989) 'Official and private violence in Roman Egypt', *BASP* 26: 201–16

(1993) *Egypt in Late Antiquity*. Princeton NJ

Baldwin, B. (1984) 'The Testamentum Porcelli', in his *Studies in Late Roman and Byzantine History, Literature and Language*, London Studies in Classical Philology 12: 137–48. Amsterdam

Barnes, T.D. (1975) 'The beginnings of Donatism', *JTS* 26: 13–22

(1981) *Constantine and Eusebius*. Cambridge, MA

(1982) *The New Empire of Diocletian and Constantine*. Cambridge, MA

(1992) 'Praetorian Prefects, 337–61', *ZPE* 94: 249–52

Barrow, R. H. (1973) *Prefect and Emperor: the Relationes of Symmachus, AD 384*. Oxford

Bauman, R. A. (1967) *The Crimen Maiestatis in the Roman Republic and Augustan Principate* . Johannesburg

(1980) 'The "Leges Iudiciorum Publicorum" and their interpretation in the Republic, Principate and Early Empire', *ANRW* II. 13: 103–233

(1996) *Crime and Punishment in ancient Rome*. London and New York

Beaucamp, J. (1990) *Le statu de la femme à Byzance (4e–7e siecles)* vol. I, *Le droit imperial*, (1992) vol. II, *Les Pratiques sociales*. Paris

Bergman, J. (1982) *Synesius of Cyrene. Philosopher-Bishop*. California

Biondi, D. (1952–54) *Il Diritto Romano Cristiano*. 3 vols. Milan

Borkowski, A. (1994) *Textbook on Roman Law*. London.

Bowman, A. and Woolf, G. eds. (1994) *Literacy and Power in the Ancient World*. Cambridge

Brasiello, U. (1937) *La repressione penale in diritto romano*. Naples

Brennan, P. (1989) 'Diocletian and Elephantine: a closer look at Pococke's puzzle (*IGRR* 1.1291 = *SB* 5. 8393)', *ZPE* 76: 193–205

Brown, P. (1967) *Augustine of Hippo*. London

(1992) *Power and Persuasion in Late Antiquity. Towards a Christian Empire*. Madison, WI

Brunt, P. A. (1961) 'Charges of provincial maladministration under the early Principate', *Historia* 10: 189–22

Buckland, W. (1966 ed. P. Stein) *Textbook of Roman Law*. Cambridge

Buti, I. (1982) 'La 'cognitio extra ordinem' da Augusto a Diocleziano', *ANRW* II. 14: 29–59

Callu, J.-P. (1984) 'Le jardin des supplices au Bas-Empire', in *Du châtiment dans la cité. Supplices corporelles et peine de mort dans le monde antique*. Coll. de l'Ecole française de Rome 79: 313–59. Rome.

Carney, T. F. (1971) *Bureaucracy in Traditional society: Romano-Byzantine Bureaucracies Viewed from Within*. Lawrence, Kansas

Chadwick, H. (1996) 'New Sermons of Saint Augustine', *JTS* 47. 1: 69–91

Chastagnol, A. (1960) *La Préfecture urbaine au Bas-Empire*. Paris

Clanchy, M. T. (1993) *From Memory to Written Record. England 1066–1307* 2nd edn. Oxford and Cambridge MA

Clark, G. (1993) *Women in Late Antiquity. Pagan and Christian Lifestyles*. Oxford

Clover, F. C. and Humphreys, R. S. eds.(1989) *Tradition and Innovation in Late Antiquity*. Madison, WI

Coleman, K. M. (1990) 'Fatal charades: Roman executions staged as mythological enactments', *JRS* 80: 44–73

Coles, R.A. (1966) *Reports of Proceedings in Papyri*. Papyrologica Bruxellensia 4, Brussels

Corcoran, S. (1996) *The Empire of the Tetrarchs*. Oxford

Coriat, J. P. (1985) 'La technique du rescrit à la fin du principat', *SDHI* 51: 319–48

Crawford, M. H. and others (1996) *Roman Statutes, BICS* Suppl. 64. London

Croix, de Ste, G. E. M. (1954) 'Aspects of the "Great" persecution', *HTR* 47: 75–109

Crook, J. (1955) *Consilium Principis. Imperial councils and counsellors from Augustus to Diocletian*. Cambridge

  (1967) *Law and Life of Rome*. London

  (1995) *Legal Advocacy in the Roman World*. London

Davies, W. and Fouracre, P. eds. (1986) *The Settlement of Disputes in Early Mediaeval Europe*. Cambridge

Dewing, H. B. (1922) 'A Dialysis of the Fifth Century', *TAPA* 53: 113–27

Dionisotti, C. (1982) 'From Ausonius' schooldays? A Schoolbook and its relatives', *JRS* 72: 83–105

Dolbeau, F.(1992a) 'Nouveaux sermons de saint Augustin, III', *Revue des Etudes Augustiniennes* 38: 63–79

  (1992b) 'Nouveaux sermons de saint Augustin pour les fêtes des martyrs', *Analecta Bollandiana* 110: 282–9

Duval, Y. (1995) 'Les *Gesta apud Zenophilum* et la "Paix de Maxence"', *Antiquité Tardive* 3. 2: 55–63

Elliot, J. K. (1993) *The Apocryphal New Testament. A Collection of Apocryphal Christian Literature in an English Translation*. Oxford

Evans Grubbs, J. (1993) 'Constantine and Imperial legislation on the family', in Harries and Wood (1993): 120–42

  (1995) *Law and Family in Late Antiquity. The Emperor Constantine's Marriage Legislation*. Oxford

Feissel, D. (1995) 'Les constitutions des Tetrarchs connues par l'epigraphie: inventaire et notes critiques', *Antiquité Tardive* 3: 33–53. Paris

Foucault, M. (1975/77) *Surveiller et punir. Naissance de la prison*. Paris, translated by A. Sheridan (1977) as *Discipline and Punish. The Birth of the Prison*. London

Frend, W. H. C. (1952) *The Donatist Church*. Oxford

  (1983a) 'The Divjak letters: new light on St Augustine's problems 416–428', *JEH* 34: 497–512 = Frend (1988), ch. ix

  (1983b) 'Fussala: Augustine's crisis of credibility', *Etudes Augustiniennes* 251–65

  (1988) *Archaeology and History in the Study of Early Christianity*. Variorum Reprints. London

Frier, B. (1985) *The Rise of the Roman Jurists*. Princeton

Gagos, T. and van Minnen, P. (1994) *Settling a Dispute. Towards a Legal Anthropology of Late Roman Egypt*. Michigan, Ann Arbor

Garnsey, P. D. A. (1967) 'Adultery trials and the survival of the Quaestiones in the Severan age', *JRS* 57: 56–60

(1970) *Social Status and Legal Privilege in the Roman Empire*. Oxford

Gaudemet, J. (1957a) *La formation du droit séculier et du droit de l'Eglise aux IVe et Ve siècles*. Paris

(1957b) 'Un problème de la codification theodosienne: les constitutions geminées', *RIDA* 3.4: 253–67

(1971) 'Quelques aspects de la politique legislative au Ve siècle', *Studi Volterra* 1: 225–34. Milan

Giardina, A. and Grelle, F. (1983) 'La Tavola di Trinitapoli: una nuova costituzione di Valentiniano I', *MEFRA* 95. 1: 249–303

Gleason, M. (1986) 'Julian's *Misopogon* and the New Year at Antioch', *JRS* 76: 106–19

Gonzalez, J. (1986) 'The Lex Irnitana. A new copy of the Flavian Municipal Law', *JRS* 76: 147–243

Grodzynski, D.(1984) 'Tortures mortelles et categories sociales', in *Du châtiment dans la cité. Supplices corporelles et peine de mort dans le monde antique.* Coll. de l'Ecole française de Rome 79: 361–403. Rome

Gualandi, G. (1963) *Legislazione imperiale e giurisprudenza*. Milan

Guarino, A (1980) 'La formazione dell'editto perpetuo', *ANRW* II. 13: 62–102

Gulliver, P. H. (1979) *Disputes and Negotiations. A Cross-Cultural Perspective*. New York

Hall, E. (1995) 'Lawcourt dramas: The power of performance in Greek forensic oratory', *BICS* 40, 39–58

Hanson, A. (1971) 'Memorandum and speech of an advocate', *ZPE* 8: 5–27

Harries, J. (1986) 'Sozomen and Eusebius: the lawyer as church historian' in T. P. Wiseman and C. Holdsworth eds. *The Inheritance of Historiography* : 35–42. Exeter

(1988) 'The Roman Imperial Quaestor from Constantine to Theodosius II', *JRS* 78: 148–72

(1994a) *Sidonius Apollinaris and the Fall of Rome*. Oxford

(1994b) '*Pius princeps*: Theodosius II and fifth-century Constantinople', in Magdalino (1994): 35–44

(1995) 'The philosophy of the codification of law in fifth-century Constantinople and Victorian Edinburgh' in Lewis Ayres ed. *The Passionate Intellect. Essays on the Transformation of Classical Traditions*, Rutgers University Studies in Classical Humanities vol. 7: 345–61. New Brunswick and London

Harries, J. and Wood, I. eds. (1993) *The Theodosian Code. Studies in the Imperial Law of Late Antiquity*. London and New York (= Harries and Wood 1993)

Hart, H. L. A. (1961, 2nd edn. 1994) *The Concept of Law*. Oxford

Heather, P. (1994) 'New men for new Constantines? Creating an imperial elite in the eastern Mediterranean', in Magdalino (1994): 11–33

Holford-Strevens, L. (1988) *Aulus Gellius*. London

Honoré, Tony (1962) *Gaius*. Oxford

(1978) *Tribonian*. London

(1982) *Ulpian*. Oxford

(1984) 'Ausonius and Vulgar Law', *IURA* 35: 75–85

(1986) 'The making of the Theodosian Code', *ZSS RA* 104: 133–222

(1987) 'Scriptor Historiae Augustae', *JRS* 77: 156–76

(1992) *Emperors and Lawyers*. (2nd edn) Oxford

(1993) 'Some quaestors of the reign of Theodosius II', in Harries and Wood (1993): 68–94

(1994) 'Arcadius, also Charisius: career and ideology', *Index* 22: 163–79

(1998) *Law in the Crisis of Empire 379–455AD*. Oxford

Hopkins, M. K. (1961) 'Social mobility in the Later Roman Empire: the evidence of Ausonius', *CQ* 11: 239–49

Houlou, A. (1974) 'Le droit pénal chez saint Augustin', *RHDFE* 53 : 1–17

Humphrey, J. H. (1991) *Literacy in the Roman World. JRA Suppl.* 3. Ann Arbor

Hunt, E.D. (1993) 'Christianising the Roman Empire: the evidence of the Code', in Harries and Wood (1993): 143–58

Jolowicz, H. (1967) *Historical Introduction to Roman Law*. Oxford

Jones, A. H. M. (1964) *The Later Roman Empire. A Social, Economic and Administrative Survey*. Blackwells, Oxford

(1972) *The Criminal courts of the Roman Republic and Principate*. Oxford

Katzoff, R. (1982) 'Sources of law in Roman Egypt: the role of the Prefect', *ANRW* 11.13, 807–44 .

Keenan, J. G. (1975) 'On law and society in Late Roman Egypt', *ZPE* 17: 237–50

Kelly, C. M. (1994) 'Later Roman bureaucracy: going through the files', in Bowman and Woolf (1994): 161–76

(1996) Review of Harries and Wood (1993), *JRS* 86: 235–7

Kelly, J. M. (1966) *Roman Litigation*. Oxford

Laiou, A. and Simon, D. eds. (1994) *Law and Society in Byzantium, Ninth-Twelfth Centuries*. Dumbarton Oaks. Cambridge, MA

Lane Fox, R. (1986) *Pagans and Christians*. London

Lenel, O. (1927) *Edictum Perpetuum*. Leipzig

Lepelley, C. (1979–81) *Les cités de l'Afrique romaine au Bas Empire*. 2 vols. Paris

(1989) 'Trois documents méconnus sur l'histoire sociale et religieuse de l'Afrique romaine tardive, retrouvés parmi les *Spuria* de Sulpice Sévère', *Antiquités Africaines* 25: 235–62

Levy, E. (1951) *West Roman Vulgar Law*. Philadelphia

Lewis, N. (1978) 'The Imperial Apokrima', *RIDA* 25: 261–78

(1983) *Life in Egypt under Roman Rule*. Oxford

Lewis, N. and Kraemer, C. J. (1937) 'A Referee's hearing on ownership', *TAPA* 68: 357–87

Lewis, N. and Schiller, A. (1974) 'Another Narratio document', in A. Watson ed. *Daube Noster. Essays in Legal History for David Daube*: 187–200. Edinburgh

Liebeschuetz, J. H. W. G.(1972) *Antioch. City and Imperial Administration in the Later Roman Empire*. Oxford

(1990) *Barbarians and Bishops: Army, Church and State in the Age of Arcadius and Chrysostom*. Oxford

Liebs, D. (1975) *Römisches Recht*. Göttingen

(1978) 'Ämterkauf und Ämterpatronage in der Spätantike', *ZSS RA* 95: 158–86

(1989) 'Römische Jurisprudenz in Afrika', *ZSS RA* 160: 210–47

Lim, R. (1995) *Public Disputation, Power and Social Order in Late Antiquity*. California

Litewski, W. (1968) 'Die romische Appellation in Zivilsachen', *RIDA* 15: 143–351

Maas, M. (1986) 'History and ideology in Justinianic reform legislation', *DOP* 40: 17–31

MacCormack, G. (1982) 'The liability of the judge', *ANRW* II.14: 3–28

    (1996) *The spirit of traditional Chinese law*. Athens, Georgia and London

MacCoull, L. S. B. (1988) *Dioscurus of Aphrodito: His Work and his World*. Berkeley

MacMullen, R.(1962) 'Roman bureaucratese', *Traditio* 18: 364–78

    (1964) 'Social mobility and the Theodosian Code', *JRS* 54: 49–53

    (1972) *Constantine*. London

    (1974) *Roman Social Relations*. New Haven

    (1986) 'Judicial savagery in the Roman Empire', *Chiron* 16: 147–66, repr. MacMullen (1990), 67–77

    (1988) *Corruption and the Decline of Rome*. Yale

    (1990) *Changes in the Roman Empire. Essays in the Ordinary*. Princeton NJ

McLynn, N. (1994) *Ambrose of Milan. Church and Court in a Christian Capital*. California

Magdalino, P. ed. (1994) *New Constantines: the Rhythm of Imperial Renewal in Byzantium, 4th-13th Centuries*. Variorum

Maggio, L. (1995) 'Note critiche sui rescritti postclassici: il c.d. processo per rescriptum', *SDHI* 61: 285–312

Maine, H. S. (first edn 1861) *Ancient Law*. London

Mandouze, A. (1982) *Prosopographie chretienne du Bas Empire I: Afrique (303–533)*. Paris

Martroye, F. (1910) 'St Augustin et la jurisdiction ecclésiastique', *Melanges de la Société Nationale des Antiquaires de France* 10: 1–78

    (1929) 'Une sentence arbitrale de saint Ambroise', *RHDFE* 8: 300–11

Matthews, J. (1975 repr. 1990) *Western Aristocracies and Imperial Court. AD 364–425*. Oxford

    (1986) 'Symmachus and his enemies', *Colloque Genevois sur Symmaque, à l'occasion du mille six centieme anniversaire du conflit de l'autel de la Victoire*. Paris

    (1987) 'Peter Valvomeres re-arrested' in M. Whitby, P. Hardie and M. Whitby eds. *Homo Viator. Classical Essays for John Bramble*: 277–84. Bristol

    (1989) *The Roman Empire of Ammianus*. London

    (1993) 'The making of the Text' in Harries and Wood (1993): 19–44

Millar, F. (1977) *The Emperor in the Roman World*. London

    (1984) 'Condemnation to hard labour in the Roman Empire from the Julio-Claudians to Constantine', *PBSR* 52, 124–47

    (1986) 'A new approach to the Roman Jurists', *JRS* 76, 272–80

Mitchell, S. (1988) 'Maximinus and the Christians in AD 312: A New Latin Inscription', *JRS* 78, 105–24

Modrzejewski, J. (1952), 'Private arbitration in the law of Greco-Roman Egypt', *JJP* 6: 329–56

Nörr, D. (1976) 'Pomponius oder "Zum Geschichteverständnis der römischen Juristen"', *ANRW* II. 15: 497–604

Oehler, K. (1961) 'Der consensus universorum als Kriterium der Wahrheit in der antiken Philosophie und der Patristik', *Antike und Abendland* 10: 103–29

Panciera, S. (1971) 'Ex auctoritate Audenti Aemiliani viri clarissimi consularis Campaniae', *Studi Volterra* 2: 267–79. Milan

Parente, F.(1979) 'Patibulum, crux, furca', *Rivista di filologia classica* 107: 369–76

Paricio, J. (1984) 'Notas sobre la sentencia del *arbiter ex compromisso*. Sancion contra el arbitro que no dio sentencia', *RIDA* 31: 283–306

Patlagean, E. (1977) *Pauvreté économique et pauvreté sociale à Byzance 4e–7e siècles.* Paris

Pearl, O. M. (1971) 'Excerpts from the minutes of judicial proceedings', *ZPE* 6, 271–7

Pedersen, F. S. (1970) 'On professional qualifications for public posts in late antiquity', *ClMed* 31: 161–213

Posner, E. (1972) *Archives in the Ancient World.* Cambridge, MA

Pringsheim, F. (1931/61) 'Zur Bezeichung des Hadrianischen Ediktes als Edictum Perpetuum', *Symbolae Friburgenses in honorem O. Lenel* 1–31 = *Gesammelte Abhandlungen* 102–30

(1934/61) 'The legal policy and reforms of Hadrian', *JRS* 24: 146– 53 = *Gesammelte Abhandlungen* 1: 91–101

(1957) 'Some causes of codification', *RIDA* 12: 301–11

Purcell, N. (1986) 'The art of Government', in Boardman, J., Griffin, J. and Murray, O. eds. *The Oxford History of the Classical World*: 560–91. Oxford

Rawson, E. (1985) *Intellectual Life in the Late Roman Republic.* London

Rees, B. R. (1952) 'The Defensor Civitatis in Egypt', *JJP* 6: 73–102

Rist, J. (1994) *Augustine.* Cambridge

Robert, L. (1948) 'Epigrammes relatives à des gouverneurs', *Hellenica. Recueil d'epigraphie de numismatique et d'antiquites greques*: 35–114. Paris

Roberts, S. (1979) *Order and Dispute. An Introduction to Legal Anthropology.* London

(1983) 'The study of disputes: anthropological perspectives', in J. Bossy ed. *Disputes and Settlements: Law and Human relations in the West.* 1–24. Cambridge

Robinson, O. F. (1968) 'Private prisons', *RIDA* 15, 389–98

(1995) *Criminal Law at Rome.* London

(1997) *The Sources of Roman Law. Problems and Methods for Ancient Historians.* London and New York

Roueché, C. (1984) 'Acclamations in the Later Roman Empire: new evidence from Aphrodisias', *JRS* 74: 181–199

(1989a) 'Floreat Perge', in M. M. MacKenzie and C. Roueché eds. *Images of Authority. Papers presented to Joyce Reynolds*: 218–21. Cambridge Philological Society. Cambridge

(1989b) *Aphrodisias in Late Antiquity.* London

(1993) *Performance and Partisans at Aphrodisias in the Roman and Late Roman Periods.* Roman Society Monographs 6. London

Rouland, N. (tr. Planel, P. G., 1994) *Legal Anthropology.* London

Rozenberg, J. (1997) *Trial of Strength. The Battle between Ministers and Judges over Who Makes the Law.* London

Salway, R. J. B. (1994) 'The Making of the Roman State, AD 200–350', D. Phil. thesis, unpublished. Oxford

Schiller, A. A. (1971) 'The courts are no more', *Studi Volterra* I: 469–502. Milan

Schlag, P. (1996) *Laying down the Law. Mysticism, Fetishism and the American Legal Mind*. New York

Schlumberger, J. A. (1989) '*Potentes* and *Potentia* in the Social Thought of Late Antiquity', in Clover and Humphreys (1989): 89–104

Schulz, F. (1946 tr.) *Roman Legal Science*. Oxford

Scott, R.D. (1985) 'Malalas, the *Secret History*, and Justinian's Propaganda', *DOP* 39, 99–109

Seeck, O. (1919) *Regesten der Kaiser und Päpste für die Jahre 311 bis 476 n. Chr.* Stuttgart

Selb, W.(1967) 'Episcopalis audientia von der Zeit Konstantins der Gr. bis zur Novelle 35 Valentinians III', *ZSS RA* 84: 162–217

Simon, D. (1971) 'Zur Zivilsgerichtsbarkeit im spätbyzantinischen Ägypten', *RIDA* 18: 623–57

 (1994) 'Legislation as both a world order and a legal order', in Laiou and Simon (1994): 1–25

Sirks, A. J. B. (1985) 'Observations sur le Code Theodosien', *Subseciva Groningiana* 2: 21–34

 (1986) 'From the Theodosian to the Justinian Code', *Atti dell' Accademia Romanistica Costantiniana VI Convegno Internationale*: 265–302

 (1993) 'The sources of the Code', in Harries and Wood (1993): 45–67

Skeat, T. and Wegener, E.P. (1935) 'A trial before the Prefect of Egypt Appius Sabinus *c.* 250 AD (P. Lond. Inv. 2565)', *JEA* 21: 224–47

Souter, A. (1905) *A Study of Ambrosiaster*. Texts and Studies 7.4 ed. J.A. Robinson, Cambridge

Steinwenter, A. (1929) 'Zur Lehre von der episcopalis audientia', *BZ* 30: 660–8

 (1957) 'Die Briefe des Qu. Aur. Symmachus als Rechtsquelle', *ZSS RA* 74: 1–25

Syme, R. (1972) 'Lawyers in government: the case of Ulpian', *AJP* 116: 406–9 = *Roman Papers*, Birley, A. R. ed. (1984) vol. 3: 863–8. Oxford

Talbert, R. J. A. (1984) *The Senate of Imperial Rome*. Princeton

Taubenschlag, R. (1953) 'The Imperial Constitutions in the Papyri', *JJP* 6: 121–42

 (1955, 2nd edn) *The Law of Greco-Roman Egypt in the Light of the Papyri*. Warsaw

Teitler, H. (1985) *Notarii and Exceptores*. Amsterdam

Tellegen-Couperus, O. E. (1983) '*CJ* 4.29.19: a rescript of Diocletian', *RIDA* 30: 313–27

 (1993) *A Short History of Roman Law*. London

Thomas, R. (1995) 'Written in stone? Liberty, equality, orality and the codification of law', *BICS* 40, 59–74

Turpin, W. (1985) 'The Law Codes and Late Roman Law', *RIDA* 32: 339–53

 (1987) 'The purpose of the Roman Law Codes', *ZSS RA* 104: 620–30

 (1991) 'Imperial subscriptions and the administration of justice', *JRS* 81: 101–18

Van der Wal, N. (1981) '*Edictum* und *lex generalis*. Form und Inhalt der Kaiser-
gesetze im spätrömischen Reich', *RIDA* 28: 277–313

Vera, D. (1981) *Commento storico alle Relationes di Quinto Aurelio Simmaco*. Milan

Vessey, M. (1993) 'The origins of the Collectio Sirmondiana: a new look at the
evidence', in Harries and Wood (1993): 178–99

Veyne, P. (1981) 'Clientèle et corruption au service de l'état: la venalité des offices
dans le Bas-Empire romain', *Annales E. S. C.* 36: 339–60

Vismara, G. (1937) *Episcopalis audientia. L'attivita giurisdizionale del vescovo per la
risoluzione delle controversie private tra laici nel diritto romano e nella storia del
diritto italiano fine al secolo nono*. Milan

(1987) 'Ancora sulla episcopalis audientia: Ambrogio arbitro o giudice', *SDHI*
53: 53–73

Vogler, C. (1979) *Constance II et l'administration imperiale*. Strasbourg

Volterra, E. (1959) 'Quelques remarques sur le style des constitutions de Con-
stantin', *Mel. H. Levy-Bruhl* : 325–34. Paris

(1981) 'Sul contenuto del codice teodosiano', *BIDR* 84: 85–124

Index